TALKING FOOTBALL
(HALL OF FAMERS' REMEMBRANCES)
VOLUME 3

AUTHORS:
DAVID SPADA & ELLIOTT HARRIS

EDITOR:
MELINDA SPADA

TALKING FOOTBALL
(HALL OF FAMERS' REMEMBRANCES)
VOLUME 3

Copyright © 2016 by (David Spada & Elliott Harris)

All rights reserved. No part of this book may be reproduced or transmitted in any form or by any means without written permission from the authors.

ISBN-13:
978-1534734425

ISBN-10:
1534734422

Printed in USA

Cover photo copyright Associated Press

Table of Contents

About The Authors 5
Chapter 1 Ron Wolf 6
Chapter 2 Bill Polian 14
Chapter 3 Dan Dierdorf 32
Chapter 4 Ray Guy 40
Chapter 5 Jack Youngblood 54
Chapter 6 Franco Harris 64
Chapter 7 Joe DeLamielleure 70
Chapter 8 John Hannah 74
Chapter 9 Dan Fouts 82
Chapter 10 Fred Dean 88
Chapter 11 Lynn Swann 98
Chapter 12 John Stallworth 104
Chapter 13 Randy White 112
Chapter 14 Mike Haynes 120
Chapter 15 Harry Carson 130
Chapter 16 Tony Dorsett 140
Chapter 17 Steve Largent 148
Chapter 18 Earl Campbell 156
Chapter 19 Tony Dungy 164
Chapter 20 Lee Roy Selmon 176
Chapter 21 James Lofton 180
Chapter 22 Warren Moon 188
Chapter 23 Dan Hampton 200

Chapter 24 Dwight Stephenson 210
Chapter 25 Rickey Jackson 218
Chapter 26 Anthony Munoz 226
Chapter 27 Mike Singletary 234
Chapter 28 Ronnie Lott 242
Chapter 29 Howie Long 250
Chapter 30 Jim Kelly 260
Chapter 31 Eric Dickerson 268
Chapter 32 Richard Dent 276
Chapter 33 Chris Doleman 286
Chapter 34 Gary Zimmerman 292
Chapter 35 Kevin Greene 302
Chapter 36 Bruce Smith 312
Chapter 37 Charles Haley 320
Chapter 38 Andre Reed 328
Chapter 39 Randall McDaniel 334
Chapter 40 Dermontti Dawson 346
Chapter 41 Thurman Thomas 354
Chapter 42 Tim Brown 362
Chapter 43 John Randle 368
Chapter 44 Aeneas Williams 378
Chapter 45 Willie Roaf 384
Chapter 46 Will Shields 392
Chapter 47 Larry Allen 400
Chapter 48 Jerome Bettis 404
Chapter 49 Derrick Brooks 412

Chapter 50 Walter Jones 420
Chapter 51 Orlando Pace 430

ABOUT THE AUTHORS

David Spada is a successful attorney whose dream was to become a sports talk show host. Elliott Harris is the former Chicago Sun-Times Quick Hits columnist who has covered the worlds of sports for decades.

David and Elliott teamed up in 2011 to host the sports podcast "Sports & Torts" on talkzone.com. "Sports & Torts" was a finalist for Sports Podcast of the Year in 2013 by the website podcastawards.com. David and Elliott have interviewed over 200 Hall of Famers from the world of football, baseball, and basketball since 2011. They are pleased by share their interviews with 51 Pro Football Hall Of Famers who talk about their careers in this book.

Chapter 1

Ron Wolf

> College:
> Maryville College in Tennessee, University of Oklahoma
>
> As Executive:
> Oakland/Los Angeles Raiders (1963-1974, 1979-1989)
> Tampa Bay Buccaneers (1976-1978)
> New York Jets (1990-1991)
> Green Bay Packers (1991-2001)
>
> 2015 Inductee Pro Football Hall Of Fame

<u>Early Years With Raiders</u>
I had finished taking my last final at the University of Oklahoma when the phone rang. It was Al Davis. He had just been named head coach and general manager of the Oakland Raiders. He said he was looking for somebody who could work in his talent department and asked if I would be interested in coming out on a trial basis. I said, "Certainly." I went to training camp with the Raiders, and from there I was hired full-time.

It was a wonderful experience for me, because at that time, being in the American Football League, there were eight teams with thirty-three players each for a total of 264 players. Every night Al would sit with his coaching staff, which consisted of four people and two scouts. They would study each position of their opponents in the American Football League. They had the opportunity to watch all the left tackles, and then rate them one through eight. The theory is a picture is worth a thousand words, which in fact it is true. By listening and seeing what a good player was versus a bad player, really enabled me to get a big insight into what it took to play professional football. That was kind of how he did things. He did things by comparison.

After being hired, I was doing pro scouting. Everything was done from a pro perspective, and then we delved into college scouting the next year.

Early Drafts With Raiders

In those days, the draft was in November, so the bulk of your scouting was done in the spring. That's when all the staffs went out, which included the coaches and scouts, and could really get a handle on who the good players were during colleges spring practices. In those days during spring practice, they really practiced. They had scrimmages, and they were a lot looser then, because there were no games coming up. It was about building their football team. You had a lot of information available to you, and it came down to the ability to pick the player. What you would do in the fall is just follow up on injuries and things of that nature.

Importance Of Offensive Linemen

The offensive line is the only position in the game, if you don't have five guys, you can't play. You could lose your receivers, you could lose your tight end, lose your backs, you could lose your defensive linemen, but if you don't have five offensive linemen, you can't play the game. There was an emphasis on that.

Comparison Of AFL vs. NFL

The AFL was a little more wide-open game. No question about it. There was more single coverage in the American Football League then. I know a lot of people in the NFL said at that time, and some still maintain, that the AFL couldn't play defense. The AFL did okay in Super Bowl III and Super Bowl IV playing defense. Then there was the merger of the two leagues. It's no different than the game today. If you have good players, you're going to be a good team, and there's no question about that. The object is to get as many good players as you possibly can. Our whole basis with the Raiders was size and speed.

Recruiting Against NFL

It was very difficult recruiting against the NFL the first couple of years. Then what happened in 1965, was Joe Namath signed with the Jets. Suddenly the whole image of the American Football League changed. It changed because of the money that Joe Namath was paid. It was difficult up to that point, but it became just like college recruiting or recruiting in any sense. The big recruiting tool is dollars. If you had more dollars than the other team, the guy was going to sign with you.

Ken Stabler
Ken Stabler was a pinpoint passer. He was very accurate and very smart. He was a terrific runner in college, but got hurt in college and that was taken away. He got the nickname Snake with how he ran.

We used to have practices where the ball was never on the ground. That's how accurate he was. He was, until Tom Brady did it, the first quarterback ever to take his team to the championship game in the Super Bowl era in five consecutive years. He was calm, cool, and collected, which is a perfect demeanor for a quarterback. He was very, very talented.

Transition From Al Davis To John Madden As Coach
The team got better, so it was a big transformation. We had better players and John Madden was a superb football coach. When you have really good football players, suddenly you're a lot better off. I think that's what happened there. John really had some quality teams and tremendous players. John Madden came and Gene Upshaw and Art Shell followed. Ken Stabler came in 1968 and although he didn't play '68-'69, and hardly played at all in '70, it was a big difference.

Daryle Lamonica & Jim Plunkett
Daryle Lamonica was a tremendous long passer and perfect for what we were trying to do. Jim Plunkett was a tough guy. He won two Super Bowls as a quarterback with the Raiders. I've been told that the problem with Plunkett getting into the Hall of Fame is he didn't win enough games. I don't know. I'm not a big fellow with stats.

Tom Flores Not Being In Pro Football Hall Of Fame
I think it's a shame that Tom Flores is not in the Hall of Fame. He was 6 and 1 against Don Shula, and I think 11 and 4 versus Don Coryell. Don Coryell gets nominated all the time. Tom won two

Super Bowls. Coryell never even won a championship. I guess Tom has gotten lost in this whole process, which is a shame, because he was a very, very talented, good coach. He won two Super Bowls as a head coach. That has to speak volumes, but he's overlooked for some reason.

Reason He Went To Work For Tampa Bay Buccaneers
There was an opportunity for an expansion team. I thought that I was ready to leave. I thought I could lead. Once I got there, I discovered that, whoa, I'm not as smart as I thought I was. I'm not as polished as I need to be. Things just didn't work out.

The Buccaneers are the only true expansion team that ever, within four years of starting, played in the championship game. You had Paul Brown, Tex Schramm, and Tom Landry— all those guys and they weren't able to do that. The Buccaneers were able to do that with 15 of the players I had a hand in getting there. I'm very, very proud of that.

Lee Roy Selmon
Lee Roy Selmon is probably still the best player they've ever had with the Tampa Bay Buccaneers. I know this from my 38-year career; he's the best player I ever personally drafted. He was just a fabulous football player, but unfortunately for him, he played in a three-man front in Tampa. If he had been in a four-man front as a defensive end, there's no telling what records he would have broken as a pass rusher. He was a superb football player. They do not come any better than Lee Roy Selmon as a person and as a football player.

Importance Of A Quarterback
I saw how important it was for the Buccaneers. I believe firmly that if you do not have a quarterback, you do not have a chance in the National Football League. When I went to the Packers, I knew what I had to do. I had been through the experience in Tampa, so I knew all about that. I knew what I had to do in order to be successful in Green Bay. The chips kind of fall as they may for me. I was able to hire Mike Holmgren and able to trade for Brett Favre. Those two things turned that whole franchise around.

Brett Favre
The first game I ever went to as Executive Vice President and General Manager of the Green Bay Packers was in Atlanta. We played the Falcons. Ken Herock, whom I worked with at the Raiders for many years, was the person that ran the Falcons football operations. He told me up in the press box that if I wanted to see Brett Favre throw, I'd have to go down before the team came out, because when the team came out, he wouldn't be permitted to take any throws. Right away, I knew I had an opportunity to get this guy. I started working on it at that point, and then finally we got in done sometime in February.

Convincing Players To Play For Green Bay
The addition of Mike Holmgren, coming in from San Francisco, kind of changed that a little bit. Then the emergence of Brett Favre helped. Plus, we started really doing a heck of a job, I thought, of selling Green Bay throughout the league. We showed all the advantages of being a part of the Packers. I started a system where we would have honorary captains. Each game we'd bring an honorary captain back. Think about all the great names in the lore of Green Bay Packers football. It was a thrill to bring back Paul Hornung, Ray Nitschke, Willie Davis, Bart Starr, and others.

We started to win. Everybody likes to be involved in winning. There's no question about that. Plus, we had some great facilities up there. The only thing we ever asked our guys to do was to conduct themselves properly, and be professional football players. That was all the guys were ever asked to do as members of the Green Bay Packers. We didn't have socials they had to go to, like dinners. That was all we ever asked our guys to do, and they bought into it. When I went with the Packers, the Packers had the poorest record in the National Football league. With the advent of free agency, and when I left, the Packers had the best record in the National Football League. I'm very, very proud of that.

Brett Favre was a phenomenal player. They say the old Yankee Stadium was the house that Ruth built, but that new Lambeau Field is obviously the house that Favre built.

Guys were being threatened that they would be traded to Green Bay, or told, "You keep this up, and we'll send you to the Packers." Well, suddenly it became a pretty good place to go play football. We won 25 straight games in Lambeau Field and it worked out very, very well for us. There were a lot of people that made that happen, but it was a great. It was a great thrill to win that title.

Leaders On Packers
It was Brett Favre on offense and LeRoy Butler on defense. Reggie White played an enormous role, don't misunderstand me, but LeRoy Butler was the real leader of the defensive group. LeRoy took control. He could cover, he could tackle, and he could dog, a perfect safety.

Favorite Moment In NFL
My favorite moment in the NFL was when the Green Bay Packers beat the Carolina Panthers for the right to go to the Super Bowl. That's the best moment I ever had, because it happened in Lambeau Field. Everybody said the Packers would never go to the Super Bowl again. When free agency came to pro football, people said teams like Green Bay would die. Well, we won the title in Lambeau Field, and that was a big, big thrill to me.

Pro Football Hall of Fame Induction
It was unbelievable. There are so many people that I'm deeply indebted to for their contribution to the fact that I am in the Hall of Fame. To be recognized with those great names of the people that are legendary figures of the game, it's an awesome responsibility, and an awesome feeling.

Ron Wolf holds the Lombardi trophy as he sits on the team plane next to his wife, Edie, after Super Bowl XXXI.
Photograph copyright Associated Press

Chapter 2

Bill Polian

> As executive:
> Montreal Alouettes (scout)
> Kansas City Chiefs (1978–1982) (pro scout)
> Winnipeg Blue Bombers (personnel director)
> Chicago Blitz (personnel director) (1984)
> Buffalo Bills (1984–1992)
> (1984–1985) (Pro Personnel Director)
> (1986–1992) (General Manager)
> Carolina Panthers (1995–1997)
> (General Manager) Indianapolis Colts (1998–2011)
> (1997–2009) (General Manager)
> (1998–2011) (Team President)
>
> 2015 Inductee Pro Football Hall Of Fame

<u>Kansas City Chiefs</u>
I had been scouting for the Montreal Alouettes in the CFL. The head coach and general manager there was Marv Levy. When he took the Kansas City Chiefs head coaching job, he brought me over there as an advanced scout.

The Chiefs were in a rebuild situation. We actually got pretty good. I think we got to 9-7 our fourth year with the team. We had a terrific young back named Joe Delaney, who unfortunately drowned in a tragic accident trying to save a child at a picnic just prior to training camp.

I remember reading about what happened. Joe was at a picnic. He didn't know how to swim. All of a sudden he heard kids were in trouble. He didn't wait; he just jumped in and tried to save the kids. I think he saved one of them.

Joe dying was devastating and on top of that, we had the players' strike, which ate up 8 or 9 games. Because of the way upper management, not Lamar Hunt but people working directly for him approached the players when they came back off the strike, we were badly, badly fractured. Even though we beat the Jets who actually went to the conference championship that year in the last game of the season, it was too little too late. We were fired.

Chicago Blitz
Well, when Marv and I left Kansas City, I went to the Winnipeg Blue Bombers of the CFL. I was the player personnel director there. Marv got hired by the Chicago Blitz of the USFL and called me. He told me to come work for the Blitz, and I did. I was the player personnel director and eventually the acting general manager.

I thought the opportunity was a bit better in the USFL than the CFL. I enjoyed my time in the CFL and had some overtures from folks that were thinking about me as a possible general manager. I just felt like the opportunity to go to Chicago and be in a growing league like the USFL was a better one. Obviously when Marv was with the Blitz, there was a comfort level there that was off the charts.

We had to start from scratch with the Blitz. The previous years team had all gone to play for the Arizona Rattlers. The only thing we had was the Blitz name and the geographical rights to certain players from Notre Dame and other local schools. That was the situation, but in professional football and really in professional sports, you can't pick your battles. You've got to go where the opportunities are and it was an opportunity. We tried to make the best of it.

We were in training camp in Arizona and Steve Ehrhart, the Deputy Commissioner of the league, came out to see Marv and me to inform us that the doctor who had been the Blitz owner had simply pulled out and wasn't going to put any more money into the team. He returned the franchise back to the league. So we were in essence working for the league office. Steve indicated that Marv and I should carry on in our executive capacities. We were told to keep going, and that the league would get back to us with a budget relatively soon.

The budget obviously was bare bones. Subsequently, it got worse. At the end of the season, we ended up just existing on fumes, really. We are very fortunate in the sense that they were able to sell the team soon after the season ended to Eddie Einhorn, Jerry Reinsdorf, and a wonderful man from Chicago named Gene Fanning.

Despite having no highly paid players, no budget, and basically having to trade things like jerseys and memorabilia for towels for the last game of the season, we ended up winning 5 of our last 7 games. It just goes to show you what kind of a coach Marv was. He kept the guys going and focused in that kind of situation. It was amazing.

Joining Buffalo Bills
Don Lawrence was the defensive coordinator of the Bills and had been one of Marv Levy's assistant coaches in Kansas City. Don and I were good friends. In 1984, the Bills had just hired a Personnel Director. They had not had one prior to that. They hired a gentleman in January, and in the spring he sustained a debilitating spinal injury that didn't allow him to work. Ralph Wilson, the owner of the Bills, had grudgingly funded the position but this gentleman wasn't working. He was on disability. They decided to try to fill the position. Don Lawrence went to Kay Stephenson who was the head coach and said, "Listen, I've got just the guy for you! He's the acting GM of the Chicago Blitz. He's been in Canada and was with us in Kansas City."

Kay asked me to come in for an interview and I did. We hit it off immediately. He called me back and told me he could offer me the job, but it's going to be for a very reduced salary because they didn't really have the funding for it. The amount was even less than I was making in Chicago. I talked about it with my wife and she said, "Listen, it's a chance to go back to the National Football League. You can't pass it up no matter what the circumstances are. We'll figure out a way to handle the finances." We did. Fortunately it worked out okay.

Signing Bruce Smith

Signing Bruce Smith was my first major signing. Terry Bledsoe, the general manager, had suffered a very debilitating heart attack and was out of work for the better part of about six months. Pat McGroder, who was a Senior Executive with the Bills, was in his early eighties. He had been with the Bills and with Ralph Wilson from the inception. Pat told Mr. Wilson we have a guy here who can do this. He's signed guys in the USFL. He understands what the USFL challenges are all about. He can negotiate contracts.

They had me fly over to Detroit, which is where Mr. Wilson lived, and meet with him. He gave me my marching orders and said, "Go ahead, and let's see if we can get him signed." So in conjunction with Mr. Wilson's CFO Dave Olsen, who is as fine a man, as you'll ever have the opportunity to meet, we negotiated with Bruce's representative. We were negotiating against the Baltimore Stars who had his rights in the USFL.

At that point, the USFL was still a growing concern. Donald Trump had not taken it under at that point. The Stars were located very close to where Bruce had grown up, which was in the Tidewater area of Virginia. It was a tough negotiation and a long one. We had to beat both the Stars financial offer and convince Bruce to come to Buffalo, which was coming off a 2 and 14 season. Buffalo had a downtrodden reputation both in professional sports and society in general, because of the weather and the economic downturn that had taken place there. We had to convince Bruce to come and we had to convince him that he was going to be the first step in the road to the ultimate success.

Signing Jim Kelly

I didn't really feel any pressure to sign Jim Kelly. You go to work and you do your job. The following January after we signed Bruce Smith, I was well prepared for the job. I was absolutely unknown outside of a small segment of the pro football industry, but I was well prepared. I'd been an advanced scout in Kansas City and signed players there. I'd done some minor league coaching. I'd signed players in Canada and helped build two championships teams there. I had gone through the experience of the USFL which, to say the least, was unique.

It wasn't any pressure. I knew what I had to do and set about to do it. I had been through situations. The money was a little bit more in the NFL and certainly the exposure was greater, but the job was essentially the same. I've said on numerous occasions when young people ask me how they can get to be a GM in the NFL, or how they can get to be an executive in the NFL, the answer is get as much experience at lower levels as you can, because that's what helps you. That's what prepares you.

I didn't feel any inordinate pressure. It was a situation that we had to take advantage of. We owned Jim's rights. The USFL, thanks to Mr. Trump, was in a position where they were not going to go forward, and as a result we were in a situation where we had a great opportunity to get a player who was going to make a huge difference for us. Mr. Wilson said, "Go do it," and that's what we did.

I explain to Jim what the rights situation was. We held his rights. Jim's agents and Jim said, "What if we force a trade?"

I said, "Well I don't know how you can force a trade other than by going to court, and even that's not probably going to work. Let's assume that you can force a trade. You can't force us to trade him just anywhere. What we'll do is trade him to the last place he wants to go which is probably Green Bay." At that time Ron Wolf had not made Green Bay competitive, so they were maybe football wise a step below the Bills. I said, "You are not going to the Raiders under any circumstances."

It was the Raiders who had contacted them, and the Raiders with whom they had negotiated. I said, "You will not go to the Raiders under any circumstances. This is not the USFL. Al Davis doesn't have the right to decide what players he is going to sign and not sign. We have your rights and you are not going to the Raiders."

I said to Jim, "Here's who we have on this team. We built it with you in mind. This is how we are going to do it going forward. This is not a situation where we want to sign you because we want to sell tickets, or we want to get the newspaper off our back, or anything of that nature. It's because we want you to be a quarterback who takes us to the Super Bowl. That's our vision. That's our drive. That's our dynamic."

We had a long discussion about what things were like and what commitment Mr. Wilson was willing to make. He'd already made a significant commitment by signing Bruce Smith, Andre Reed, Frank Reich, and others. I said, "He's prepared to make an incredible commitment to you and then we are going to go ahead and continue to build the team. If you want to be with a winner, if you want to go to a place that really cares about football, this is the place to be. It will take a leap of faith, I realize, but if you feel that way, we can do it."

For that I am really grateful. The folks, the fans at Buffalo, took a chance on me. The support came pretty quickly.

I've often said there was a black cloud over the franchise but the day Jim Kelly signed, that black cloud lifted and there was nothing but blue skies from there on out. The prodigal son came home. He had finally chosen Buffalo after he had initially rejected it. He was here to lead us to the Promised Land. I realize I'm mixing my biblical metaphors here, but that's the way it was. That's the way it was; not only portrayed, but we lived it.

On the flight to Buffalo after he signed the contract and we were going into the press conference, I said to Jim, "You've never experienced anything like this in your life. You are going to see a reception the likes of which you have never experienced."

As we exited the plane there had to be 15 or 20 media crews there. People from all over western New York, Canada, etc. We took an expressway into the city. We had to hold the press conference at a downtown hotel because the Bills facility could not accommodate the number of people. It was so large! We had to drive down a freeway that had any number of overpasses on it. About every quarter of a mile there was an overpass. From the overpass, people were standing with signs— Welcome Back Jim! Thank God Jim, You're Here!
Let's Go Win A Super Bowl! People 4 or 5 deep on the overpass, just waiving at the motorcade.

He was dumbfounded. He couldn't believe it. When we got to the hotel, it was as if it was a Presidential press conference. There had to be at least 250 media people there. They preempted the networks' evening news in Buffalo, nearby Canadian cities, and in Rochester, to carry the press conference live. It was a big, big, big day. People there were simply rejoicing. This great quarterback that the Bills drafted, who had chosen not to come, was there and we were on the right road. That was the catalytic moment where once again everybody said, "Hey. The Buffalo Bills are back!"

Marv Levy's Coaching Prowess

Marv Levy along with Tony Dungy, are the best teachers I've ever been around in this business. Marv has a way of boiling things down so everybody can understand him. He's got a firm grasp of what it takes to win and how to teach players to do that. His greatness was pretty evident in Montreal, and even more so in Kansas City.

First of all, he's the greatest communicator I've ever been around. Keep in mind that's high praise because I've been around Tony Dungy, Cal Murphy in Canada, and hall of famers. He's incredible in that regards. Secondly, he's a tremendous organizer. Third, he is the greatest teacher I've ever been around. He's able to boil things down and get them across to the players in a way that both instructs and inspires. Finally, he has a vision that is unique in terms of how to prepare a football team, how to treat professionals, and how to create a culture of inclusiveness. He's caring and honest. That's the kind of person he is. In terms of understanding what it took to win and the ability to do that immediately, I had no question that he was the right man.

Lamar Hunt told Mr. Wilson, who called for a reference, the greatest mistake I've made in my entire football career was letting Marv Levy go. I think that cinched it for Mr. Wilson in terms of making the hire. Marv's everything you want in a football coach. He's the measuring stick I've used from that day on. Everything you want in a coach—vision, strategy, organization, and inspiration—he's got it all.

Scouting Success With Buffalo Bills
We didn't get lucky. Former Texas Coach Darrell Royal said, "Luck is when preparation meets opportunity." That's what occurred there. We knew exactly the kind of player we wanted. Knowing that made it relatively easy to scout. We didn't concern ourselves with outside forces, noise, consensus, or other peoples' opinions. We simply took the players that we felt were the best for our team. We used every avenue we could to try to unearth those players, the college draft, collegiate free agency, USFL, waivers as is the case with Steve Tasker, and trades. Leonard Smith, Kenneth Davis, and Cornelius Bennett all came through trades.

Improving Buffalo Bills Image
When I first took the job in Buffalo, the first person I saw after I got back from the press conference was the ticket manager. He said, "Congratulations we have 12,000 season tickets sold in a 80,000 seat stadium." I was a bit floored by that number. I could understand it given how bad the team had been, not signing Jim Kelly after drafting him, and the loss of Joe Cribbs. It was a snowball rolling in the wrong direction.

Our general manager and I went out and tried to meet with as many groups as we could. A, to try to take their temperature—why were you not supporting the Bills? And B, what can we do to make it better? I would always introduce myself the same way I did at the press conference. I'm a guy whose name nobody knows but here's my background. Strangely people almost all accepted me as a football guy. I was told we trust you; you'll get it done.

I was told here's what you need to do. You need to make tickets more available to us. We need to have better seats and customer service, and by all means we need to have better security at the stadium. At over 200 events I attended, that was an absolute consensus. I guess because my football background was so extensive and my notoriety was so limited, people just assumed this guy's a blue-collar guy who knows football. He'll get the right players.

Marv Levy's Initial Meeting With Buffalo Bills Team
Jim Kelly's arrival was part 1 of the puzzle. Part 2 really was Marv Levy. When Marv came in the morale was really, really bad. Jim was

playing, but he didn't have a good relationship with his position coach or with the head coach. The offensive line guys were really out of sorts. The defensive was not performing well. Everybody was more down in the dumps then when we were 2-14 because the players' expectations were higher. Constant harping and criticism beat down the players.

Marv came in and called the team together. He spoke for about 7 or 8 minutes. One of the things he said was, "What it takes to win is simple, but it isn't easy. We're going to do the following things. We're going to play smart football. We're not going to be dumb, and we're not going to be dirty. We're not going to beat ourselves. We're going to pay attention to detail; the devil was in the detail. We are going to expect adversity, but we are also going to expect to overcome it. No one is preordained as a loser; no franchise is preordained as a loser. Finally, we're not going to have a lot of rules. I want you to be on time, I want you to be a professional inside and outside this building, and I want you to be good citizen. Those are our rules. Now, let's take the first step. Our goal here is very simple. We're going to win the Super Bowl. We take the first step this Sunday against the Pittsburgh Steelers. Let's get ready to go beat the Steelers!"

The players stood up and applauded! Unbelievable. I have never seen it before or since. They simply stood up and applauded! It was though they had said to themselves, "Okay. We finally have the guy who can take us where we want to go." The very first time he stepped up to the podium, he had them in the palm of his hands.

<u>January 3, 1993 Houston Oilers vs. Buffalo Bills ("The Comeback Game")</u>
At halftime I said, "Oh boy. What a way to end. This is awful." You know, given all we'd accomplished.

In those days, I used to sit out on the photo deck, and fans sat directly in front of me, within an arms distance of me. All during the first half, the 5-7 guys in front of me were just furious, yelling, "You guys stink! This is awful! It's terrible!" They got up at halftime and walked out, as did many of the people in the stadium.

By the way, the game was not a sellout. People forget that now. We didn't even televise it in western New York because it wasn't a sellout.

After halftime, we got scored on right away and things were looking even worse. Then bingo, Kenneth Davis ran for a touchdown. Frank Reich through a touchdown pass to Don Beebe. We were still, I think, 3 scores down at that point but it was obvious we were going to onside kick. Marv got the onside kick group together on the sideline. You could see that. I turned to Bob Ferguson, our assistant general manager, and said, "You know what? If we get this onside kick, we're going to win the game."

He said, "You've lost your mind! You have finally gone over the edge." We just kind of laughed, and boom! We get the onside kick. On the very next play, Frank threw a touchdown pass to Andre Reed, and now the route is on. Houston is in a position where they are now saying to themselves, "Uh oh! We've awakened this giant and here they come!" Naturally, the fans went bonkers. Our security director, who was seated next to me, said that people were trying to get back into the stadium. Our policy was to close the gates at halftime after people left and not allow them back into the stadium for obvious reasons. You don't want people coming in without a ticket halfway through the game. He wanted to know what to do. People were trying to climb the fence! I told him to open the gates.

People came flooding back in. We scored again, and then quickly scored again to tie the game. Then here come these guys who were really letting us have it before they left the stadium, come running up, high fiving us, and going, "Wow! What a great team! This is unbelievable!" At halftime, I don't think any of us thought we had a chance except for the players and Marv.

<u>Chances Of Another Team Playing In Four Consecutive Super Bowls</u>
Well it's going to be awfully difficult. I think it's like Joe DiMaggio's 56 game hit streak. There may be people who come close, but it's going to be awfully difficult to match it or beat it. The rules have changed dramatically with the advent of the salary cap. Teams turnover so much, particularly teams that are fortunate enough to make the Super Bowl. They turnover so much, it's hard to have the

kind of continuity that you need to go to the Super Bowl consecutively as many times as we did. Also, I think the grind of the season and the grind of going back to the Super Bowl time and time again, is really difficult. It wears on a team after a while.

Not Winning A Super Bowl
I regret it for the fans. For me, that was the most important thing. The fans who had supported us so loyally throughout that whole run, who had made the Bills story number one, 24/7 365 days a year. For us not to win a Super Bowl for them was pretty frustrating. When you are in the business you realize that the Super Bowl is just one game, it's not a 7 game series. A game can turn on luck. It can turn on a break. It can turn on anything that you, in many respects, can't control.

For example, if we had one more time out in Super Bowl XXV, Thurman Thomas probably could have run for another 15 yards, and we could have taken that time out and kicked a field goal. The results I'm sure would have been different but we didn't have that extra time out. That's the way it goes. From the standpoint of the fans, I still feel very sorry that we didn't get it for them.

Interestingly enough, what makes Buffalo so special—when I was with the Indianapolis Colts and we went to our first Super Bowl, I heard from upwards of 75 or so fans, who called or sent messages saying, "We're rooting for you. This is our Super Bowl."

Carolina Panthers Playing In NFC Championship Game In 2nd Year Of Existence
It was a unique situation with the Carolina Panthers. We were able to take advantage of the NFL rules because any veteran contracts that we had inherited through the expansion draft were simply counted dollar for dollar against the cap.

With maybe two or three exceptions, we took the lowest contracts we could in the expansion draft and left ourselves with as much salary cap room as we possible could. The first two years of the franchise's existence, we were able to sign any number of free agents who could really make a difference for us. That first year we had a 7-9 record, which was the best record of any expansion team in any sport.

We had a veteran defense with guys who really could play. Coach Dom Capers had just a phenomenal defensive mind. By the end of the first season, we were able to build a defense that was as good as any in the league.

By adding Kerry Collins, Tim Biakabutuka, and Muhsin Muhammad in the draft along with a darn good offensive line, we were able to grow the offense the second year. In addition, we had another great free agent acquisition in Wesley Walls.

We had gotten Anthony Johnson and Mark Carrier in the expansion draft. We were able to put together an outstanding team quickly. Had we run up against anybody other than Mike Holmgren and the Green Bay Packers, we might have gone to the Super Bowl. We had to go to Green Bay and play against what was a very special Green Bay team with Brett Favre and company. Green Bay went on to win the Super Bowl, but we deserved to be there. It wasn't a fluke by any means.

Joining Indianapolis Colts

Jim Irsay had taken over from his father Bob. Jim and I had worked together on the NFL Management Council. We negotiated and executed the bargaining agreements from 1989 to 1993. We'd gotten to know each other, respected each other, and became friends.

He told me if there is ever a time when I feel like I want to leave Carolina, to let him know. There'd been some changes in the management in Carolina. I just felt like maybe we'd gone as far as we could go there. The players were getting a little old and there wasn't quite the commitment I thought to rebuild the team that I thought was necessary.

Jim Irsay asked me, "How's everything going?" I said, "Well if you are interested in making a change, I might be interested in coming." He went and called Jerry Richardson and they worked out a trade for my rights. When I found out what the price was, I was shocked and chagrined. I was traded for a 3rd round draft pick. That was unbelievable. In any event it worked out and I had 14 great years in Indianapolis.

Reason Didn't Hire Marv Levy As Head Coach Of Indianapolis Colts

Marv was still coaching the Buffalo Bills and I wasn't going to disrupt that. Mr. Wilson had been too good to me and Marv had been too good to me for me to go in there and do that. That wasn't going to happen. We hired Jim Mora and subsequently, Tony Dungy, as head coaches. Tony led us to a Super Bowl victory.

Decision To Hire Tony Dungy As Head Coach Of Indianapolis Colts

It was an amazing situation. Tony Dungy and I knew each other. We'd chaired on the competition committee for 4 or 5 years before the head coaching position opened at Indianapolis. Mr. Irsay had posed a question for me. He asked, "What would happen if Tony Dungy is fired by Buccaneers?" I said, "All bets are off! Call the airport, get the plane ready, and I'll go to Florida and get him done. He's our first and only choice!"

Jim said okay, and low and behold, that's exactly what happened. I flew to Tampa and met with Tony for about six hours. Neither of us, even to this day, can believe that it was that long. Our meeting went so quickly and so swimmingly. He had to leave to fly to Carolina. He had promised Mr. Richardson that he would interview there. I asked Tony a question about how he would prepare the team and what his practice regiment and organization would be doing, going from training camp to the Super Bowl.

About 1/3 of the way through he stopped me and asked, "Have I said something funny?" I said, "No. Why?"

He said, "Well, you are smiling and nodding your head ..." I said, "Oh, I am sorry. I've heard this all before, verbatim from Marv Levy. This is all ... You are channeling him."

Then we had a little side bar discussion. Have you ever crossed paths with Marv? Have you ever been in a situation where you'd been exposed to his teachings?

He said, "No. No, I haven't. I know of him very well." Ironically enough, we tried to sign Tony in Montreal when Marv was there, but he elected to go to the Steelers. He was a quarterback in college and would have been a great Canadian quarterback but he elected to go play defensive back with the Steelers. In any event, he said, "I've never had any real up close exposure to Marv."

I said, "Well, it's just incredibly amazing that you two are so alike philosophically." I knew then and there that this was going to be a match made in heaven. We saw things so alike in terms of how you should build and run a program.

Deciding To Draft Peyton Manning
When I got to Indianapolis, I met with the scouting staff. That was in early January. They were split right down the middle 50/50. Fifty percent wanted Peyton Manning, 50% wanted Ryan Leaf. I said, "Okay. Let's go back to ground zero."

We had our film department put together every pass that both guys had thrown as college players. We had a number of people go through the films—scouts, coaches, even Bill Walsh. I asked them to take a look at it and give their opinion. Of course, I went through it on numerous occasions.

We finally reached a decision around March 1st. I would say the decision was clear among Tom Moore our offensive coordinator, Bruce Arians our quarterback coach, and me. There was a clear consensus that Peyton was the guy for a number of reasons. The conventional wisdom was that Peyton had a week arm, he wasn't very athletic, and he was "a product of the system". To this day, I don't know what that means. The opposite was true in every aspect. Peyton was, by far, the better choice. From a psychological and maturity standpoint, it wasn't even close. It was Peyton hands down.

The No Huddle Offense

It takes a special quarterback to operate it. It is very difficult to defend. It dictates to the defense. But it takes a while to learn and different quarterbacks have different personalities. Jim loved the up tempo part of it. He wanted to go, go, go. That fit his personality perfectly. Fast break football; that was Jim to a T. Jim Kelly, Frank Reich, and Ted Marchibroda had a signal system worked out. They would simply signal at one another, the play would come in, and away you go!

Peyton, when he first started with Tom Moore and Bruce Arians in the no huddle, wanted to go much more slowly because he wanted to make sure that every blitz that could possibly come at us was picked up. That was good because things had changed. Carolina and Pittsburgh came to the floor with the zone blitz. They were the two biggest proponents of it at the time. You better make sure you know who's picked up because if you don't, you are liable to get the quarterback killed. We went at a much slower tempo in the early days in Indianapolis.

When Peyton and our offensive line became comfortable with the blitz pickups, we were able to go at a much higher tempo.
Peyton learned to master and control the tempo of a game like an orchestra leader. If he wanted to go fast, he would go fast. If he wanted to go slowly, he would go slowly. When we became a mature team 3 or 4 years in, we all recognized that we could control what the Patriots, among others, did to us in many ways by simply using tempo. We could wear them out. That was true with virtually every 3-4 team we played. Those big guys can't go at that tempo. They aren't conditioned to do it. Tempo became a very important thing for us, although it wasn't at the beginning.

Winning Super Bowl

I've always believed that if you get there, it is a marvelous thing. Unfortunately, the media down plays what a terrific season the Super Bowl losers had. Often the media treats that team as though they were 2-14, when in fact they've had a great season. Obviously it's great to win, but my life wasn't going to end if we didn't win it.

It's only one game and there is a lot that you cannot control or cancel. That particular game was the only foul weather game there has been in the history of the Super Bowl. Rain poured from start to finish, in Miami of all places! Not just a mist, either. It was a pouring hard rain. We were fortunate to come out on top, but that's one game and there's a lot you can't control. Having said that, there is no loss like the Super Bowl. It stays with you forever, really. You can't get it out of your system until you tick it off the next year.

Winning is obviously the opposite. You have to be careful not to let it hang on too long. We came back and had a great season the following year. It's wonderful to win, no question about it. For me, going to the White House was the most special part of it. I wouldn't trade that for anything in the world. As I said, I wasn't going to go out and run in front of traffic if we had lost the game.

Pro Football Hall of Fame Induction
I was dumbfounded. I had written a book and I was in Buffalo, of all places, promoting the book. I had just gotten back to my room. It was around three in the afternoon, when I got a call from David Baker, the president of the Hall of Fame. When the call came in on my cell phone, it was a California number. I almost just let it ring. I don't know anybody in California who would call me other than the media, and I wasn't getting those calls anymore.

I answered it and David said, "It's my honor to tell you that you've been nominated as one of the two candidates in the Senior category." He explained that I still had to be voted in. The nomination would stand alone and it would be an upward bound vote, not in competition with any players or anybody else. I didn't have a response! I was completely dumbfounded. In fact, I think I said, "Holy shit", to be very honest. David said, "There are others in the room here. This is an open line." I apologized and said, "Never in a million years did I ever think that this would come about. Never!"

I had been there for the induction of many players. And, I was fortunate to be with there with Marv for his induction. In fact, I presented Marv when he was inducted, so I knew exactly what was going to take place. It was extremely surreal. It's almost as though it's happening to someone else.

I got into this business hoping to be a small college head coach. That was the extent of my dreams, if you will. I grew up watching Frank Gifford, Charlie Conerly, and Andy Robustelli and the New York Giants. They were always my heroes, but I never thought I'd make it into the league. I mean it's always an ambition you have, but it's something that's way off in the distance. I never thought that I'd become friends with Frank Gifford and talk football with him, or get to know Don Shula or Paul Brown, or any of these giants that I had admired from afar. Many times I just thank the Lord that I've had the opportunities that I have had. It's amazing to be a part of such a good thing. I never envisioned it, that's for sure.

Bill Polian, right, poses with his bust and presenter, Hall of Fame coach Marv Levy, during inductions at the Pro Football Hall of Fame. Photograph copyright Associated Press

Chapter 3

Dan Dierdorf

> College:
> Michigan
>
> Career History:
> St. Louis Cardinals (1971–1983)
>
> 1996 Inductee Pro Football Hall of Fame

Hometown Canton, Ohio
I grew up about a mile from the Pro Football Hall of Fame. If you're from Canton, Ohio, your DNA is mixed with the DNA of the Pro Football Hall of Fame. Everyone in Canton is involved, in one way or another, with the Hall of Fame. I'm a little more fortunate than most to actually be a member.

Being One Of Two Hall of Famers From Canton
Alan Page is also from Canton. I went to Glenwood High School, and Alan went to Canton Central Catholic. We are both from Stark County. Canton is the county headquarters. Stark County actually has five members in the Hall of Fame. Lenny Dawson is from Alliance, which is a city that actually touches the city limits of Canton. Paul Brown is from Maslin, Ohio, which is right next door. Marion Motley, a former fullback who played for the Cleveland Browns in the '50s, is also from Stark County. We're well represented.

College Choice
I was an okay player in high school, but never really a great player. I was one of those guys that were a little late to blossom. I wasn't offered a scholarship by Woody Hayes to Ohio State. I like to say that they didn't offer me a scholarship because they offered one to a linebacker on my high school team. I don't have to make excuses to anybody in the state of Ohio as to why I went to Michigan. It was my best offer.

Playing For Bo Schembechler

I was actually recruited by Bump Elliott, the head coach at Michigan at the time. Bo Schembechler came to Michigan my junior year. I started with one coach and then I played my final two years for Bo. It was the best thing that ever happened to me. He was a huge influence in my life and I'm honored to have had that opportunity.

Transition From Coach Elliott to Coach Schembechler

The transition from Coach Elliott to Coach Schembechler was about 180 degrees. Bob was a fatherly figure. He was just a wonderful man. He is still alive, and till this day, he's just a gentleman personified. Bo was like a tornado coming right through. He came in and wanted to change the culture, and boy did he. We had guys quitting left and right. I'd never worked as hard in my life as I did for Bo Schembechler those two years that I played for him, but he got results. He taught us that we were capable of doing much more than we ever envisioned. We are capable of pushing ourselves farther than we ever though possible. If you've never been exposed to that kind of motivation, that kind of teacher, I feel sorry for you because you learn an awful lot about yourself.

Playing Against Ohio State

When you played Ohio State you were fulfilling your mission in life. There was no other reason to be at Michigan other than to beat Ohio State. It's the same way in Columbus. When you're a part of a rivalry of that magnitude, you realize that the other games are great, but the only game that really matters is Ohio State. It would be interesting to ask a Michigan guy, "Would you rather be 11 and 1 and lose to Ohio State, or be 6 and 5 and beat Ohio State?" You'd be surprised how many guys would settle for 6 and 5. The rivalry was everything. It's fun to be apart of something like that.

Looking back, I've always taken it for granted. It's like my last name. Michigan is part of me. Every now and then I sit down and it dawns on me that, wow, I was really part of something special. Just to be able to say I played in front of all those people in Ann Arbor is special. I know what it's like to run out of that tunnel with over 100,000 people on their feet cheering. It's an experience that I can cherish my entire life.

Playing For St. Louis Cardinals

It was a little bit different culture. I lost more football games my first year in St. Louis than I'd lost in high school and college combined. It was a tough transition. I was thrilled to be in the National Football League. You don't have a say so in where you go. Some guys get drafted by Dallas and some guys don't. I was one of the don'ts. It's funny how your life works out. I've been in St. Louis ever since. It's my home.

It's kind of interesting when you're a professional football player. Somebody calls you and tells you, "You've been drafted by a team." It circles around somebody else's choice.

When I played for the Cardinals my paychecks were from the Chicago Cardinals doing business as the St. Louis Cardinals. We were still an Illinois corporation. My first couple years in the league we had training camp in Lake Forest, Illinois. We didn't go back to St. Louis until after training camp was over, six weeks later. That's how long training camp lasted back then. We were playing football in St. Louis, but in many ways there were a lot of strong Chicago ties.

The Bidwell brothers owned the team. Billy lived in St. Louis, but his older brother Stormy, lived in Winnetka, I believe. For the first twelve or thirteen years after moving to St. Louis, the club continued to have training camp in Lake Forest. Ultimately the Bears took over the training facilities at Lake Forest College and the Bears trained there until they built their own new complex.

When Billy bought out Stormy, he made the decision to no longer go back to Chicago. He kind of severed the Chicago ties, and we starting having training camp in Bloomington Normal at Illinois State.

Jackie Smith

The Cardinals had a lot of talent. I lined up next to a Hall of Famer Jackie Smith. Jimmy Hart was our quarterback. We had Terry Metcalf and Jim Otis in our backfield. We had Mel Gray, who might have been the fastest man in the National Football League, at one of our receiver spots. We had a great offensive line. In fact, we had the best offensive line in football. We were a pretty good offensive football team.

Larry Wilson

Larry Wilson and I were teammates my first two years in the league. Larry stayed with the club and became General Manager. Larry Wilson is a dear friend and has been for a long time. He was the first great free safety.

His defensive coach in St. Louis, Chuck Drulis, was still there when I first joined the club. He was the originator of the safety blitz. That wasn't a staple back then. He realized there was a tough guy in Larry Wilson. He'd bring Larry in on a safety blitz and let me tell you, a lot of quarterbacks were sorry. They weren't used to having the safety come up the middle. A lot of times he had a free run at the quarterback. The league was a little different back then. If you had a free run at the quarterback, you hit him any way, as hard as you wanted to, and just about any time you wanted to.

Cardinals Offensive Line

Conrad Dobler was a lightening rod. It seemed like I was the guy playing next to a tornado all the time. There was yelling and screaming, people cursing and what not. All of this was happening about 18 inches away from me. He was a piece of work.

We led the league in the least number of sacks allowed approximately five years in a row. Jimmy Hart enjoyed great protection and he delivered. A lot of that was to Jim's credit. He was a quick decision maker. He had a quick release and he was a rhythm quarterback. It was nice from an offensive linesman perspective, having a quarterback that you knew wasn't going to move a lot and put you in a bad position. I always liked blocking for a guy who I knew where he was going to be.

Playing Offensive Line

There is a huge difference in the offensive line positions. There is a different skill set involved in the positions. First of all, many times the centers and the guards are interchangeable because they're passing guys off from one to another. In other words, the majority of the time, if you can play one you can play the other. Playing tackle is unique. For the most part, you're out there by yourself. You're dropping and giving more ground than the guards do. It's a completely different skill set playing tackle than either center or guard.

Position Change
I started out playing guard my first couple years in the league because that's where the Cardinals had a need. Both of their starting tackles had been in place for a number of years and they didn't really need a tackle, so I started out at guard and played left and right guard. At the beginning of my third year in the league, they moved me to tackle. That's where I played the majority of my career. I moved to center my last couple of years in the league because of a pretty serious knee injury that I thought had ended my career. I wasn't capable of playing tackle anymore. I didn't have the moves necessary to play tackle the way I wanted to play it so I moved to center where I didn't have to move as much.

Toughest Defensive Lineman Faced
I played against a lot of great players. I broke in playing against guys like Bob Lilly, Deacon Jones, Willie Lanier, and Buck Buchannan—a long list of Hall of Famers. I didn't play them very often, maybe three or four times during my career. One of my really good buddies, Jackie Youngblood, was always a challenge for me. We were teammates in the College All Star Game. He was a smaller guy, and he wanted to run around me. I would have preferred if he tried to run over me, but he never obliged me in that request.

I went two whole seasons without giving up a sack. It's something I was kind of proud of. I never did a lot of pass blocking in college. We were predominately a running team. I was always a better run blocker than a pass blocker, but I worked hard at it and I got to the point where I thought I was pretty good at pass blocking.

Being Elected Into the Pro Football Hall of Fame As A Player and A Broadcaster
Winning the Pete Rozelle Award is a thrill. This award is a real treat for anybody in broadcasting, if you're fortunate enough to be chosen by the Hall. I'm one of the few people, who are in the Hall as either a player or coach and also in the Hall with the Rozelle Award.

There are four of us—John Madden, Frank Gifford, Lenny Dawson, and me.

Photograph copyright Associated Press

Chapter 4

Ray Guy

> College:
> Southern Mississippi
>
> Career History:
>
> Oakland/Los Angeles Raiders (1973-1986)
>
> 2014 Inductee Pro Football Hall Of Fame

College Choice
I had an assistant coach that actually played at Southern Mississippi when Thad Vann was the head coach. One day when I was doing visits at different schools, the assistant coach asked me if I would like to visit Southern Miss. I went there one weekend and just fell in love with Southern Miss. I fell in love with the program, the campus and everything about it. It wasn't a hard choice because I'd get to come right in and play freshman football. I was also going to play baseball, so it wasn't a hard choice.

It was kind of a small school at that time, probably 7,000, maybe 8,000 students. They were on a mission you might say, to rebuild and make the school and its program bigger and better. I felt like I could be a part of that. I had no regrets going to Southern. In fact, I'm still here working. I work at the University with the Athletic Department and the Alumni Association, giving back and trying to help increase enrollment and make it bigger and better than it is now. I love every minute of it.

Being Drafted By The Cincinnati Reds
It might sound a little awkward compared to what the younger generation is doing now. Today athletes start at a young age. They kind of train themselves or are being trained to reach that higher level in athletics. Their goal is to one day become professional

athletes, which is a very good way to look at things. It gives them something to work for. I wasn't really that way. I enjoyed playing many different sports. I didn't weigh one against the other or compare one to the other. I just took what came and went with it.

When I was in high school, the Reds came to me. They offered me money to play baseball for them in the summer, and pay for me go to school. I had already signed a scholarship with Southern. Once I make a decision and tell somebody I'm going to do something, I do it because that's the way I was raised.

If you tell somebody that you're going to do something, don't back out. You go ahead and fulfill that obligation. I went to Southern and I was fortunate to play baseball and football. I still got drafted in college by major league baseball teams. I made the choice to go with the Raiders because I thought I got a good deal out of it and I've never looked back. I mean, I always think about what it might have been if I'd have chosen the baseball route, but I don't think there'd have been any difference. I'd have given it my all in baseball just like I did in football.

Southern was a small school and they didn't have a big budget. In fact, when they started recruiting, many of the football coaches actually had to pay a lot of expenses out of their own pocket. Coach P.W. Underwood took over the year I came in and organized the Big Goal Club. It's a booster club that raises money to help the coaches go out and recruit players, and then bring them to Southern.

I don't think there were any players that we had strictly on baseball scholarships. If there were, I didn't know about it. It seemed every year Coach Taylor, who was the baseball coach then, would actually have tryouts for players. He'd pick his team from that group of kids. We were a scrappy little bunch, I can tell you that. I don't think there was really anybody on a full scholarship in baseball.

Better Baseball Or Football Player

I could throw the ball. I was averaging 98 miles an hour and had really good control. I knew exactly where the ball was going instead of just roaring back and letting it go. I could position that ball where I wanted to. My key role at Southern in football was starting free safety.

That's what I played. I was able to do all the kicking phases, so I just continued with that. I never set out to be just a punter.

In 1973, the Raiders drafted me strictly as a punter. I knew my job was kicking, but I was still prepared to do other things during the game. I was more involved because I wound up being the third string quarterback with the Raiders. I got involved in practice. I wanted to be involved so I knew what was going on in a game situation. I wanted to know what we were trying to do against certain teams, and being involved in practice kept me in the game.

I think my active participation made me more accepted by the team veterans. I guess they looked at me as more than just a punter. I was an actual player.

I wanted to get my head in the game. That stems from playing defense. Your body's trained. It's hard to break something that you have been doing for so many years. I wouldn't shy away getting in there and busting somebody. Believe me, it made me mad if somebody even got a yard return on me. Hell, I'd do the same thing again if I were young enough. I'd show these young ones how to do something.

Starting Out As Punter and Placekicker

It was just something I did growing up as a young kid, at about 6 years old. I'd go out in the backyard and play with different balls, depending on what sport was in season. I didn't want to stay in the house; I still don't. I'd rather be outside doing something constructive. I'd just go out, a lot of times by myself, and punt in the fields behind the house. I would break windows and do all that good stuff that kids do before getting your butt tore up when your dad got home.

I give all the credit to the good Lord for my ability to do anything and do it well. I guess you'd say I had a natural ability to understand the mechanics behind what I was trying to do. I understood how to take those mechanics and work for me. It's like playing golf. I just picked up a set of golf clubs and started playing. I finally got it down to a scratch but realized I wasn't going to make a living playing golf.

I might as well put the clubs away. I had accomplished what I was after.

The good Lord has always been good to me. Even though this old body doesn't move fast anymore and it takes a lot more Bengay at nighttime, it works.

Being Drafted In the First Round
I really don't think any owner beside Al Davis would have drafted me in the first round. I think Al understood the importance of the kicking game.

Looking back, the Raiders always had great special teams. They put a lot of emphasis on that because a game is determined on the amount of field positions you gain during the course of the 60 minutes. Whether it's running the ball back on a kick off or a punt, or the punter making a long directional-type kick to gain some field position back, it all goes hand in hand.

Over the years, I've heard John Madden mention me in interviews. He has said that when the Raiders drafted me, it was the first time he was sitting in a draft where everybody agreed on one thing—to draft me. I think John understood the importance of kicking too.

Once I joined the Raiders in spring training camp and started kicking the ball, John told one of the managers, Bobby Romanski, to get him a stopwatch. Romanski brought him one that was still in the package.

Apparently, they'd never used it before. John opened the package and asked, "How do you work this damn thing?" Maybe that was the first time he used one.

I guess John came to realize, hey look, we've got us a weapon here. We took a lot of pride in playing special teams. I took a lot of pride in it, as did the guys who were protecting me and covering after the ball was punted. That's why we were so successful all those years. We made a lot of playoff games and won a lot of championships and Super Bowls. The special teams of the Raiders were dominating too. It made a big difference.

Being Named MVP Of College All Star Game

To me, everybody is an MVP regardless of their position and the game plan. The kickers and the punters are MVPs too, but they just don't get recognized a lot. I was very proud of being named MVP, but I was also proud of the class of 1973 that came out of that game. We had Burt Jones and John Hannah. I think three quarters of the guys on that all-star team are in the Hall of Fame, if I'm not mistaken. We had a great class that year and we gave the Dolphins fits in the game. The Dolphins only won 6-3. That tells you something about the class of 1973.

Hang Time On Punts

Hang time was natural with the kicks, but with each punt I found ways to make the hang time longer. I knew I could probably get it a little bit higher and maybe a little bit longer. I'd focus on the position of the ball and my foot to make it feel better. That gave me a more solid impact. I learned there was very little I could change with each punt to make it better. The kind of distance and hang time I had at the time was a just natural.

I think one of the things that helped me so much was my flexibility. That flexibility helped me achieve the extension I needed to get my leg far above my head after each punt. I had people wanting to know if I took ballet. Hell, I didn't take ballet. You weren't going to catch me in a tutu. I was just fortunate to be very flexible. It's just one of the gifts that the good Lord gave me.

Hitting Video Screen During 1976 Pro Bowl At Louisiana Superdome

I hadn't even thought about hitting the screen until I walked out on the field. I knew I could hit it. During the game I called whatever play we were going to do; which way I was going to punt it. My ten teammates turned and walked toward the line of scrimmage. I got 15 yards from the line of scrimmage, which happened to be on the 2-yard line, and I stood there waiting. Everybody was set for the snap. I just looked up and thought to myself, I'm at the right angle; I'm going to try to hit the video screen. I didn't even tell the guys. Jim Tunney, the Head of Referees for many years, was the referee. He was standing there and I heard him say, "Ray, you're going to try this aren't you?" I said, "Yup."

Of course, trying and making it happen are two different things. In that situation you've got to have everything just working together. You've got to keep yourself under control with your steps, and you've got to make good solid contact with your foot. When I hit it I knew I hit it good, believe me. The ball released from my foot and took off. I always followed it off my foot up to the height of it. I just kept watching and that ball hadn't even peaked yet, it was still climbing. I said, "Uh oh, here we go." Sure enough the ball hit the top edge of the screen and fell right down so we had to come back and punt again.

I don't think the players were very happy because the majority of the cover team was made up of guys who never played punt coverage. Here's the funny thing, the second punt almost hit the screen again. If I had hit it again, I would have just left the Superdome. I would have gone to the locker room and got dressed.

The Pro Bowl is a fun game. The rules are a little bit different. I had the opportunity to try that without technically getting the ball blocked, because that's one thing they couldn't do. The only time they could really hit me was when I actually fumbled the ball or had a bad snap. I was able to take my time and hit. I said, "Well, let's go for it and see if we can do it."

The first thing people typically ask me is, "Did you hit the roof?" I say, "No, I didn't hit the roof. This isn't a fishing story." You know how fishing stories go, you catch a little bitty minnow and 25 years later it's a whale. Yeah, I hit the thing, but mom said never to play inside a house anyway.

Al Davis

You hear so much about people, but you can't really judge them until you've been around them, conversed with them, and watched them in certain situations. You have to spend time with someone to really know what that person is like on the inside. Al Davis was a businessman. He was a very smart man. He knew exactly what he wanted to do and he knew how to go about doing it. If he didn't, he wouldn't have been so successful all those years.

It's like anybody that starts from scratch and goes on to create a dynasty. Whether it's in sports or in a corporate environment, there are going to be things that you do that technically may not look right, but it usually works out. I'm sure some of the players did not always see eye-to-eye with him. In those days, if you had a gripe with the coaches or the owner or anyone else, it was pretty much behind closed doors. It wasn't out in the open.

When players wanted to renegotiate contracts, nobody else really knew what was going on. We weren't that concerned with each other's salary. All we wanted to do was play. We wanted to go practice, play the game, and win. We all stuck together. There was no inner distinction between the players. We were just like big families. We backed each other up, kind of like brothers. We got into little squabbles like families do, but we got over it. We did what we had to do to work it out, brushed each other off, and went down to the pub for a beer. That's just the way we were.

Reason For So Few Blocked Punts

I credit it to the center and the line up front because you've got to have protection up there. You've got to have guys that are dedicated and really want to block the opposing team because you know they're going to try to block it. The center is 50% of a punt or a kick. I was fortunate enough starting in high school,
then in college, and in my career in the pros, to have great centers. I could probably count on one hand all the bad snaps I had. You're going to have bad snaps because people are going to make mistakes. But, you don't want them to happen a lot. I never had to worry about where the ball was going, whether it was going to my right or my left, or wherever it went on the field.

When we practiced the center always asked, "Where do you want it?" I'd tell them where I wanted the ball and very rarely would it be offline. My job was a lot easier because I didn't have to worry about it. What I had to worry about was trying to generate too much power into the ball, which in turn makes the steps that I take a little bit longer than I should take. With that kind of security up front, knowing that the ball is going to be where I want it, I didn't have to rush it. I didn't have to overpower it. I just did my thing and kicked it under 2 seconds. That's fast enough from the time it was snapped to the time it left my foot.

There were times there was a missed block, a missed assignment, or something went wrong up front. I don't hold any grudges against anyone I know. Mistakes happen because we're human. I made a lot of mistakes, but I took the mistakes and analyzed what went wrong and I corrected it, which in turn made me better.

Changing Punting Scheme Toward End Of Career

Toward the end of my career, the return guys were getting faster and the return schemes were getting better so I had to come up with another scheme. I reassessed why I wanted to kick the ball down the middle of the field as far as I could, all of the time. That was only going to hurt me and hurt the team in general. I changed by not punting down the middle of the field anymore. I started punting directionally, whether it was punting out of bounds inside the 20, or punting it out of bounds before the 20. It just depended on where I was on the field. I also hung the ball between the numbers on the sidelines to eliminate a lot of the return area for the return guy.

It got to be a strategy for me and it got to be very important to my team, They knew when I told them where I was going to punt, they didn't have to worry about chasing the ball all over the field once they got down there. They knew the ball was going to be in that position or in the area I told them. It made their job a lot easier. When you've got to change, you've got to change. That's just the way it is. You learn to adapt to the changes in football.

Waiting 22 Years To Be Elected Into Pro Football Hall Of Fame

It was very hard all those years. There are guys out there who have waited longer than I did. You know, some of them need to be into the Hall of Fame. It's tough. After being passed over a few times, you realize that's how it works sometimes, and you learn to accept it. You just wait until the next year and see what happens. Of course, the more you wait and the more it does not happen, the more frustrating it gets. But you have to realize that it's not the end of the world. I would have liked for it to happen the first time around, but who wouldn't? Sometimes those things don't happen.

As the saying goes, good things are worth waiting for. You just hope that you're still around when it does happen. All of the finalists had to be in their hotel room before 5:00 p.m. on the Saturday before the Super Bowl, and wait for the announcement of that year's enshrinees. We were told we would get the announcement call at 5:30 p.m. We were sitting there and it was 5:35 p.m., then 5:40 p.m. I was thinking, well, maybe not this year but at 5:42 p.m., the phone rang.

I almost didn't answer it. The previous September, Joe Boykin of the Veterans Committee for the Hall of Fame said he would be the one calling me if I got in. I put his number in my cell phone, which is a 330 number, the area code for Canton.

I took a deep breath and said, "Well, maybe it's not going to happen this year." I looked down at the phone and the area code was 714, a California area code. Now I'm thinking, it's probably a reporter. After the third ring, I reached down and picked it up.

It was Dave Baker, who is now the president of the Hall of Fame. He said, "Ray? I'm Dave Baker, President of the Hall of Fame. I personally wanted to make this call to you and let you know that you are now a member of the Class of 2014." I said, "Dave, you're kidding me aren't you?" I asked him three times before it hit me. You wait all these years and when the phone call comes and you don't know whether to really accept it or not.

My legs got weak and I just kind of sat back in the chair, trying to let it soak in. It took about a week to a week and a half before it really soaked in. It was after I got back home. Now it's a reality. I'm in there. It's hard to explain how it feels being placed in the Hall of

Fame beside all of the other football legends. That's the final game. There are no more records to set. There are no more games, championships, or Super Bowls to win. The Hall of Fame is where we sit forever. I am proud to be part of that.

When I got back to Southern Miss, I spoke to some fans at a Meet and Greet held during halftime of a basketball game. I told them, as I tell everybody I talk to, even though my name will be enshrined in the Hall of Fame, this is for all of you. You are the ones who stood behind me. My supporters and friends kept the push going to get me in. I said, "It's for you, it's technically mine but it's not mine. It's ours."

I'm really proud to be the first one from Southern Miss to go into the Hall Of Fame. I bleed black and gold, black and silver. I'm going to help Southern Miss. It's going to be a great boost to Southern Miss from the standpoint of recognition too.

Brett Favre
I was a player at Southern Miss before Brett Favre played there. I taught Brett everything he needed for three years. I was a volunteer coach at Southern Miss Brett's last years there. I knew then what everybody knows now—how great he was going to be and how much of a competitor he is. But, I would never let him know that. He always wanted to wear my Super Bowl ring and I said, "Well, Brett, what do you want it for? He said, "Well, me and a couple of the guys we're going down to such and such a place." I said, "You're not going with my ring, and you're not taking my 4x4 either."

He was a great kid; still is. I don't see him very often around here. He's kind of like me. He does his thing and stays on the west side of town, and I'm on my south side of town. We run into each other once in a while but I don't bother him. I don't really want to bother him. He's been there, he's done that, and now it's time for him to sit back and relax and enjoy life. That's what I do. I want to do what I want to do. Some of the things that I haven't done I want to do now. I'm just being myself.

Raiders Who Should Be In the Hall Of Fame

One of the objectives now is to start campaigning for Tom Flores and a bunch of other Raiders that need to be in the Hall Of Fame. We've got Cliff Branch, Jim Plunkett, and a ton of deserving Raiders.

Tom Flores is great and he should be in there. He was very intelligent. He was John Madden's offensive coordinator. He had been around a while then he got the opportunity to step forward and be the Head Coach of the Raiders. I knew he was going to be a successful coach. Just the way he was with the players; that was the key to it. He had the player-coach relationship just like John had.

There was no changing. We didn't have to change anything. We just kept the same flow going.

He was a brilliant offensive coach and he was a brilliant head coach. He knew how to handle the players without getting upset and screaming. He just talked about the different problems, what we needed to do, and how we needed to handle things. Once we came to an agreement then we just left it alone and went on. We're going to have a big campaign for a lot of those guys.

1984 Game Against Chicago Bears

Jim Plunkett was on injured reserve. Marc Wilson was our starting quarterback and got hurt. Then we had to bring in Dave Humm, who we drafted years before out of Nebraska. Of course they had me. That was a very brutal and a bloody game because Jim McMahon got hurt. Shoot, we were falling on both sides of the ball like flies. It looked like the MASH unit. They were taking the army cot out there and carrying players off the field. Dave Humm got knocked out. Marc was already in the locker room because [I think] he had hurt his thumb or something on the helmet of somebody. Head Coach Tom Flores, already had me get ready. We were discussing what play to call, and of course, Marc came back out. I had one foot on and one foot off; you know what I'm saying?

That defense made no difference to me. I'd have given it my best. Heck, I might have got knocked out too who knows. We had other objectives to worry about then. We were going to roll that pocket, man, and give me time to throw that ball.

Stickum
It wasn't only Lester Hayes using stickum. Fred Biletnikoff used it too. Mark van Eeghen was the worst, in my opinion. After running the ball, the ball would still be stuck to his chest it had so much Stickum on it.

They took lighter fluid and washed the ball down after every play because they had so much pine tar on it. Every once in a while they would miss a spot and for of my fingers would always touch that spot when I got ready to release the ball. One day I said, "Mark, would you get away from me? Go on down to the other end where you belong. That's where the running backs are. Let me stay up here by myself, man." It's like the wind blowing pollen; that stuff gets blown all over you.

It didn't bother me that much. That's what they wanted to do, and I let them do it. Lester did kind of abuse it a little bit, though. It looked like he was having some kind of seizure when it was dripping out from under his helmet. Freddy used a whole jar of that pine tar stuff before every game. No wonder they could catch the balls.

Faking A Punt
We always had an audible to fake a punt if the opportunity was there, by the look of the defense. They would always say on the sideline when we went out, just be alert. What that means is if the return team had a certain look with a certain player somewhere then the option would be there. We ran a couple. We ran a couple and threw a couple. You don't want to do it too much because it becomes too obvious. Teams look at those films and they say wait a minute now, they don't normally do this but there's a chance there might.

One year, I think it was a Monday night football game against Seattle at the Kingdome; the Seattle end guy was real quick off the corner. He had just come off the corner and just laid himself out trying to block the punt.

The ball was somewhere around midfield and Tom Flores said, "Look, if he's sitting out there and you see that, go ahead and catch the ball, and go through your routine and let him lay out." I said, "Okay." Man, I was excited. I was ready to go. Sure enough, I look over there pre-snap and he had his weight forward on his down hand, which told me he's coming. The ball was snapped and I took my time a little bit. I took about a step forward, and sure enough he laid out trying to block it and I pulled it back in. Hey, I made 25 yards on that run. I'd have still been running if the edge of the field hadn't got so close to me.

Photograph copyright Associated Press

Chapter 5

Jack Youngblood

> College:
> Florida
>
> Career History:
> Los Angeles Rams (1971–1984)
>
> 2001 Inductee Pro Football Hall Of Fame

College Choice:
I had only one opportunity to go and play college football. Florida State was 25 to 28 miles from my backdoor, and they had no interest in me. In fact, Bill Parcells was scouting for Florida State at that time and made a stop at my high school. He told my coach, "That kid will never play college football."

We won the Class B state championship. We were cheering and carrying on, celebrating on the field, when a gentleman grabbed me by the elbow. I turned and looked at him not knowing who in the world he was. He said, "How would you like to play football for the University of Florida?" I said, "Let me think about it. Yes sir." It didn't take me long to figure out that might be my only opportunity to play college football.

I was a center and middle linebacker in high school. During the first game of my senior year, I think I had 45 yards in holding penalties in the first half. That's the last time I touched a football on the offensive side.

Florida State University was in my backyard, so I kind of followed them and knew what was going on. I didn't follow Florida when I was in high school that much. I knew that they had an historic program down there, the oldest program in the state. I was thinking that maybe I would get the opportunity to stay at home and play in Tallahassee for Florida State. Anytime Bill Parcells and I run into each other at social events, he tells the story about not recommending me as a player for Florida State.

Position Change In College
Once I got to Florida they looked at me as this 6'4", 205-pound kid and said, "He's got some room to grow. We got an All-American middle linebacker we just signed in Mike Kelley. Let's see if we can make him into a defensive lineman."

It hurt my feelings at first because I thought that I was going to be the next great middle linebacker for the University of Florida. I loved to play, loved to control the game, and all of the signals. Then you become one of the big and ugly and you've got to put your hand on the ground and get into the real mix of it in the pit. I walked around with a fat lip for about two or three weeks. I realized that if I was going to have the opportunity to play, I needed to make the most of it.

College Coaches
I had Doug Dickey as coach for one year, my senior year. In 1969, we went to the Gator Bowl and beat Tennessee. Doug became our head coach and coach Ray Graves was just the fulltime athletic director at that point.

It was a change that somewhat upset the applecart a little bit for the football team. We didn't quite understand the change because we loved coach Graves. He was like a father to us. I mean we really did love him. Then Doug came in with a different philosophy. At first he was not nearly as personable. It seemed like he didn't want relationships with the players. I don't know why he didn't come in and embrace us, especially the seniors who were going to be the foundation of his football team.

Teammates John Reaves and Carlos Alvarez
They were superstars my junior year. We got to practice against them and you could see that we had some talent there. We had talent at quarterback, wide receiver, and running back, all sophomores.

There were a couple offensive linemen who were pretty good too. We could see that we had some talent to work with.

NFL Draft

I think it seemed as though there was some divine intervention going on. In 1971, the draft wasn't publicized like it is today. I didn't know that I was going to be drafted in the first round. My line coach, Jack Thompson, told me that I might get drafted in the 10th - 12th round. I think there were 16 or 17 rounds back then. He said, "You'll probably have the opportunity to go to summer camp with a team."

Draft day came and I wasn't expecting anything. In fact, I had already been to Georgia and accepted a job at a bank. I was preparing to move on to my next job after graduation in June. Low and behold, the Teletype started going off and I saw Jim Plunkett, Dan Pastorini, John Riggins, and all those boys come off with the first 10 or 12 picks. I was sitting and all of a sudden one of the boys at the newspaper said, "There's a phone call for you." I said, "Who in the world is calling me down here?" He said, "It's the Los Angeles Rams." All I could think was, "What?"

I have a series of pictures of that moment where I have my hand over the receiver. I was asking the people I was with, "Who is the coach?" I had no idea who the man calling me from Los Angeles was on the other line. In 1970, we didn't get to see much Rams football in Gainesville.

Tommy Prothro, the Rams coach said, "Youngblood, we're going to draft you." I was thinking to myself, thank you very much coach. As I was talking to Tommy on the phone, I saw on the Teletype, "First round, 20th pick, University of Florida, Jack Youngblood." The words over the telephone didn't seem real. Seeing it in print, you think oh my goodness. There was a whole different world I was about to step into.

I had no idea what it would be like. I had heard about the Fearsome Foursome, so I started doing some reading about the guys. I saw stuff about Deacon Jones and Merlin Olsen. Rosey Grier and Lamar Lundy had already moved on. Coy Bacon was there along with two or three different right tackles. I thought I was a left defensive end, and I wanted to know who was in that position ahead of me. I discovered it was Deacon Jones. I didn't think I'd make the football team. In fact, I thought it might be a short trip. I kept my contacts with the bank because I did not know how long me I'd be with the Rams. Fortunately, I got there and by the grace of God, both Merlin and Deacon put their arms around me during training camp and said, "Son, you can play. We're going to teach you how to play our style," and they did.

I was playing behind Deacon that first year. He got injured and I had to fill his shoes. Not only did I have to fill the shoes of Deacon, I also had a responsibility to Merlin. I was playing with two of the best that ever played the game, and I had a responsibility to them to play up to that level. Certainly I didn't play up to that level, but I held my own and didn't hurt the football team.

Rams Trade Deacon Jones

During the offseason before my second year, I was in Orlando with my family. We took a trip to Disney World. We were watching the news in our room when we heard that Deacon Jones was traded from the Los Angeles Rams to the San Diego Chargers.

I thought did I just hear that right? I said, "Whoa, wait a minute here. Now what?" I was on the phone for the next couple of days trying to figure out what was going on, and what position I'd be playing. Tommy Prothro tried his best not to let me be the left defensive end. He tried everything. For whatever reason he just did not like me.

Deacon Jones Head Slap

Deacon Jones taught me the head slap. We used it for another four or five years, I think. Everybody thinks that's a malicious act, but it's not. It's not intended to hurt anyone. It's intended to turn the opponents head. It makes his eyes blink so he can't see you. He can't react to you at that moment. You make your move when he's got his head turned, or you made him blink. Actually, you could fake it and get the same effect. The offensive linemen hated it. They would come out almost in a boxing stance so they could block your left hook. It was funny. I got cussed at several times. Offensive linemen did not like that little maneuver.

Acting Career

I tried a little bit of acting. I did some cameos during the off seasons. I was on television a couple of times. When I retired, I got a call from Billy Friedkin. He wanted me to be a character in his TV movies.

I did two movies, one that spring and the other the next spring. I didn't like the undisciplined part of it. They're never on time. I know you have to practice and rehearse like in sports, but the timing of the things took so long. It was never sharp and to the minute. Coach Chuck Knox used to say, "You're on my time. When I say 8:00, I mean 7:55. Don't be late for anything." That's not the nature of show business.

Freddie Dryer and Merlin Olsen were natural at it. I wasn't a natural. Freddie actually went to acting classes during the season. He was looking forward to being an actor, as was Merlin. Merlin was a natural as a commentator for the ballgames, and that turned into acting as Father Murphy and on Little House on the Prairie.

Playing With A Broken Leg

It's not that I don't like the fact I did this, it just seems like people always go back to the fact that I suffered through the pain to compete and contribute to my football team. That's what it was all about. It wasn't because I was this big, ugly, mean, tough character. I wanted to play and if I could, I was going to contribute to the football team. The coaches trusted me enough that I would not go out on that football field and be a detriment to the team. If I couldn't play and I didn't play up to my level, I was probably 20% off. To this day, I still think that maybe if circumstances had been different, we might have won Super Bowl XIV.

Adjustment From 4-3 To 3-4 Defense

I hated it. It was absolutely not one of my skills. I played at 250 pounds. You play the 3-4 straight up the field. You play the 4-3 from an angle. You take advantage of position in the 4-3; you take away the running game and the vertical running game.

In the 3-4 all you're doing is mass on mass. You're pushing an offensive lineman who's trying to push you. You're trying to push him backward and he's trying to push you backward. That's not the philosophy of the 4-3. I couldn't play the 3-4. I felt it was the wrong concept, but I wasn't the coach then.

To this day, every time I see former Rams Head Coach John Robinson I say, "You're the reason I didn't play three more years." I couldn't play the 3-4.

Decision To Retire
I think that after you've had the success that I was fortunate enough to have, deciding to retire is as big of a decision as deciding to get married. You have a relationship with your career and what you've established. The reward is being successful, being good, and being able to work at your craft. The decision to retire was a huge, huge one.

What really drove me was that I knew I had a job. There was no question that I was going to work in the front office. I had blown out L5-S1 in my back in the Tampa Bay game the year before. I had trained the entire offseason to see if I could come back from the injury. I came back and was fine.

In my mind, I question whether I could play at the level that I wanted from a physical perspective, for the full season. I did not want to play and then five games into the season, injure my back and get put on injured reserve. If I was going to play, I was going to play from game one to game sixteen, and then into the playoffs.

I did not want to go into the season thinking that something may go wrong some place along the way, although that's the mindset you start with every year. After 14 seasons, you realistically wonder if you can play the 3-4 defense being 34-years-old, the same way you know that you can play the 4-3. That is why I had to make the decision, and it was a tough one.

Best Players
One of the best players I've ever seen play was my teammate, Nolan Cromwell. He was one of the most athletic players who ever stepped on the field. Unfortunately, he got hurt too. He blew out his knee.

In today's game, Adrian Peterson is a pretty good football player. Some of these big, tall receivers are fantastic athletes. There's no question about that. I enjoy watching them. I enjoy watching not so much what they're doing, but how they do it. Adrian Peterson is so smooth. He's going in one direction, and the next minute he's turned 90 degrees, and going in a different direction.

It was a pleasure sitting on the sideline watching Eric Dickerson play too. He was one of those players that didn't look like he was going as fast as he was. He loved to touch the football. I like to see a player who wants to play, and be on the field, a guy who doesn't want to come off the field.

One time the coach sent somebody out there to replace Eric, and I saw Eric wave him off. He wanted to touch the football. That's the difference with the game today. I believe there are a lot of players who don't have that attitude.

Toughest Offensive Lineman Faced
There are three of them—Dan Dierdorf, Ron Yary, and Rayfield Wright. They're all in the Hall with me. I knew they were going to bring out the best in me because I was playing against the best. Gene Washington is another one I remember. He has not gotten the recognition I believe he should have. He was a nightmare for me. He just wouldn't go away. He was a shadow and he was a big shadow at that.

Waiting To Get Inducted Into Pro Football Hall Of Fame
I was the Susan Lucci of pro football. I kept getting nominated but never elected. I was nominated ten times. There was nothing I could do about it. All I could do was hope that at some point, the voters would recognize that I had a career that qualified for the Pro Football Hall Of Fame.

When I got elected into the Hall Of fame, it was one of those surreal moments. I thought, really, after all this time? Now? The monkey is off my back. It was a shining moment.

Georgia Frontiere

The players all had to sit back for a while and see how much influence Georgia Frontiere was going to have on the management side following her husband's death. We didn't know if she going to try and follow Carroll Rosenbloom's way. Carroll loved us. He was at practice every chance he had. He'd fly his helicopter down and land it on the field.

We didn't know what kind of influence she would have on the team, or if she possessed the same desire he had, to be around us. It would have been difficult to have her in the locker room. We didn't know how that was going to work. We had to wait and see.

She loved us. She did not surround herself with people that really wanted to win. The key to success in any endeavor is having people who are smarter than you, around you.

I wasn't convinced that those who were giving her advice really wanted to win. They wanted to continue to be a valuable franchise but there's a difference in that and really having a drive to win a championship.

University Of Florida & Gatorade

The Florida players were the guinea pigs. The first Gatorade was horrible. One of the inventors, Dr. Robert Cade, used to stir it up in a steel washtub.

We were practicing and it was hot as blue blazes, as it often gets in Gainesville. We came off the field and Mike Kelly, our middle linebacker, reached down and grabbed a can out of the ice. He threw it back and fainted. He just went down.

We were all looking and thinking, "Damn. I'm not drinking one of those." I don't think it was the Gatorade as much as it was the cold. I think the cold got him. We were the guinea pigs for it. It changed the whole concept of training, how to hydrate the body, and what it takes to hydrate the body. There was real science behind it.

In my high school days, it's a wonder half of us didn't die. I mean we were literally taking salt tablets. Then for the discipline part of it, we couldn't have water more than twice during practice. That's how we were conditioned. We adapted, but looking back, it could have been tragic.

Favorite Play

There was one play in Gainesville. We're playing Georgia and the game was close. They were driving the football on us. They were inside our 10-yard line. I literally remember saying we've got to take the football away from them. They ran a running play right at me and a guy got both hands around the ball. I literally reached in and snatched the ball out of his hands. That turned the ballgame around and we beat Georgia. That's one play that stands out.

Another time, I intercepted Jimmy Hart's outlet pass. It happened in the 1975 Divisional Playoff Game. I went 45 yards and scored. I knew I could run that far and I knew that I was not going to get caught by Dan Dierdorf or Jimmy Hart. I would have never lived that down. That was a good moment.

Los Angeles Ram Jack Youngblood recovering the Dallas Cowboys fumble in the NFC championship game in Los Angeles on Sunday, Jan. 7, 1979. Tony Dorsett and Pat Donovan of the Cowboys couldn't get their hands on the loose ball. Photograph copyright Associated Press

Chapter 6

Franco Harris

> College: Penn State
>
> Career History:
> Pittsburgh Steelers (1972–1983)
> Seattle Seahawks (1984)
>
> 1990 Inductee Pro Football Hall Of Fame

College Choice
When I was being recruited, I visited ten colleges. I visited Notre Dame, Ohio State, Michigan, Syracuse, Pittsburgh, and Cornell. All of them were good schools, but in the end I had to make a decision. It was a tough decision, and went with my gut. In the end, my gut told me Penn State, and boy did that gut feeling work out well.

A lot of times that's what you have to go by. We really weren't a college family. My mother and father didn't go to college; none of my relatives went to college. There was pressure, but as I mentioned, my gut said Penn State and my gut was right.

Joe Paterno
Joe Paterno was out on that field everyday. If you were on the other side of the field running a play, all of a sudden you would hear from way across the field, "Hey Harris, what are …" You know what I mean. You wouldn't even think that he'd be watching you. You'd think wow, how did he see that? He was really aware of what was happening on the football field. He went on to build great programs there, and have one of the highest graduation rates for football players in the country. It was just an incredible experience.

Lydell Mitchell

With Lydell Mitchell and me in the backfield at Penn State, there was a great balance. We both had a lot of opportunity to show our talents and to help the team. There really wasn't a competition where I wanted it more than him or he wanted it more than me. We ran in spurts of "Hey, who was doing well?" Our senior year, Lydell had a phenomenal season. I believe he scored 26 touchdowns and set a new NCAA record. I believe he held that record until Barry Sanders broke it.

My sophomore year, I had a great year. We complemented each other very well, because I was in the fullback position and he was in the halfback position. It worked so well that both of us were drafted into the NFL the same year.

Joe Paterno's History Of Wanting Recruits To Change Their Positions Like Tony Dorsett

Joe Paterno didn't ask me to change positions from high school to college. I know you hear many stories about that happening with Joe Paterno. Joe Paterno wanted to make Jim Kelly a linebacker. In the end, I like it when things work out well for people. As we know, Tony Dorsett ended up going to University of Pittsburgh and being an All-American, Heisman Trophy winner, and Pro Football Hall of Famer.

Look at Jim Kelly. They wanted to make him a linebacker, now he's in the Pro Football Hall of Fame. I'm glad those guys made the decision to say, "Hey, you know what? I want to stick with my position," and I think that worked out well for both. I have to say there were many times when the Penn State staff would think that a player would be better at a certain position, and they would make that switch. Once again, that player turned out to be an All-American at Penn State in that new position, and went into the NFL in that new position. Sometimes it works and sometimes it doesn't.

Pittsburgh Steelers Drafting You and Not Lydell Mitchell

I was surprised. I definitely had no inclination that I was going to be drafted in the first round or by the Pittsburgh Steelers. As a matter of fact, I had never thought about playing in the NFL. During my senior year in college people were telling me, "Franco you are going to be drafted," and it kind of surprised me. It was a complete shock and a surprise that I was the first running back taken.

Coaches

I had a great high school coach in Bill Gordon. During my journey in football from high school, college, and the pros, I had the right coach at each level. I can't tell you how lucky I was to have great coaches, at each level. Coaches need different talents, different skills, and have to handle players differently at each level. In each level I was at, I had a great coach and great teams.

Pittsburgh Steelers Pro Football Hall Of Famers

The Pittsburgh Steelers have nine Pro Football Hall of Famers and I feel that a couple of guys are on the bubble, like L.C. Greenwood and Donnie Shell. We were so well balanced in every area; it was incredible. When you think about offense, we have a Hall of Fame quarterback, two Hall of Fame receivers, a Hall of Fame lineman, and me at running back. You look and say, "Wow!" That covers everything offensively. You look at our defense and you say, "Wow." We have a Hall of Fame defensive lineman, two Hall of Fame linebackers, and a Hall of Fame defensive back. You look at all those different segments of offense and defense and it just blows your mind. We had Hall of Famers in each segment, which helped us win four Super Bowls.

Mike Webster set the tone for the lineman, but for the offense, it was Terry Bradshaw. He was the quarterback. Mike Webster was an unbelievable guy and a great leader on and off the field with our lineman, and it was great to see because our lineman really jelled. That's what really made things happen for me; it started with the line.

Controlling Players

There were not a lot of people that needed control. You don't win four Super Bowls with things being out of control. When you look at our defense and with our guys playing with the intensity that they had, I guess you would say they'd be out of control sometimes with some things that they would do. When you have two guys like "Mean Joe" Greene and Jack Lambert, phew! Man!

You didn't worry about them being out of control. You liked it as a matter of fact.

Steelers Practice
Practice was very physical. The defense wasn't allowed to touch me but believe me, they wanted to. It frustrated a lot of those guys. I just loved frustrating those guys, because then they would take it out on the opponents running back come Sunday.

Favorite Super Bowl
The Super Bowl that's dearest to me is the first one, which was down in New Orleans. It was just so unbelievable realizing that, "Wow! We made it to the Super Bowl, and our location is New Orleans." It's an unbelievable town, and to be there, wow! That first one was pretty incredible. It was so good, we said, "Hey let's do it again. Let's do it again. Let's do it again." We enjoyed going to the Super Bowl. That was a big goal of ours every year.

Immaculate Reception
The Immaculate Reception has gotten bigger, what can I say? When you look at the whole situation, it still seems so unbelievable. The circumstances, the timing, what it meant, all those factors added together it just keeps getting bigger and bigger over the years. It's almost 43 years later, and that play is still considered the number one NFL play of all time. It makes you feel special. It still brings recognition to our team and was the start of our incredible run.

Great Running Back In Football History
I appreciate when people say I'm in the category of great running backs, but to me Jim Brown will always be number one. He was number one since I was in high school. I was always a big Jim Brown fan and of what he accomplished in those days.

How can you not be a Walter Payton fan? That guy was so amazing, incredible, and extremely talented in many ways. You have to rank those guys number one and two as far as I'm concerned. You also have Barry Sanders, Gale Sayers, and Emmitt Smith, all great guys who did unbelievable things.

I was in a system that worked great for me. I was on a team that was great for me. With that, I was able to accomplish some things personally, but beyond that, I was able to be in four Super Bowls. Being in four Super Bowls, is more important than individual rushing accomplishments. When I look at the whole picture, we were balanced offensively, which helped in our greatness along with our defense. The scheme that the Steelers used at that time was perfect for me, and allowed me to show my talent.

Pro Football Hall Of Fame Induction
That was an incredible feeling. I look back on my career, the Super Bowls, Pro Bowls, and individual accomplishments—what could be better than that? When you put that Gold Jacket on, phew! It's like the whole history and the whole universe of football just went inside of you. It's an awesome, awesome feeling.

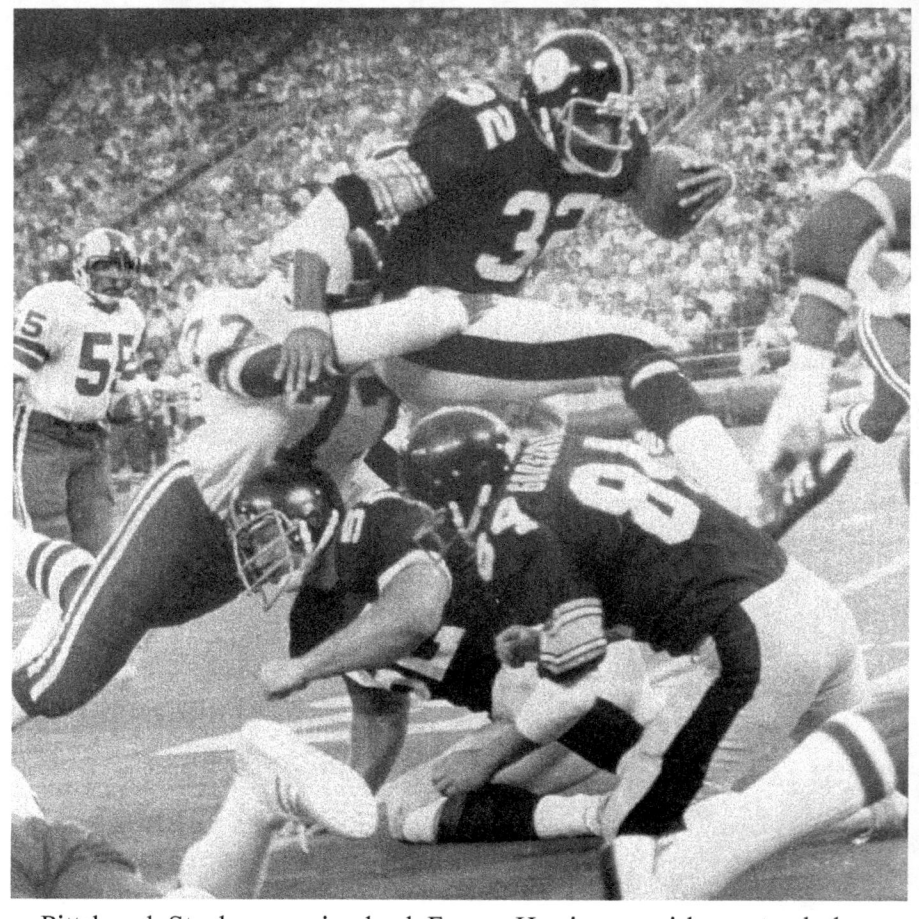

Pittsburgh Steelers running back Franco Harris goes airborne to elude Buffalo Bills left end Ben Williams. Photograph copyright Associated Press

Chapter 7

Joe DeLamielleure

> College:
> Michigan State
>
> Career History:
> Buffalo Bills (1973–1979)
> Cleveland Browns (1980–1984)
> Buffalo Bills (1985)
>
> 2003 Inductee Pro Football Hall Of Fame

College Choice
I'm from Detroit, and I wanted to go to the University Of Michigan. I was Bo Schembechler's first recruit at Michigan. Then I wanted to go to Notre Dame. Notre Dame coach Ara Parseghian's defensive coach was Johnnie Ray, who coached both of my high school coaches. I was going to go there because of Johnnie Ray. I'm the ninth of ten kids, so obviously we were very Catholic. My dad said, "You go to Michigan State because Duffy Daugherty is Catholic and I want you to be coached by a Catholic." That's how I ended up going to Michigan.

My dad said, "That Parseghian guy is a phony. He's not even Catholic and he's coaching at Notre Dame." I said "Alright dad." At that time you did what your parents told you to do, no matter what. I did what he told me and that was a good move for me. I loved it there. I had great friends and attended a great school.

Duffy Daugherty
Duffy Daugherty taught me a lot. He would always tell the guys at the beginning of the year that it takes three bones to play football—a backbone, a wishbone, and the most important bone of all, a funny

bone. I lived my life like that; you have to have a backbone, you got to wish for things, and last, but not least, you have to have a good sense of humor. Life can be kind of humorous.

Being Drafted By Buffalo Bills

Paul Seymour, who also grew up in Detroit, and I were both number one draft picks of the Buffalo Bills in 1973. The Bills drafted Reggie McKenzie, who's also from Detroit, the year before us. Jim Ringo, who was our offensive line coach, had played center for the Green Bay Packers when they ran the famous Green Bay sweeps. He said we were going to run the Green Bay sweeps just like he did in Green Bay with Jim Taylor and Paul Hornung. We had Jim Braxton and O.J. Simpson as our running backs, and we did really well. He put the team together to do just that. We had two guards who could really run, Reggie and me. We were pretty quick for that era.

Transition From College Game To NFL

Jim Ringo was a great coach. I played in the Senior Bowl for the Buffalo Bills' coaches. I was comfortable going to Buffalo when they drafted me, because Coach Ringo coached me the week of the Senior Bowl. When I got to Buffalo, the coach said we weren't going to throw the ball a lot. Four out of five of the offensive linemen had played in the Big 10, where all the teams primarily ran the ball. Mike Montler played at Colorado, but he was from Columbus, Ohio. The rest of us all played in the Big 10—Donnie Green, Dave Foley, Reggie McKenzie, and me. Coach Ringo would say he had a great play, and we would just run it over and over. Nobody could stop us.

O.J. Simpson's and My Head Size

O.J. Simpson and I had fat heads. O.J. has a bigger head than I do. I used to tell people, "All the better to block you with," like the Big Bad Wolf. It was a different game back then. You hit with your head. If you didn't put your face on guys and block with your head, you weren't going to be in the league very long. One of the first things they'd say is, "That guy is a wuss. He won't put his face in there."

The next thing you know, that guy was gone. We were the guinea pigs for the current players right now. We had head slaps, now there are no head slaps; we had the wedge, now there's no wedge, and there's no chop block either. We used to practice every day on AstroTurf, which is basically colored concrete.

O.J. was embarrassed about his head size. I heard when they made his bust for the Hall Of Fame the girl that measured his head said, "Oh my God!" and the guy who was making the bust said, "Don't ever say that to him. He is really conscientious about his head size." If you watched him during his trial, he was always moving his head so the camera didn't get a good shot of it.

Favorite Moment
I'm the ninth of ten kids. When I was born my dad was 43-years-old and my mother was 41. No one went to college except me. I thought to myself, my mom and dad are sitting in Detroit watching this game saying, "Holy cow! My son is starting in the NFL." I was thrilled they were able to see me. You see, my parents had the guts to have kids when they were in their 40s. They made us go to school. They sacrificed to send us to Catholic school so we had discipline and learned what to do, and how to treat people. My mother always said, "Treat the President like the janitor, and the janitor like the President, and you'll be successful in life." My biggest thrill was just being able to start in the NFL.

Joe Greene
Nobody wanted to go against Joe Greene. When I flew into Pittsburgh, I would get butterflies thinking about Joe Greene; he was a great player. We did the smart thing, we ran away from him. We'd run sweeps and plays like that. O.J. had over 188 yards rushing in one game against the Steelers. We rushed for 303 yards in a 1975 game against the Steelers. Joe Greene was frustrated a lot in that game because he didn't get to pass rush much.

Photograph copyright Associated Press

Chapter 8

John Hannah

> College:
> Alabama
>
> Career History:
> New England Patriots (1973–1985)
>
> 1991 Inductee Pro Football Hall Of Fame

<u>College Choice</u>
My dad grew up pretty rough. He was a sharecropper. My parents met when my dad was in Naval Preflight School. After he got out of the Navy, one of his good Navy friends talked Dad into going to college. Dad said, "Who'd take me?"

His friend was a big Clemson fan so Dad went to Clemson and said, "I got half of a VA scholarship, but if ya'll give me a half football scholarship, give me a bed to sleep in, and three meals a day, I'd love to come play football for ya'll." They said, "Herb, we can give you the half scholarship and we can give you a bed to sleep in, but we only give you
two meals a day."

Dad went down to the University of Alabama and there was a guy there who had coached Dad when he was in the Naval Preflight School at Georgia, Hank Crisp. Hank basically agreed to Dad's terms. For the price of one meal Dad went to the University of Alabama. Not only that, my Uncle Bill played there, I played there, my little brother Charlie played there, and my brother David played there. For the price of one meal, they got five Hannahs! While he was at Alabama, Dad continued dating Mom. After graduating, my mother was a teacher and a professor at the University of Georgia.

My dad gave me no choice of which college to attend. My uncle was coaching at Cal State Fullerton and said, "If you get to thinking about some other place beside Alabama, you ought to think about Southern Cal." I said, "Okay." I ended up talking to Dad about it and Dad said, "That's great. You can go to any school you want to, but you just got to worry about where you're going to eat supper when you come home." I guess it was pretty well decided.

Bear Bryant
I had a high school coach who played for Bear Bryant and said it best. He said he wouldn't take a million dollars for the experience, but you couldn't pay him a million dollars to go through it again. Coach Bryant was very tough. He demanded a whole lot from his players. When I was there, he basically ruled by fear.

Bear Bryant Said John Hannah Greatest Lineman He Ever Coached
The last time I talked to Coach Bryant was when I was in college. We were getting ready to play Texas in the Cotton Bowl. It was the first day of meetings. I had been getting a lot of letters from the NFL. I went up to Coach Bryant and said, "I don't want to talk about this now because I don't want you to worry about getting my mind off the game, but the draft is in January. When this game's over, I was hoping I could come and talk to you and you might advise me in hiring an agent." Coach Bryant looked me square in the eye and said, "John, you ain't good enough to need no damn lawyer." I think that's what he really thought of me, not what he said later on!

NFL Draft
I didn't think I'd go where I was drafted. I thought I'd be about a second or third round pick. I am short for a lineman at almost 6'3". Everybody thought I was too short.

Even though I am only 6'3" I have a 37-inch sleeve length, which means I'm probably the only guy who can scratch his ankle without bending over. That abnormality in my physique, allowed me to keep the pass rush away from me, once I finally learned how to use it.

The New England Patriots Head Coach, Chuck Fairbanks, realized that and was willing to take a chance on me. Basically, he took a lot of ridicule for drafting me so high.

Joining Patriots

The Patriots weren't much of an organization. It was like a step down from the University of Alabama. I was used to playing in Birmingham in front of 80,000 people in college. I went to the Patriots and their stadium only held about 50-55,000 people. When we played the Giants at home, there were more New York Giants fans than there were Patriot fans. The facilities were just awful compared to what we had at Alabama. It was really a step down. I was shocked that it was so bad.

Chuck Fairbanks

Chuck Fairbanks was the best coach I ever had. He wasn't intimidated by anybody. He surrounded himself with people who were smarter than him and he listened to them. He didn't have a big ego. He had great organizational skills—probably the best I've ever seen. He just had an eye for talent, not only in players but also in coaches.

He listened to his players. Even if he disagreed with his players, he'd listen to them and take their thoughts into consideration when he made decisions. However, he'd eventually do what he wanted. He liked offense, which was something unusual for me. With Coach Bryant, offense for him was a necessary evil. Coach Fairbanks liked offense. That suited me fine.

Patriots Drafts

The 1973 Patriots draft was a great draft. Sam Cunningham, and Darryl Stingley, and I were first round picks. It was reinforcing to play with both of them. I think that the 1973 and 1976 drafts were probably the best drafts that the Patriots ever really had. In 1976, we drafted Mike Haynes, Tim Fox, and Pete Brock in the first round. That was a pretty good draft, too. We drafted Steve Nelson in 1974, and drafted Steve Grogan in 1975.

Darryl Stingley

Darryl Stingley was a great player. As a matter of fact, he was really just coming into his own when he got hurt. Not only was a great ball player, he was a really good human being. It was a devastating blow for our team. Coach Fairbanks did what he always does. He went out and traded for Harold Jackson. Harold Jackson came in and filled in pretty good. We had Harold Jackson on one side and Stanley Morgan on the other at the wide receiver position. It was pretty good. Coach Fairbanks had an eye for talent. He knew how to bring it in.

Russ Francis

We had a real good tight end in Russ Francis. When Russ wanted to strap it on, there wasn't a better tight end in the league.

Toughest Defensive Linemen Faced

Joe Klecko and Howie Long were the two toughest all-around ball players I ever played against. There are a few others. Doug English and Mike Reid were really good, too.

Alan Page and Randy White were awfully good pass rushers. Gary "Hands" Johnson wasn't too bad either. He played for San Diego. William "The Fridge" Perry, was like trying to move a side of a warehouse, he was so darn big.

Jim Plunkett

Jim Plunkett was a great guy and a great quarterback. The problem was we were running four- and five-man patterns, which meant that the quarterback needed to get the ball off in 2.8 to 3 seconds. Jim was pretty slow, but he had an arm. He could hit the eye of a needle at 50 yards. So what happened was, he went to the San Francisco 49ers and had the same results. The reason why? They were running four- and five-man patterns.

When he got to the Raiders, they were running three- or four-man patterns, which meant they always had another guy in there to help block. That basically bought him another second. Now you're talking about 3.5 to 4 seconds to get rid of the ball. When Jim found that extra half a second, he tore people up. He was that kind of a quarterback. He fit into that scheme.

His talent finally got displayed. He just didn't fit into that quick release type of offense we had. With our offense you had to get it back, set, and throw. When he could sit back there in that rocking chair with the Raiders, he tore people up.

Steve Grogan

Steve Grogan probably was the best quarterback I've ever played with. He was a great quarterback. It was a travesty the way his career ended. A lot of the coaches and assistant coaches who came in afterward tried to put faith in another quarterback that we had drafted. He probably had great skills, but maybe didn't have the courage that Grogan had. The reason being, maybe they felt the owners had invested so much in the draft pick.

Super Bowl XX Against Chicago Bears

The Chicago Bears had a unique defense because the Bears Defensive Coordinator, Buddy Ryan, realized that you could always send one more guy that an offense can block. It gave everybody a lot of headaches until they started figuring it out. They had great talent. Richard Dent was a great pass rusher and Dan Hampton was a great ball player. Steve McMichael used to be with us, but the dumb coaches had traded him away.

That was a great defense. They had great linebackers. They had great defensive backs. That year the only team that beat them was the Miami Dolphins. The reason they beat them was Miami dropped back and they ran what they called turmoil. The quarterback would drop back, everybody would shoot (that's in the blitz), and then Dan Marino would basically roll away from the blitz. That bought him an extra second, so Mark Duper and Mark Clayton were able to get open.

Buddy Ryan said, "I can cover anybody for two seconds man-on-man, and you ain't going to have but two seconds because I'm going blitz more than you can pick up." Don Shula said, "No you can't, because I'm going to roll my quarterback out and you won't get to him in two seconds." The Dolphins were able to beat the Bears that way.

One thing that hurt us in the middle of the week leading up to the Super Bowl there was an emotional letdown for our team. Rumors spread throughout the offense that Steve Grogan was going to be ready to play. The whole offense got excited about it. We were lifted up that Grogan was going to be back.

The coaches came in after a practice one day and said Grogan is ready, but Tony Eason's got the starting nod. I think a lot of the guys basically were let down because of that. I think that hurt us emotionally.

Plus, there were a lot of things going on. There was an article a *Boston Globe* reporter had written regarding drug issues and things like that. Everybody was thinking about that being in the newspaper the day after the game. It was just kind of crazy.

We got there, but we weren't all there when the game was actually played. Not that we could have beat them, but I think we could have probably got it a lot closer.

Leon Gray

Leon Gray and I had the closest of bonds. When they traded Leon away, I was madder than a hornet. That was 1979. I loved Leon. I thought the world of him. It was the worst thing they could have done for our team. It was the worst thing they could have done for Leon. I wasn't happy and I let it be known. I was very, very upset. I was very angry when I found out about it.

Almost Being Traded To Los Angeles Raiders

In '83, I was trying to get traded. Robert Irsay, the Colts owner, had talked to the Sullivans, the owners of the Patriots. The Colts were going to trade John Elway to the Patriots for me and possibly another draft choice. The Patriots wouldn't trade me.

My brother Charlie was with the Tampa Bay Buccaneers. He wanted to stay in Tampa, but wanted to make a little more money. One Friday or Saturday night in Alabama, we were going to a catfish place to eat some catfish and hushpuppies, and Charlie was late. Finally he came in. He was all 'hang dog' (his head was bowed). I said, "What's wrong?" He said, "I've been traded." I said, "Where have you been traded?" He said, "The Raiders." I said, "You sorry son-of-a-gun. You stole my job." He went out to the Raiders. They changed his number to 73, moved him to left guard, and he won the Super Bowl.

Al Davis came up to Charlie and said, "Charlie, you know why we got you, don't you?" Charlie said, "No." He said, "Hell, the Patriots wanted two number one picks for John." He said, "He's good, but he's not worth two number ones. Tampa Bay only wanted a fourth-rounder for you!"

Decision To Retire
I was very good friends with an orthopedic surgeon. In 1977, the Patriots trainer and the doctors basically told me that I had a leg strain. Anyway, it never got better, so when I went to a legitimate orthopedic surgeon, he told me it was actually a tear.

Back then they couldn't do what they could do now. They were going to have to reroute the hamstring to the front of the knee. He said it was only about 50% successful. I went to the orthopedic surgeon and I said, "Here's the deal. If you ever see a situation where you think I could cripple myself for life, I want you to tell me." He said, "All right."

After the Bears game I'd already had both my shoulders operated on. Once that healed up to where I was able to get around a little bit, they decided to work on my knee. I went in for my knee surgery. After I got out, he called me down to his office. He said, "John, you remember what you asked me?" I said, "Yeah." He started telling me about everything and I said, "Well, what does that mean?" He said, "Well, John, I'll tell you. You could play. But if I had another job that I could make a living at, I think I'd do that instead."

So that's what it was. It was my left knee that caused me to end my career. I was hoping I'd get at least three more years in. Because they had lied to me and told me it was a strained ligament instead of a torn one and not let me get it fixed during the season, it cut my career short.

Photograph copyright Associated Press

Chapter 9

Dan Fouts

> College:
> Oregon
>
> Career History:
> San Diego Chargers (1973–1987)
>
> 1993 Inductee Pro Football Hall Of Fame

University of Oregon
Oregon was the only major football program that offered me a scholarship. We had a very good football team at St. Ignatius High School. Eleven of the guys from our 1957 Championship Team received college scholarships. There was a lot of attention given to our team. We won the city title and we had a great running attack. A couple of running backs attended USC. My job basically was to hand the ball off. The Oregon coaches were in attendance at a game where I threw a lot and had some success. Two of the coaches, George Seifert and John Robinson, recruited me because they were from the area.

They were outstanding coaches and I think that goes a long way. Our head coach, Jerry Frei, really put together a great staff. We were underdogs a lot because at the time, there was no limit on the amount of football scholarships a school could offer. In those days, it was difficult to compete with the big schools. We competed as well as we could.

Oregon vs. Missouri Game
We had a screen pass go for a long touchdown and the referee said we had a man illegally down the field. When I look at the tapes all these years later, we still didn't have that man down the field. It was a little home cooking there in Columbia, Missouri. I didn't need to

keep the tape. That play is in my mind with all the other close controversial plays that happened during my career.

NFL Draft

I hadn't heard a word from any team prior to the draft. In those days, there weren't the combines or the 24/7 NFL news coverage. There had been a lot of teams going around working guys out. When the Chargers drafted me, I was completely surprised.

First Training Camp With Chargers

It was great because Johnny Unitas was there and I learned a lot from him during the short time he was on the team with me. He was such a great guy. I don't know why he took a liking to me, but we hung out a little bit and had a couple of cold beers after practice. For a 22-year-old kid to be able to look across the locker room and see Johnny Unitas, it was pretty awesome.

Johnny Unitas Routine Of Throwing To Raymond Berry After Practice

That's pretty much what you've got to do. That is the secret to success, but I think with Johnny Unitas and Raymond Berry, it was like a science. They were so good and they played together for so long. I eventually developed that type of rapport with Charlie Joiner, and then with Kellen Winslow, John Jefferson, and Wes Chandler. If you want to be good on Sundays, you better be good the other six days of the week.

Don Coryell

When Don Coryell came in as coach, our team was in disarray. We had some pretty good talent on the team, but we just couldn't seem to get it together. Don Coryell basically relaxed us a little bit, gave us some good plays, and put in his system. The rest is history. We had the talent of John Jefferson, Kellen Winslow, and Charlie Joiner—three outstanding individuals. They were All-Pros and the offensive came together.

Chargers Receivers

The receivers were dependable. They were all very tough going over the middle and enjoyed playing the game. We had a good time in practice because we were throwing the ball around and the guys were making catches. It's not drudgery. It's upbeat. That's the way we played on Sundays. I describe the four top receivers I had in all different ways. I just knew where Charlie Joiner was going to go every time he ran down the field. He was so reliable. Kellen Winslow set the standard for tight ends because of his versatility, and he could make the most spectacular catches in a crowd, or with one hand. Wes Chandler was a guy who could run to an inside defense if you got him the ball in the right space. I was just the luckiest guy in the world to have four receivers like that.

San Diego Charger Offense Under Don Coryell
It's hard to describe how enjoyable it was to play in Coach Coryell's offense. We would have such a good day of practice on Wednesday when we would practice the game plan. We couldn't wait to get to Sunday because we knew were going to be successful against certain teams and
against certain defensive schemes. Coach Coryell's time, his plan, and the way he coached us, was up-tempo. You hear a lot now about teams and how they practice, but we practiced as fast as we played. I think that really helped.

Our offensive system was based on timing, flooding zones, looking for the two-on-one, and eventually the one-on-none. The receivers all knew that. I was just reading the defense and the receivers were reading at the same time, pretty much every time. If we were on the same page, the defense would dictate to us where the ball would go. It really wasn't a matter of egos or playing favorites. It was really very mature on the part of our receivers knowing that I was not playing favorites. The defense was telling me where to throw the ball.

Toughest Cornerbacks Faced
There were so many good ones in my era. Mike Haynes with Raiders and Louis Wright of the Broncos were great. When I broke into the league, Willie Brown of the Raiders, a Hall of Famer, used to pick me off once a game until I got smart and quit throwing the ball in his direction. Look at the Hall of Famers from that era. Those were the guys I had to face.

Don Coryell's Greatness

I think it was his adaptability, his steadfastness going about things, and his belief that we could win games throwing the ball, and be fearless doing it. The commitment that he had to his system, permeated throughout the team. It gave us all the feeling that we were going to be successful. Any great coach makes sure his team has the confidence to go out and win every Sunday.

Bill Walsh Chargers Offensive Coordinator

I certainly missed Bill Walsh when he left the Chargers. He was in San Diego with me in 1976, Up until that point, I really never had an offense coordinator or quarterback coach of his caliber. He and I had a great rapport. He left after one year because the Chargers decided not to hire him as a head coach. He went up to Stanford and turned that program around and then of course, the 49ers. Walsh meant a lot to my career. He rebuilt my game from the ground up as far as footwork and reading defenses went. Then it all came together two years later when Coryell came to San Diego.

1981 AFC Championship Game

It was windy. I think that was the biggest problem for me. It was cold, but the Bengals played better than we did that day and they handled the weather a little bit better. They deserved to win. We had a rematch the following year in San Diego that we won, but that day they were better than us and you've got to give them credit.

Toughest Defenses Faced

I think teams with great players always gave us problems. Playing against the Raiders was always an adventure. We played Oakland twice a year. Once a team has familiarity with you, it is difficult to come up with new ways to beat them, but the Raiders were great at times. The Steelers obviously, in their hay day, were awesome because of the great players they had.

Decision To Retire

My body told me it was time to retire. You've got to be honest with yourself because you don't want to embarrass yourself. I knew that after 15 years, I had enough and I was anxious to get on with my second career.

Pro Football Hall Of Fame Induction

I was absolutely thrilled. I was with my family when I found out. We were sitting around waiting for the phone to ring. When it did ring, the emotions that I felt … the gratitude of all the people that helped me get where I got … the support from my family and friends, was overwhelming. It's the most humbling experience, even to this day 20 years later, to realize that I am in the Hall of Fame with all these great players. It's an awesome feeling.

It's fun to go back to the Hall Of Fame every year and reminisce with guys about how great we used to be, even if we weren't that great.

Decision To Become A Sportscaster

My dad, Bob Fouts, was the long time voice of the San Francisco 49ers when I was growing up. I spent a lot of time in the broadcast booth with him keeping stats or spotting for him. As a kid, it looked like a really cool way to make a living. Fortunately, when I retired from the Chargers, I had an audition with CBS and it worked out well. I'm going on my 27th year as a sportscaster. It's a great job.

Photograph copyright Associated Press

Chapter 10

Fred Dean

> College:
> Louisiana Tech
>
> Career History:
> San Diego Chargers (1975–1981)
> San Francisco 49ers (1981–1985)
>
> 2008 Inductee Pro Football Hall Of Fame

College Choice
Louisiana Tech was right in my backyard. My grandmother lived a block from the school, so I was able to watch them play. I'd go watch from the top of the hills at the stadium. That's how close it was. I really enjoyed that.

1st Training Camp With San Diego Chargers
My first training camp was interesting. I had to go out and prove myself. It was an experience like I'd never had before. It was different than high school and college because I was playing with actual men. I had to be able to sustain and go through the necessary pressure that comes with football. It was an interesting time for me.

I think that training camp in San Diego had a lot of advantages, but there were also disadvantages. First of all, I was used to the heat in Louisiana. Whenever we went to play in a climate similar to Louisiana, I always seemed to fair pretty well. The weather is great in San Diego. Here in Louisiana it's hot and humid. That's a big difference. It was an advantage to me in so many ways.

Don Coryell Being Named Head Coach of Chargers
I would say Coach Coryell was mostly committed to the offense, but we had real good defensive coaches. They made a difference overall for us. Coach Coryell was more offensive mined and concerned about putting points on the board. When he came to San Diego, our defense got the opportunity to expand and try different things in

order to stop opposing teams' offenses. It was a proven fact to us at that time.

Changing Positions With Chargers
In college, I was a linebacker and defensive tackle. Once I went pro, I was more of a defensive end. I was drafted as a linebacker because of my size. I wanted to play. I wanted to be a down lineman. I guess you could say it panned out for me.

Chargers Defensive Line
We had the defensive linemen in Louie Kelcher, Leroy Jones, Gary "Big Hands" Johnson, even Wilbur Young, and later on Charles Dejurnett. There were a lot of guys who came along that were instrumental in our success. I would say the years that we led the league in sacks, were our more dominant years.

Coach Bill Walsh was in San Diego as an assistant coach for a short time. While he was there, he saw how I put pressure on the quarterback in practice. He liked that. I guess he felt that I could be instrumental to him when he was the head coach with the 49ers.

Practicing Against Dan Fouts
I didn't really go after Dan Fouts. You couldn't hit the quarterback even back then. You would be able to just get close to him and be in his face every now and then. I would make him look at my face and he'd probably get tired of looking at me. The goal for me was to work on my skills. We had great defensive units in San Diego when I first went there. I looked up to the older players because of their skills. I thought maybe I would hone my skills by watching them and practicing with them.

San Diego Chargers Defensive Line With Louie Kelcher & Gary Johnson
We had each other's back and it kind of clicked. The thing is we were very motivated. My thing was always to go after the passer. When you stop the run, you can go after passer at a free pace and normally, you would come out victorious if you were successful.

San Diego Chargers Never Playing In The Super Bowl During His Time

I can't really say why we didn't make it. We had the personnel to have made it there. I know that at the time I was traded, I felt that we had an opportunity. After I got traded to the 49ers, my hope was that we would meet the Chargers in the Super Bowl. We didn't because unfortunately, they had lost to Cincinnati in the playoffs. We had the personnel and game plans to get into the Super Bowl and actually win it, but we weren't able to do that with the Chargers.

Reason For Trade To San Francisco 49ers

It boiled down to a contract dispute; the business aspect of it. I guess that the owner, Mr. Gene Klein, didn't feel that I was deserving of what I was asking for, like John Jefferson wasn't, or the rest of the players he let go. The bottom line is that it panned out pretty good for me.

Trade To 49ers In Mid Season

Coach Walsh had been in San Diego and saw me play. He witnessed me disturb the offense in some shape, form, or fashion. When he brought me to San Francisco, I guess he felt that I was the final link in what he needed to get some things done. I remember the first game I played in was against the Dallas Cowboys. The 49ers hadn't had much success in been beating them.

When I came to the 49ers, Coach Walsh told me that he was concerned about my conditioning and I wouldn't play against the Cowboys that week. I hadn't really played against the Cowboys much prior to joining the 49ers, but I played against the Cowboys that week.

I didn't really have anything to prove. I wanted to advance my skills as far as rushing the quarterback. Being traded was a good thing because Coach Walsh gave me the opportunity to do that.

I left a good quarterback in Dan Fouts. When I first went to the 49ers, Joe Montana and I went to do an autograph session together. We drove together to the session and we had a pretty good chat.

There were a lot of adjustments for me just going to San Francisco. I found that Joe was very cool, and I enjoyed being around him. His humor was really good for me because he made me feel like I was a real part of San Francisco. He was a good guy.

Difference Between Dan Fouts and Joe Montana

Both guys were pretty good quarterbacks. I'll say it like that. When you look at them now, you can see why both of them are in the Hall of Fame. As far as their differences, they were different people with different styles. Joe was much more mobile than Dan. Dan was more of a pocket passer and had great receivers around him. Joe had great receivers, but he was able to get out of the pocket and make things happen. Dan was more of a pocket passer. That was the difference in itself; but they both were good.

Second Game With 49ers Against Rams

I knew that I was a halfway decent. I knew that I could have a big impact in various games. With the guys beside me, Lawrence Pillers, Dwaine Board, Keena Turner, Ronnie Lott, Eric Wright, Dwight Hicks … all those guys made me feel comfortable playing. I had adjusted to the Chargers defensive line, but I just felt at home with those guys. My attitude was to always give other players their due. It was overall a good situation.

Dwight Clark Catch Against Cowboys In NFC Championship Game

It was a great feeling being in San Francisco my first year because that catch caused us to move on deeper into the playoffs. It was an exciting moment for me to see Dwight make that catch. The Dallas defense was doing well and had won a lot of different ways, but the bottom line was the 49ers were destined to be champions. We were sort of the Cinderella team. I think we did things to really surprise people. All along the way, we had something to prove. The great players that we had, Ronnie Lott, Hicks, and all those guys … those DBs set some precedent.

Winning A Super Bowl In First Year With 49ers

It was a place you could very easily fall in love with. It was kind of lonely in the beginning because I didn't know my teammates that well, but they made me feel at home. There was camaraderie among the guys in the locker room. There was a connection there that you really can't describe. People weren't tense like I had witnessed in the past with the Chargers.

In some places the tension is so strong, you could cut it with a knife. We were so relaxed going out to play because we had people like Hacksaw Reynolds, Keena Turner and those guys. They made it about going out and hitting.

We all came together as one. It's kind of difficult to describe because we had leaders across the board. My thing was, I didn't have to say a whole lot. You go out there and you hit them in the mouth and we can be successful. We had guys go through their rituals, their routines. It was a combination of everything. Everybody wanted to win. We did or said whatever it took to get to that next step, that next stage.

Ronnie Lott Cutting Off Part Of His Finger To Continue Playing In A Game

I didn't realize that took place until after the game. For him to do that and to finish the play, spoke volumes about Ronnie, his heart being in the game, and his desire to win. A lot of things like that happened. It makes everybody realize that you've got people beside you that have your back. That's the interesting part of playing the game of football. Some people make mistakes and there's someone there to compensate for that. When we made mistakes there were others who would always compensate. It was an overall team effort.

Offensive Linemen Competed Against

I was smaller than the majority of the offensive linemen I competed against. As far as I'm concerned, the offensive linemen whom I played against were all pretty tough. The linemen who really gave me a good game every time we played against each other, were the Raiders Art Shell, Rams Jackie Slater, and later in my career, Anthony Munoz. These guys were good and it was always a good game. It was always a chess game to play against those guys and try to achieve your next goal against them. Those guys are in the Hall of Fame. They were pretty skilled players and they would give me a hard time. I had my share of success against them, but they did vice versa against me. Those guys were pretty tough. I would say that it all balanced out in the long run.

Pro Football Hall Of Fame Induction
I didn't really picture myself going into the Hall of Fame. I never really thought about it. I just heard of it and knew there were some great players in there. I didn't let it bother me at all because I knew how good I was. I didn't need to get into the Hall of Fame to understand that. I got a stamp of approval when I did get in, though. It's a great pleasure to be among those guys.

Jerry Rice Joining 49ers
When you look at some people and their work ethic, you know that they're going to be successful. When I looked at Jerry, he didn't have that true speed, but he worked at running good routes. He would work on the way that he ran them continuously. I looked at some of the greats when they played. I'm quite sure that Jerry did too, and he was inspired by the greats. I knew that he would be good. I just didn't know how good he would be. You could see that in Ronnie Lott and those guys. You knew that they'd be good and they were, but you couldn't really say this person or that person was going to be that good.

Bill Walsh
Bill Walsh was a great coach. He knew successful plays, to get the job done. That's what he did. He mastered doing those things. Some coaches in the league handle situations better than other coaches. The bottom line is getting the basics down and then going forward with it and he did that. He knew how to keep his players relaxed going into the game. If he wasn't relaxed, he didn't always show it. I guess there were certain things he tried to keep from the players. They would be relaxed, go out and do well, and play for you regardless of the circumstances.

Edward DeBartolo
Mr. D was a top-notch owner. He was the guy who called for Bill Walsh and everyone else to put forth their best effort to get the job done. He was behind you 100%. Mr. D. gave off positive energy for the guys who played for him. He was interested in the players and how they felt about things. He would talk to you on a level that

would make you want to play for him and go out and be as successful as you could be.

The success has shown throughout the years. There are going to be times when players have disputes with owners, but the bottom line is, the majority of them didn't really have disputes with him because he did a lot of great things for people.

He was a players' owner. He helped you in every way. He chose smart people to get the job done to be successful. He made the fan base feel comfortable because of the extra things that he did. A lot of times, he was doing things to make it easier for the players to play.

Even though we'd go through periods that were rough, he would always do things that made the players feel comfortable. It shows to this day. I look forward to him going into the Pro Football Hall of Fame one day because people like that deserve to be there. He is a great man. You could see it in his organization—everything he did and how he did it.

Favorite Player Growing Up
I had a variety of them from running backs to linebackers, and every now and then, a quarterback. Growing up, Jim Brown was one of my favorites. Lineman Deacon Jones was another one of my favorites, and then there was Dick Butkus. Those were the ones that I grew up really knowing and understanding. I know they put forth their best effort on the field. Their skills were really impressive.

Being In Hall Of Fame With Players Watched Growing Up
To see them and be around the guys you once idolized was incredible. I never ever thought that I would meet them, but the bottom line is, one day I did. My thing was always to grab some of that success that they had for myself because I wanted to be as good as they were. I wanted to just change the way the game was played in some form or fashion. That's what all of them did. They changed the way the game was played. They were successful at football and made me feel really special whenever I could go out and play at the kind of level that they had played at and be as successful as they were.

If they ask me for a favor and it's in my ability to be able to do it, there's no question in my mind that I won't go out to go out of my way to try and do something for them. I'd do that because they are guys I looked up to. These are the same people that established the game the way they played in the past and are getting rewarded for it. That's something very special.

Just to be in that echelon, makes you feel special because there's a brotherly feeling among those guys. You see all the different personalities, the things they did, and the way they are today. It is just a feeling that I will never forget. I'll always have that feeling until the day I die. It's something that I want to pass on to kids … to let them know that if you work hard, you can change things.

San Francisco 49er Fred Dean brings down Tampa Bay Buccaneers quarterback Steve DeBerg. Photograph copyright Associated Press

Chapter 11

Lynn Swann

> College:
> Southern California
>
> Career History:
> Pittsburgh Steelers (1974–1982)
>
> 2001 Inductee Pro Football Hall Of Fame

Marv Levy
I remember when Marv Levy was coaching early on. I was actually working in broadcasting during the offseason when he was named coach. I went down for a press conference and one of the members of the media pointed me out and said, "Hey, maybe you'd like to have a receiver like him." He looked at me and he said, "Well, I don't know if you can play but we may have an open try-out. You're welcome to come." Someone said, "I think he's already played a little bit of football." He responded, "My apologies, I'm sorry." Good guy though, good guy.

Chuck Noll Not Becoming A Media Member After Retiring As A Coach
Chuck Noll was not a guy who was going to be a broadcaster. He was not looking to get into the media. As a matter of fact, if you recall Chuck's demeanor and personality, he gave it all to the players and to everyone else. He didn't have a coach's show or any of those things because he chose not to have a life in the media beyond being the coach of a championship football team.

Ronald Reagan
He began as a sports announcer at Iowa covering football games. His ability to articulate a message that people could understand and

grasp was one of his greatest assets as Governor of California, and eventually President of the United States.

He loved football and broadcast football. He had teams come to the White House. He was in Los Angeles in the '90s and was giving a speech at a luncheon. The next day he went over to the stadium and flipped the coin for the USC & Notre Dame football game. I think he understood the value of sports, the life lessons you learn in sports, and what it means to be a part of a strong team. Certainly those things were practical for him in his roles.

Favorite Moments While Playing
I mean payday was a good day. Then of course there were Super Bowls, the day I was drafted, and the day we won the national championship. Some other memorable moments were the day Willie Brown walked into my hotel room and told me I made it to an All American Team my senior year, the first catch I made as a professional, and catching a touchdown in the Rose Bowl. I consider myself beyond lucky. I consider myself to be extraordinarily fortunate to be able to have more than one moment that I can look back on and think it was a great moment.

Will There Be Future Dynasties In Football
I think it's possible, but winning four in six years? You may see teams, like the Patriots, that win championships over a longer period of time without necessarily the same people. The 49ers were multi Super Bowl winners but over a longer period of time. I think there were only five players from that team who had all four Super Bowl rings. I think it is possible, but it's not easy. We may not see four Super Bowls in six years again. I think we'll see teams that are consistently strong and considered dynasties. Look at the Steelers and the success that they're currently having. They didn't win the last Super Bowl, but they got there and they continued to press on to be competitors, to be in a position to win Super Bowls.

More Pressure To Win At USC Or With Steelers
There was pressure to win everywhere. Sometimes it's not really pressure that anybody else puts on you, it's the pressure you put on yourself. Championship caliber players and individuals always want

to win and always want the best. When you look at the amount of pressure they put on themselves to make things happen, it's incredible.

Look at the guys at USC now and guys in college. There is pressure on them because they want to win for that school, and the pressure is on them to win because they want to get drafted. They want to be one of those guys who signs a contract and plays for a pro team for a million dollars. I'm not sure if that's not more pressure than the guy who is already on the team and playing professionally experiences.

Terry Bradshaw Becoming A Media Personality
Terry gave no indication that was a direction he wanted to go in when he was a player, but it's something that evolved. It happened for him. He was in the right place at the right time, with the right skills, with the right kind of personality, to make it work. He has done well and continues to do well.

Mister Rogers
Fred Rogers started his broadcast at WPGH I believe, a public broadcasting station. He was phenomenal in terms of his talent and the impact he has had on kids and adults around the country. Being on his show was a lot of fun.

Becoming A Politician
I think essentially it is the fact that I view politics and being an elected official as volunteering. You give your time to help in a big way and a strong way. That's what I was doing. I was never looking to be a professional politician. I was never looking at it as a career. It was always my intent to actually try and win, have an impact in Pennsylvania, and then step back and go back into the private sector.

Running for office is certainly much more difficult than playing football. What's required of you in terms of responsibility and getting things done has more impactful on people. Football is entertainment. Football is a competitive sport. In politics, like being governor of a state, you're in a position to change and alter lives in positive and in negative ways depending on the decisions you make or you don't make.

Big Brothers & Big Sisters

I have work with Big Brothers and Big Sisters for more than 35 years. I'm on the national board. Mentoring has always been important to me. I think everywhere we look around the country, in any job all of us have been helped by people along the way. Sometimes it's important to have that direct mentor who can help us grow from an adolescent into a responsible adult.

Pittsburgh Steeler Lynn Swann goes up to make a catch over Dallas Cowboys cornerback Mark Washington in the Steelers 21-17 win over the Cowboys in Super Bowl X on January 18, 1976. Photograph copyright Associated Press

Chapter 12

John Stallworth

> College:
> Alabama A&M
>
> Career History:
> Pittsburgh Steelers (1974–1987)
>
> 2002 Inductee Pro Football Hall Of Fame

College Choice
It was a different time; it was the early '70s. My last year in high school was 1970 so it was before some changes took place at the university. I actually got one offer to go to college on scholarship and that was at Alabama A&M.

Alabama A&M
It was a great experience for me. Black college football was certainly a different experience. I went to a predominately white high school. Sometimes the approach that we took in high school was different than the approach that was taken at Alabama A&M, but that was good. It was the first time I was in a passing offense. My forte, I've always thought, was catching the football. In high school we didn't have a quarterback that could throw the football. So, I was a tall, skinny, running back. When I got to Alabama A&M, I had an opportunity to do the thing that I thought I was good at. Football was a good experience. The academics at Alabama A&M was good for me too. And, I met my wife at Alabama A&M. A lot of good things happened there.

NFL Draft
Alabama A&M had not experienced a lot of players being drafted. The Pittsburgh Steelers drafted me in the fourth round. At that time, I was the highest draft pick out of Alabama A&M in their history. I

felt being drafted by the Steelers was probably going to be my kiss of death. At that time the one thing Pittsburgh did really well was run the football. They had a great running back in Franco Harris who was entering his third year when I joined the Steelers. The Steelers played great defense. The offensive philosophy was three yards and a cloud of dust. They just didn't throw the ball that much.

Change In Steelers Offensive Philosophy
With Terry Bradshaw's development, and Lynn Swann and me coming on, we changed the offensive philosophy a little bit. Rocky Bleier played a crucial role for us in all of our Super Bowl wins.

Lynn and I both liked the big play. We liked coming up with the big play. That gave Terry the opportunity to do that, which went with Bradshaw's style of play. We all came together at the right time. Bradshaw's early years with the Steelers were up and down. Then he started playing with some consistency, and we were there for those years.

Practicing Against Steelers Defense
We never got anything done offensively unless the coaches called them off. We couldn't run the football against the defensive line. With guys like Mel Blount, Donnie Shell, Mike Wagner, and J.T. Thomas, it was kind of hard even to throw the football. Going against those guys at practice everyday was good for us because when we got to the game, it was a lot easier.

Normally the offense comes along a lot slower than the defense. You get to training camp and the defense starts clicking almost right away. The offense, because of the timing of blocks and throwing the ball with the timing of the quarterback back and receiver, takes a little bit longer to develop. The defense knew exactly what we were going to do. There wasn't going to be anything that we were going to do that was going to surprise them. So when you had guys on defense who were as talented as they were and then they knew where you were going, sometimes they'd take the short cut and get there before you.

Catching 75 Yard Touchdown Pass In Super Bowl XIII
It was my best performance in a big game—a playoff game. I think I had other games where I played better catching the football and blocking, but that was probably my best big game performance.

Super Bowl XIV
In that Super Bowl, we were not running the ball very well. Three of our coaches had left right before the season started and were now coaches with the LA Rams. So, the Rams knew what we were going to do. They knew Bradshaw's strong suit and they did a great job of game planning for that. The only thing they left us with were big plays down the field and it worked well for us. Lynn Swann had a big play for a touchdown and then the two that I caught, a 73-yarder for a touchdown and later a 45-yard catch that put us in position for our final score. As a kid you dream about having a great performance in the big game of the year. For professional football, that's the Super Bowl. So I came up with the winning catch and a Super Bowl win. It was a dream come true for me. I have a lot of great memories. For our era of the Pittsburgh Steelers, that was the last Super Bowl we played in, so it was special place for us.

Favorite Super Bowl
My favorite Super Bowl was any that I played well in. The first one against the Minnesota Vikings we played great defense and ran the football. We didn't throw it a whole lot. It was a good game and I was happy with the victory. As a receiver you like to do more and be more of a factor in the outcome of the game.

Chuck Noll
Ultimately, I think Chuck was a great teacher. He cared. He was communicating effectively so you knew not only what you had to do but also why you were doing it. I think that gave us a leg up in understanding what we had to do in the game. I think there's a part of Chuck that most people don't see when they look back. He had a lot of compassion for the guys who played for him, but he thought that a coach couldn't show compassion. So, he didn't show that side of his personality. He definitely cared about the guys who were on his team. He cared about their development not
only as football players, but also their development as human beings. There was a lot of truth to what he said about why you do certain

things and how you react when certain things happen. Those truths transcended football. They were life lessons we could take to our next job, our life's work, as he would call it. Whatever we were doing, they were applicable.

Rollie Dotsch
Rollie was a good man and an excellent coach. He had a great rapport with all of us. We really hated to lose him when he left our team and went to coach in the USFL for Birmingham. He was such a good person, not just a good coach. He was a good person and a friend.

Rollie actually had a great singing voice. I don't know if anybody has ever said that. You'd catch him in a moment when he was totally relaxed and feeling comfortable and he'd belt something out for you. You'd come away from it amazed.

Terry Bradshaw
Terry Bradshaw is a very approachable guy. He comes across as a real easy, likable guy. With Terry there was always that awkwardness of starting something new. When he came to the Steelers getting adjusted to the game at that level was new to him and it took him a while. When he transitioned into broadcasting, it was awkward. I think the first few years he was doing that, he'd only broadcast games out of New Orleans.

We joked with him about that because at that time, New Orleans wasn't a successful team. So, if you screwed up nobody would know. Terry practiced his craft. He's fully comfortable with that, so I could see him being where he is and being very successful. Nobody knows when you leave the game what you're going to do. Everybody's got something they'd like to be able to do. To what degree that we're going to be successful when we transition, nobody knows. I think all athletes ask themselves, 'What's next?' If you can answer that question, then your transition out of football is easy. You make it and you welcome it. If you can't answer that question, you tend to cling to the life that you've got because that's the only one you know.

Toughest Defensive Backs Faced
I liked playing against the tough defensive backs like Mike Haynes with the New England Patriots and then with the Raiders. Hall of

Famer Mike Haynes was an excellent defensive back. There was a guy that played a number of years with the Cleveland Browns named Hanford Dixon. I had some good battles against him. I also liked to play against Ken Riley of the Cincinnati Bengals. There were guys out there that I knew going into the game, were going to be tough to play against.

Pro Football Hall Of Fame Induction
After we settled down and the screaming stopped, I thought deeper about what it meant. You look back over my career and I was never the guy that was going to be in the paper all the time. I saw myself as a hardworking receiver who had some big plays in big games and did well. I wasn't the guy who was going to spike the football or win MVP in the Super Bowl. I felt good about my career. Going into the Hall of Fame, sort of justifies or verifies it. The way I approached the game was to keep my nose down, do a good job, and catch the ball when I was called to catch it. At the end of the day, people recognize it for having a great value. A lot of times during the course of my career, other things were going on and people on our team were being highlighted for this and that. I thought, well maybe I will change, maybe I will do things a little bit differently, but I didn't. I continued to do what I felt comfortable with. Being voted into the Hall of Fame sort of let me know that I made the right choices.

Leaders On Steelers
On defense you have to look at Joe Greene and Jack Lambert as leaders. Certainly, Lambert was the more vocal of the two. Joe's actions and words made him a leader, but Lambert was a lot more vocal than Joe. We had a group of leaders on the offense. The quarterback has to be one of the guys that stands up and does the job. At times during our heyday, we would call plays by committee because Bradshaw, in his wisdom, would listen to what Swann, Franco, and I wanted to do and what Mike Webster thought the offensive line could do. Terry had a lot of input. He was his own quarterback and he called his own plays. A number of quarterbacks had the philosophy that everyone should just shut up and they'd call the play. That was not our approach in Pittsburgh with Bradshaw. We all had suggestions of what we wanted to do and Bradshaw respected that.

L.C. Greenwood Not Being In The Pro Football Hall Of Fame

No question in my mind that L.C. should be in the Hall of Fame. Look at his performance over the years on the defensive line, the number of sacks he had, and how he influenced major games for us. Just his steadiness over the years should have put him in. Without a doubt I think he has all the credentials to be a Hall of Famer, and I'm hoping it's going to happen.

Joe Greene Nickname (Mean Joe Greene)

He was called that when I got there. He came to the Steelers in 1969 and I came in 1974, so I think those early years are when he was Mean Joe Greene in the truest sense of the word. When I got there, Joe was starting to be more Joe Greene the leader. Joe Greene was the guy who, when you wanted an assessment of where the team was, how we were doing, and how we were going to get through whatever phase we were going through, offered those words up. That was the Joe Greene I knew. I told him that back then. I never knew Mean Joe Greene, I knew Joe Greene the consummate leader. Joe Greene, the guy who by his actions and his words set the path for us. Joe owned the field. As a young guy, you kind of looked at him and thought, "What's Joe going to say? How's Joe going to react to that?" You took your cues from him in that regard. So, to me, I never knew the guy called Mean Joe Greene. I knew Joe Greene the leader.

Biggest Rivals

In the sense that we saw the Dallas Cowboys twice in the Super Bowl, they were our biggest rivals. And, we had a big rivalry with the Oakland Raiders. I had to learn to hate the Oakland Raiders when I got to the Steelers. We played a couple of championship games against them. Then, we had a big rivalry with the Houston Oilers. We had to play them a couple of times in conference championship games. As far as the big games go, our big rival was the Cowboys because there was a big difference in player style. Our player style was smash them on the field. Coach Noll said we had to hit them harder than they hit us if we were going to win the football game. In Dallas, with the flex defense and multiple sets of offense, they were going to finesse you. That was the difference in playing style. In that era, the smash mouth against the finesse won out most of the time. The Cowboys were America's team and that's how they promoted themselves. We were Pittsburgh's team--Western Pennsylvania's team, and we took a lot of pride in that.

Favorite Player Growing Up

I had a number of favorite players. I liked Raymond Berry. Raymond Berry wasn't the fastest guy, but he ran good rounds and caught the football when it came his way. That resonated with me even as a young football player. Paul Warfield was smooth, steady, and came up with the big play. He just happened to be on an offense that wanted to run the football in Miami with John Kiick, Larry Csonka, and Mercury Morris. When they threw the ball, Paul got it. I really liked to watch him play. I just liked receivers in general. I also liked Otis Taylor with the Kansas City Chiefs. He came from a black college, so I could identify with that. As for a quarterback, Johnny Unitas will always be a hero to me.

Meeting Raymond Berry

My first encounter with Ray Berry was when he was with the Detroit Lions as a receiver coach. That year, the Lion's coaching staff was at the Senior Bowl and I was there as a player. Ray came over to me to me said, "Well, I hear you've got great hands." So, he put me in a drill. Standing in front of me, he put his hands out and had someone throw the ball to me. He was right up close to me, distracting me with his hands. The ball had to go by him to get to me. I was thinking this is Ray Berry doing this, rather than thinking about catching the ball. He didn't have to move his hands; he could have just stood there. I've never told him that.

Detroit obviously didn't draft me. He probably left thinking whatever they say about this guy's hands, is completely false. He can't catch a thing.

I've read stories of what Ray Berry and Johnny Unitas did after practice. Berry would run so many yards and then cut to the outside, and Unitas knew the timing of the route. Unitas released the ball before Berry went into his cut, so when Berry came back, the ball was right there so he could make the catch. That type of work ethic breeds success.

Pittsburgh Steeler Mel Blount, left, and John Stallworth hug each other in the locker room Sunday, Jan. 5, 1976 after the Steelers beat the Oakland Raiders 16-10 for the AFC Championship. Photograph copyright Associated Press

Chapter 13

Randy White

> College:
> Maryland
>
> Career History:
> Dallas Cowboys (1975–1988)
>
> 1994 Inductee Pro Football Hall Of Fame

College Choice
I was born in Pittsburgh, Pennsylvania, and grew up in Delaware. My entire family is from Pennsylvania. Penn State never looked at me in high school. I never had an offer from them. I had three offers. They were from Arizona State, Virginia Tech, and Maryland. Maryland was the closest one to where I grew up, so that's the main reason I ended up going there.

At the time, I hadn't been to a whole lot of places. I went to Arizona State for a visit, and they had me room with Mike Hartenstine. Mike ended up being a Bear. Before that, though, he played for Penn State. I got to room with Mike again during the College All-Star Game.

Maryland Head Coaches
My first year at Maryland, Roy Lester was the head coach. My first visit to Maryland my dad and me sat down with Coach Lester. Coach Lester told me, "I don't know if you can play college football for the University of Maryland, but we're going to give you a scholarship." I said, "Well, that's good. I'm glad you're giving me one." Anyway, he was gone the next year. Jerry Claiborne was the head coach for my sophomore, junior, and senior years.

I didn't realize at the time what kind of a foundation Coach Claiborne was giving me. He gave me the foundation play on the professional level. He was a great coach and a real disciplinarian. I learned a lot about football playing for him.

NFL Draft

If the Cowboys had the opportunity to do the draft over, they probably would have taken Walter Payton instead of me. The way it worked out, I ended up a Dallas Cowboy. The Baltimore Colts had the number one pick in the draft that year. Joe Thomas was the general manager of the Colts and had been down to Maryland. Joe said, "Randy we're taking you with the first pick." Even up until the day before the draft, that's what he was telling me. At the last minute, the Colts traded their number one pick to Atlanta. Atlanta took Steve Bartkowski; Dallas acquired the number two pick by trading Craig Morton to the Giants, and chose me. That's how I ended up being a Cowboy.

The Cowboys not drafting Walter worked out good for Walter and me. Walter was a great player and a great guy. We came out of school the same year. I got to know Walter from playing in the East West Shrine Game, the College All-Star Game, and then competing against him over the years. He was the best player of all-time.

Playing Middle Linebacker For Cowboys

Lee Roy Jordan was getting ready to retire. Coach Landry was the one who kind of invented the middle linebacker spot with Sam Huff and the Giants. I guess they felt that since I was 6'4", weighed 260 pounds, and could run a 4.6 40, I would be an excellent middle linebacker. That experiment didn't work out, though. The Cowboys flex defense was a little different than playing in a conventional 4-3 defense. The moves that the middle linebacker had to make, the reaction time, and a lot of involvement in pass coverage, just never became natural to me. Most of the time I was a beat off, because I was thinking too much.

Position Change To Defensive Tackle

My third year in the league, Coach Landry told me, "Randy, we're thinking about moving you to defensive tackle. How do you feel about that?" I said, "Coach I just want to play football wherever you think I can help this football team win. That's where I will play." I had moved from middle linebacker to strong side linebacker, to weak side linebacker, and I was running out of spots.

He asked, "You want to play on the defensive line?" I said, "Sure." I was always undersized for the defensive tackle position, but it was a natural position for me. I felt like somebody took the handcuffs off of me and I could play football the way I knew how to play. It was a good moment for me when Coach Landry switched me.

We had an excellent middle linebacker, Bob Breunig. He just stepped right in there. That was his natural position. I went to the right defensive tackle spot and had some success. They started mentioning my name with Bob Lilly and I said, "Whoa wait a minute. If I can do this for 14 years like Bob did, then go ahead and mention my name with him."

Bob Lilly is Mr. Cowboy. As far as I'm concerned he's the greatest Cowboy that ever played along with Roger Staubach. We had a lot of great ones, but Bob is right up there.

Cowboys Defensive Line
We had Larry Cole and Jethro Pugh split time on the left side. After Jethro and Larry retired, we got John Dutton from the Colts, who was an All-Pro defensive end. John moved into that left tackle spot. So, we had a pretty good defensive line back then.

Playing In Super Bowls Early In Career
We had a great group with a lot of talent and we got along. We had a great team. I went to the Super Bowl my rookie year, I went there my third year, and I went there my fourth year. I thought we'd get back to the Super Bowl but we ended up playing in three NFC Championship Games after my fourth year in the league. I played for 14 years and never got another opportunity to play in the Super Bowl after my fourth season. If you get an opportunity to play in a Super Bowl, savor that moment because you never know if it's going to come back around.

Winning Super Bowl MVP
Winning the Super Bowl MVP was the furthest thing from my mind. I wasn't even thinking about that. Ed Jones had a great game that day, our strong safety, Randy Hughes, intercepted a pass and had two fumble recoveries. Roger Staubach and a lot of guys were the most valuable players in that game. That was a big day for Harvey

Martin and me. We were chosen as the MVPs. I remember I was standing on the sidelines at the end of the game and Harvey came over to me and said, "We were chosen as the MVPs in the game." It didn't sink in with me.

The big thing was winning the Super Bowl. I had played against Pittsburgh my rookie year in the Super Bowl, and the most exciting thing I remember about that was the after game party. Willie Nelson, Waylon Jennings, and Jimmy Buffet were there. We got up and sang with them on stage after the game. Having the chance to go back to the Super Bowl, win, and get a Super Bowl ring was a great experience.

As MVP, each of us was given a new car. Harvey and I went to New York and we each got a new Thunderbird. I thought they gave you the car and it was yours. Well, I found out at the end of the year that, you had the use of the car for a year. After that, you had the option to buy it at the end of the year or you could turn it back in. That was a little disappointing.

The Super Bowl definitely turned into something more than what it was. It was great back then, but now it's like the greatest sporting event of all time every year. It was wonderful; it was a great experience playing in the Super Bowls.

Transition From Maryland To Dallas
At that time, going from college to the pros, I was just concerned about having a chance to make the football team. I wasn't thinking about the fans or what it meant to play for the Dallas Cowboys, but over time you start to realize that. My main thing when I first went down there was figuring out what I had to do to stick around there for a while. That's what I wanted to do, make the football team. Playing the middle linebacker spot for the first couple of years was kind of frustrating for me. Finally in my third year, I started being able to play football the way I liked to play it.

Tom Landry
It was obvious that Coach Landry was a great football coach. He did a lot of things to change the game defensively and offensively. As far as a person, he was a great example of a real Christian. He just didn't talk the talk; he walked the walk. A lot of things about him were special

and impressive but for me, in the 14 years he was my coach, I never once saw him lose his temper or get out of control. Now he would get angry and he would not be happy, but he didn't do it by yelling and screaming. He had a way of getting his point across by just looking at you. You knew he wasn't happy. He was definitely a special person.

Jerry Jones Firing Tom Landry

It was a tough time for everybody when the ownership changed and Coach Landry was gone. That was a hard transition. Coach Landry used to tell us all the time, "One thing you can be sure of is things will change." Sure enough, they do. When Jerry Jones bought the team, he came in there and the team won three Super Bowls. It was tough when Coach Landry left, but time heals and you pull for the Cowboys. You want them to win.

Jerry is one of the best owners in the league. He really takes care of his players. He does everything he can to put the best football team on the field. It was tough back then.

Super Bowl XIII

The second time we played the Steelers in the Super Bowl, I had a broken thumb. Roy Gerela squib kicked the ball to me. I pick it up, started running with it, and fumbled the ball. Pittsburgh recovered and one play later they scored a touchdown.

Everybody thinks Jackie Smith dropping that pass in the end zone is what what made us lose, but there were a lot of other things that happened in that football game that caused us to lose. Jackie was one of the best of all-time. He was a great player and really helped our football team when he joined us. He is one of the greatest of all-time. He is in the Hall of Fame and deserves to be.

Mike Ditka

Mike Ditka was my special teams coach for two years. He also coached tight ends. I got hands on with Mike for those two years. You're never going to meet a more competitive guy than Mike Ditka. He's hardnosed.

I always liked Mike. I like the way that he coached and I like his attitude. He was an inspiration to all of us. Anybody who was ever around Coach Landry had the kind of respect for him that Mike had for Coach Landry. I've never met anybody who has one bad thing to say about Coach Landry. He was a very special person.

Coach Landry demanded a certain amount of control from his coaching staff I'm sure, but Mike was always Mike. Coach Landry didn't accept anything except 100 percent. He wasn't afraid to express his position on things. If you made a mistake, you knew you were going to hear about it, but that's what made him a great coach. Mike's a special guy too.

Any time we played against the Bears, it was always a dogfight. When Mike Ditka went to coach the Bears, they adopted his personality. You were going to be in a dogfight no matter what happened in that football game.

Toughest Offensive Lineman Faced
Bob Young from the St. Louis Cardinals gave me as hard a time as anyone in the running game. I could pretty much pass rush against the best of them. I played against John Hannah and Mike Webster.

A guy who gave me a hard time that played for the Bears was Noah Jackson. He was a left guard. He had a big belly and they called him Buddha. He was an artist at the flex. He would give me head fakes, cut me, and have me on the ground more than anybody I ever played against. They had Walter Payton running the football, which made it that much harder, but Noah Jackson was a pretty tough guard.

Danny White
Danny White had to follow Roger Staubach. Who can fill those shoes? Roger was Roger. People expected Danny to do the things Roger did, but Danny White wasn't Roger Staubach. Danny was an excellent quarterback, though. We went to the playoffs ever year and three NFC Championship games. The quarterback doesn't win or lose them by himself. It takes a whole team effort. Danny was a great quarterback.

Dallas Cowboy defensive tackle Randy White coming in for the sack on Seattle Seahawks quarterback Jim Zorn. Photograph copyright Associated Press

Chapter 14

Mike Haynes

> College:
> Arizona State
>
> Career History:
> New England Patriots (1976–1982)
> Los Angeles Raiders (1983–1989)
>
> 1997 Inductee Pro Football Hall Of Fame

<u>On Attending John Marshall High School In Los Angeles</u>
When I was going to school there, it was more known for academics than sports. We were actually called the Marshall Barristers, after John Marshall. I played football there. Our team didn't win any games my senior year. Since that time, they have played in the CIF championship, so it's different now. The demographics in the whole area have changed over the years.

<u>College</u>
UCLA came after me for track. Back in those days, I think every kid playing football in L.A. wanted to play at USC when John McKay was there. He had a lot of Heisman Trophy winners.

At Arizona State, we had a lot of good guys on our team. Some of the guys went on to have great NFL careers before me and after me. There was Charley Taylor, Hall of Fame wide receiver for the Washington Redskins, Curley Culp, Hall of Fame defensive tackle, J.D. Hill, Art Malone, and Ben Malone, to name a few. Then with me, Danny White, Steve Holden, Woody Green, and Al Harris, who played for the Bears; just a whole bunch of good players. We played in three Fiesta Bowls. My senior year, we were undefeated and beat Nebraska in the Fiesta Bowl.

When I was playing in college, not very many teams went to bowls. Playing in a bowl meant a lot more than it does today. Fortunately, the Fiesta Bowl is still recognized as a great bowl. I still think going to a bowl is pretty exciting for the players.

Playing For Coach Frank Kush At Arizona State
We could beat teams, but for Coach Kush, it mattered how we beat them. We might beat them at halftime 14 to nothing, and he'd come in and rip us like we were doing poorly. So, we'd go back in the second half and score 30 points. He was an interesting guy. I'm glad I had a chance to play for him. My senior year, we only had six seniors. The year before we had more than 20 seniors. He said the team that I was on my senior year was maybe the best team that he'd ever coached. As of today, it is still the only undefeated team in ASU history. That was back in 1975.

They've had some other teams that have come close, but they lost in a bowl game. Coach Kush was on to something. He knew a little bit about us, and off that team we had several first-round draft picks. Larry Gordon, linebacker, went to the Miami Dolphins, and Al Harris, a defensive lineman, went to the Chicago Bears. Some of the other guys, including me, went in the early rounds of the draft. We were putting up a lot of points in those days and we had an unbelievable defense. They're trying to get back to those days now, but it's not getting any easier.

Getting Drafted By The Patriots
The year I got to the Patriots, in 1976, they were coming off of a terrible season the year before. They had only three wins, but they had quite a few draft choices so they had three first-round picks. They were defensive back Tim Fox out of Ohio State, offensive lineman Pete Brock from University of Colorado, and me. We had other guys on our team from the draft that year that were all big contributors. We turned that season around and only had three losses during the regular season.

Dealing With Brisk New England Temperature

It was culture shock to play in New England and think that was where I was, hopefully, going to be spending the next 10 years of my life playing football, but I adjusted. I can remember the first time it snowed. I'd never really seen snow come down except in the movies. I'd been up to the mountains where it snows in Southern California. One of the great things California is you can drive out to the beach and go surfing, or you can drive up to the mountains and go skiing on the same day. I'd been up to the snow, obviously, but I never really saw it come down.

I'll never forget seeing it snow for the first time. Tim Fox had invited me over to his home for dinner. I went out to my car then I went back inside and called him. I said, "Hey, Tim. It's snowing, man. I can't make it." He started laughing. He laughed so hard. I don't think I'll ever live that down.

Getting Eight Interceptions His Rookie Year

One of the things I loved to do was to have the ball in my hand. I liked to run with it. Being a rookie, every team picked on you. When you are trying to figure out where the weakest area of the defense is, you think, let's go after the young guy. I did make a lot of mental mistakes that year. I probably led the team in mental errors, but I would self-correct in the middle of a play. For instance, if I was lined up outside the receiver, back pedaling on the outside, and then remember, "Oh, wait a minute, if both the backs go away, I'm supposed to switch to the inside."

Because I was on the outside and the quarterback recognized I was on the outside, he thought I was going to stay on the outside. But, I would just seem to switch back to the inside just as he was throwing the ball and consequently, I'd be in great position for an interception. I almost led the league that year in interceptions. I did lead the league in punt return yards. I had a thing back in those days. I never used to fair catch, so my average probably wasn't as high as it could be, but it was one of the higher averages in the league that year. I led the league in total return yards.

Giving The Patriots Their First Punt Return Touchdowns

I thought it was kind of strange they had that record and no one had ever returned a punt for a touchdown. I knew early on that we would break that, because of the commitment that the guys had on special teams. We had a lot of guys who were just really awesome special teams players, like Dickie Conn and Jess Phillips. We also had a lot of starters on our punt return team. It wasn't like taking guys who weren't playing. These were guys who were excellent athletes who wanted to score. I'm kind of lucky to be the guy who was chosen to be the returner. It was a lot of fun. I think people used to love to come see if I was going to fair catch or not. It was just a good time to be back there and a good time to be a Patriot fan.

Ending Up With The Raiders

I was having some contract problems. The way I got there is a long story. I jumped on an airplane, flew out, and signed a contract with the Raiders. Technically the Patriots still owned my rights, so I played out my contract. The league challenged my situation, but in the end everybody decided that it might be the best thing to happen and they let me go to the Raiders. They gave the Patriots a couple of draft choices for me, so I was happy because it got me back home into Los Angeles.

It was pretty difficult. It was October and my wife was pregnant. It was pretty hard to be home wondering if I was going to play that season, but everything worked out in the end. It was one of the better decisions I made in my life.

Playing In The Super Bowl After Playing In Five Regular-Season Games

It doesn't get any better than that. The Raiders had a great team. They had a young corner, a guy named Ted Watts out of Texas Tech, and he was playing great. Just like when I was a rookie, they would pick on him. I think even though the Raiders would still win the game, they felt like they wanted to take that off the table, you might say, for other teams, and brought me in. They didn't pick on me. I wish they had, but they didn't. That helped the defense and we went on to win the AFC Championship, defeat the Seattle Seahawks. Then we went on to the Super Bowl to play the defending champions, the Washington Redskins.

Playing With Lester Hayes

The only difference between the two of us was just the spelling of our names. We both loved playing corner, loved playing man-to-man, and liked getting after people. Lester was a little bit more aggressive in the way that he approached the game than I was. I wouldn't really call anybody out and say, "I'm going to shut you out." I wouldn't say anything like that, because I wouldn't want to say anything that was going to amp up your testosterone. For me, I tried to just keep it low-key, but with Lester that was hard to do. I think as a result though, we would always get the best effort from our opponents. It made us bring out our "A" game more often.

Use Of Stickum

It didn't last for very long. They had to outlaw Stickum, not only because Lester was using it. Other guys in the NFL started using it. Lester led the NFL that year with interceptions. In fact, he was the MVP of our league because of that great year.

When Stickum gets on a football, you can't get it off. You have to take it in the back and use some kind of special chemical to get if off. It ruined a lot of footballs. They were going through too many balls for a game. So, Stickum was outlawed.

A 97-Yard Interception Return For A Touchdown

That was against the Miami Dolphins and I was covering Mark Duper. A quick little three-step-drop type play, and I stepped in front of it. It's really kind of funny. I've seen him a million times since then and never asked what he was doing. You would think that one of them made a mistake. Either Dan Marino made a mistake or Duper made a mistake, because Dan threw the ball and Duper was breaking out. I looked, took a little peek, and saw the ball coming, so I just grabbed it and ran with it. I tried to get to the other end zone before he caught me. That guy was one of the world-class sprinters, a Cliff Branch type. He could really run.

I knew I had six as long as he didn't catch me, and that was my only concern. When I'd caught the ball, I really lost sight of him. I didn't know where he was. I didn't know if he was right behind me, or deep in the end zone. I had no idea, and I didn't want to take a look to my right to find him there, so I just kept looking downfield and kept going.

Going From The Raiders To Working For The NFL

It was a great change, because I became educated with what the league was all about. I think as a player during my era, we didn't really think that the league cared about the players, and didn't care about the game as much as it should. I found out that was totally wrong, and probably the biggest thing that the players and the league needed to do was communicate with each other. If both sides were just able to talk about common issues, they would have come up on the same side of the table every single time. Commissioner Tagliabue, who was Commissioner when I joined the league, was really good at doing that and so was Roger Goodell. Roger, the current Commissioner, is also very good at getting information from all the sides before he takes a position.

It was probably one of the best things that ever happened to me. I know that when it comes to the game, the players and the safety, a lot of times when we think they maybe didn't care, it's that they just didn't know what was going on. Everybody assumed that they did, and I know from being there that wasn't always the case. Today there seems to be a lot of polarization between sides on many topics. There are a lot of safety issues, you have replacement officials and things like that, and it's sort of an organized chaos. You would think an enterprise as big as the NFL, with all of the money involved, could somehow get all their ducks in a row and have things run smoothly.

It does amaze me, but sometimes I don't have all the facts. I'd like to see the referees, the officials, taken care of. They are big contributors to the game. I don't even know, to be honest with you, what their real issues are and why they're not on the same page.

I know that those guys really, really work hard to be the best officials they can be. I worked in the league office and I saw them do their work firsthand during the season and during the off-season. There is a commitment to the head official in football operations and to getting it right. They want the coaches and players to communicate with the league office about different penalties and situations, all with the idea of trying to get everybody on the same page. They want to be sure that they're making the right decisions in the best interest of the game.

As a consequence, things are much better. Safety is extremely important and looked at completely different now than it was when I played, in the '70s and '80s. They're constantly looking at equipment and all kind of other things, which I think is important for the future of the game. For me, because it was my sport, I'd like to see the game played all over the world and continue to grow. When you look at where it started and where it is now, that has a chance of happening during my lifetime. I'm excited about it. It's not perfect. It will probably never be perfect due to the evolution of the game. Overall, it's all been going in the right direction, and a good direction for the growth of the game.

People's Criticism Of Gene Upshaw

For me it was very hard because Gene was also a friend of mine. I never really played with him as a Raider, but I did play with him in Pro Bowl games. I got to know him well. Even when I got the job in management for the Player Development Department with the NFL, I had a lot of interaction with the Players Association and I saw Gene quite a bit. I knew where his heart was and what he was trying to do. I can't say that I always agreed with what he did, but I knew where he was focused. I really didn't understand why he said some of the things that he said. He really upset a lot of the guys. We all had a lot of respect for him, so he put himself in a situation where there was a lot of room for criticism. But, there was also a side of him that was very good and did a lot of good things for players.

The thing I hate is that all of the good things he did will be forgotten. People will remember the things they wish he had done, but I totally understand that. I can't really say that the way a lot of former players are looking at him is wrong, because I understand their point of view. I see what they're seeing, and I wish it wasn't that way. I wish Gene would have done things a little bit differently, but he's not here to tell us why he did them. He was constantly trying to defend himself.

I would see him in different situations and talk to him privately, and he would share a different side of the story that he could not share publicly. I still think people should remember him as one of the great players of all time, and one of the guys who really led change for the Players Association. It's just unfortunate he didn't get things done the way that we all would have loved him to. Hopefully, that'll happen in time. Let's just say he got the ball rolling. He'll be judged by a lot of people, by how his decisions impacted them individually. I think there's a real good reason for criticism from a lot of the pre-'93 guys.

Decision To Retire
I thought I had a couple more years left in me. Once you've been in the league for a while, you can see how guys are being moved around and how they are getting ready to play. I could see that. I wasn't ready to stop playing. I really didn't feel like I got beat out, so that made it a little bit tough to leave. When they asked me to step down and let the other guys play in front of me, it was hard. How do you say, "Sure, great, this is wonderful?"
In hindsight, I wish I had done that. Maybe I would have gotten three more years in and I would have been able to do a lot of things that I wanted to do anyway. My attitude, I guess, with the end of my career and how it was going to end, was ... no one knows this, but I wish I had done things differently. I had a chance to do things differently and I think I may have made the wrong choice, but I'll never know.

Owner Al Davis
I don't think there could possibly be anyone like Al Davis. One, it's just the era that he was a part of, the friends that he made, and the impact that he had on the league. All the great things that he did as the owner have been adopted, really, into the NFL. He did different things that were really special. When word got out that he was doing it, other owners started doing it. I think they probably owe him a lot, but his personality was one where he walked alone a lot. I hope he'll go down in history the way he should go down in history, as one of the greatest owners of all time.

Pro Football Hall Of Fame Induction
The first time in Canton was very tough, because I was being inducted into the Pro Football Hall of Fame. That was my first time there, and it was whirlwind. You're going from one banquet room to

the next, celebrating something, either a terrible cause or being introduced as the next guy who's going to be inducted this weekend. It was a blur. You don't really get to enjoy too much time with your friends until after the ceremony. You had your little party, and you got a chance to be with your family and friends. For the most part, before that, it's very difficult to enjoy it. You have to come back and enjoy it the following year.

Involvement In National Prostate Awareness Month
At the Pro Football Hall of Fame, the NFL and the American Neurological Association had partnered up for free screenings for retired players, and they kicked it off at the Hall of Fame. At that time, I was an employee of the NFL. They asked me to go down to where they were doing the screening because they were going to do a Public Service Announcement. While I was there, the ladies that were working there ... I now call them the angels ... convinced me that I should take this simple blood test and told me I might encourage other guys to do it, so I did.

Then the doctor called me in and started asking me about my PSA (Prostate Specific Antigen) and asking what my baseline PSA was. That was the first time I had heard of PSA for blood tests. Anyway, the doctor scared me when he gave me all the statistics about one in six men will be diagnosed with prostate cancer in their lifetime, and when you compare that to one in eight women will be diagnosed with breast cancer in their lifetime.

I was diagnosed with prostate cancer and was successfully treated. It's important for men to know about the PSA test and prostate cancer screening.

Seattle Seahawks wide receiver Steve Largent is covered by Los Angeles Raiders cornerback Mike Haynes..Photograph copyright Associated Press

Chapter 15

Harry Carson

> College:
> South Carolina State
>
> Career History:
> New York Giants (1976–1988)
>
> 2006 Inductee Pro Football Hall Of Fame

College Choice
I wound up following friends who were attending South Carolina State. I wasn't heavily recruited coming out of high school because I quit the football team during my senior year. I had a little disagreement with my high school coach.

South Carolina State
I knew that I was going to be playing football at South Carolina State. I didn't know what I was in for in college. Even though I played in high school, college was a completely different situation. The competition was more intense than I thought it would be. I had to adjust very quickly to fit in.

As it turned out, I wound up being a starter as a freshman. I was able to sort of adjust to the program. I thought I fit in very well.

We had a pretty good team. During my first year Donnie Shell and Barney Chavous, who played for the Denver Broncos, were on the team. Willie Mays Aikens was primarily a baseball player but he was also my backup on the football team.

I had the opportunity to play with some really talented guys during that era. Outstanding athletes surrounded me. I think Willie Mays

Aikens and Gene Richards were one or two in the baseball draft in 1975. There was a lot of talent at South Carolina State.

NFL Draft

I really didn't have a whole lot of expectations about what round I was going to be drafted in. Being chosen to play in the NFL was good. Scouts, GMs, and personnel people had scouted me. Some had projected me to be drafted as early in the second round. Others projected me to go later than the fourth round.

I was drafted and quite frankly, I was a little disappointed when the Giants drafted me. They wanted me to play middle linebacker, but I had never played middle linebacker before. I was comfortable playing right defensive end and being able to get after the quarterback from blindside.

Marty Schottenheimer drafted me and taught me how to play the middle linebacker position. I had to adjust whether it was in high school, college, or on the Pro level as a rookie. I had to learn a new position, middle linebacker. Middle linebacker in the 4-3 defense at the Pro level, is probably the toughest position to learn.

It was a challenge but I think that I validated Marty choosing me in the fourth round to be the player to play that position.

The transition was hard and entailed a lot of studying. I used to work out at the University of South Carolina. Carolina gave me the freedom to come to their facility and work out.

Their coach was Jim Carlen. I remember engaging in a conversation with Coach Carlen. He said, "When you're in college, it's about 80% physical and 20% mental. When you get to the pro level, it's the reverse. It's 80% mental and 20% physical."

I heard what he said, but it didn't dawn on me until I got into NFL training camp. The playbook that I got was about 10 times thicker than the playbook that I got when I was with South Carolina State. There's a lot more intellectual work that you have to do, a lot more studying. It's more mental. People look at the NFL game and they see the physical side of it. They have no clue as to the mental aspect of the game you have to be able to deal with once you come into the National Football League.

Sam Huff
Sam Huff had retired years before I got there but I was certainly aware that Sam Huff had played with the Giants. Quite frankly that was the other thing that I liked about the Giants at that time, the rich history and tradition of the players who played before me. It gave me something to shoot for, to basically follow in the footsteps of an iconic player like Sam Huff.

Giants Linebackers
I'm not going to go so far as to say that we had the best linebacking group in NFL history. I like to think that, but I'm not going to say it out loud. The guys who I first played with, Brad Van Pelt and Brian Kelley, were very good players. Then when the Giants chose Lawrence Taylor and we went from a 4-3 defense to a 3-4 defense, we became a very dominant group of defensive players. We couldn't have been as dominant as we were without a strong defensive line.

After Brad and Brian left, Carl Banks and Gary Reasons assumed their roles, so it was Carl, Lawrence, Gary, and me. We wound up being a pretty good quartet of linebackers in the mid-'80s.

Being Named To 1978 Pro Bowl
It was gratifying. It was even more gratifying for me to come in and make the all-rookie team playing a position that I'd never played before. A couple of years later I made the Pro Bowl. It was before Lawrence Taylor got there and I sort of made that on my own merit. I was named NFC Linebacker of the Year twice. Those were tremendous honors.

When Lawrence arrived we got even better. He just elevated our play the way that he played the game. It took some pressure off of the other players, put a lot more pressure on him, and it gave us an opportunity to make plays. We all worked together and it worked out well.

Lawrence Taylor

Lawrence Taylor was an outstanding player. We were good but he was better. You want to focus on the best. He established himself as being the best. Again, we were able to infuse our game with the way that he played and it just elevated our play. There was no jealousy of the attention that Lawrence was getting.

For us, it was just about bottom line ... the production that we were able to produce on the football field. That was ultimately the bottom line. Each guy understood his role. I knew that my role wasn't to rush the quarterback. My role was to stop the run so I tried to pursue my role as best as possible. Lawrence did a great job and the other linebackers on the defensive line did their job.

The spotlight is always on the flashy guys. Lawrence was one of the flashy guys. He deserved the attention that he got as a player. If a player has a problem with the media attention then that could be a problem for the team. The player can sort of lash out at any time when it becomes a bit too much for him.

It didn't bother me because I had to deal with the media anyway as a captain. It allowed the other payers to just focus on playing the game and not have to deal with the media. They just flew under the radar and did not have to deal with cameras, microphones, and so forth. In some ways, that can be a plus for your teammates. In other ways it can be a negative for your teammates.

Lawrence Taylor Breaking Joe Theismann's Leg During A Monday Night Football Game

Every Friday the team would sit down and go over our goals as a defensive unit. The one thing that I remember saying during the meeting was, "Don't knock Joe Theismann out of the game." We knew everything about Joe. We wanted him in the game. If we had him in the game, there was a very good chance that we were going to win the game.

The play was a flea flicker. It initially looked like a running play where Joe Theismann handed the ball to John Riggins. Ultimately my responsibility was to stop the run. When I saw Riggins pitch the ball back to Theismann, I was already up into the line, trying stop the run. I was sort of in this no man's land where I didn't know whether I should go back to my pass coverage spot or go ahead and rush the quarterback.

I decided to react as a football player and I rushed the quarterback. Theismann sidestepped me. When he sidestepped me, Lawrence Taylor came in for the kill shot and went down on Joe's leg. If Joe was not as nimble as he was at that time, I would have tackled him. That was probably the most gruesome injury people have seen watching NFL football.

It was a situation that nobody wanted, but it happened and you reacted. As a humanitarian what you do is you stop being competitors and combatants and you take on a more humanitarian role. Both teams started to talk to Joe because we didn't want him to go into shock. Football just wasn't that important for those minutes that he was down on the ground.

Bill Belichick
Bill Belichick was a very headsy coach. It was about thinking. It was about creating new situations on the defensive side of the ball to disguise coverage. He utilized the strength of different phases of defense. Bill Belichick started us rushing two linemen, which was unheard of.

A lot of times when Bill would write things on the board, just diagramming as a coach does, we'd look and say, "Bill, that won't work." We'd go out on the field and incorporate it into our practice sessions, and it would work. During games we'd do things our opponents hadn't seen before and it would throw them off. We got to a point where we really began to trust Belichick.

We sort of looked at him as this mad scientist who could come up with all kinds of coverage and all kinds of fronts that would help us tremendously if we just bought into it. At that time, we all bought into it full tilt.

Bill Parcells
Bill Parcells came in and tried to coach a certain way. He treated guys like men and gave them a certain amount of freedom and

flexibility. It didn't work for him. We had a disastrous season. We had a lot of injuries. His first season as head coach we went 3-12-1 and Bill almost got fired. The next year he decided that he was going to do things his way.

When he did that he let some players, like Brian Kelley and Brad Van Pelt, go. He got players who were younger and had a hunger for playing. He experienced success in '84 and '85. Then in '86, we went to Super Bowl.

After Winning Super Bowl

I was an older player when we won our first Super Bowl. I was going into my 11th year and I could tell that I didn't really have much longer to play. As it turned out, after we won in '86, I played two more years and then that was a wrap for me.

I just wanted to move on with my life I wasn't really thinking about how many Super Bowls we could go to. I just felt very fortunate that we were able to get to at least one. One was better than none. There are a lot of great players who have never gotten to a Super Bowl.

Origin Of Gatorade Shower For Head Coach

It was Jim Burt's idea and started in 1985. Parcells had been riding Burt all week prior to the Redskin game. He was really getting under Burt's skin. We were playing the Redskins and as time was winding down, Burt came over to me and said, "You know that Parcells is a real S.O.B. We should get him." I said, "What do you mean 'we'?"

He said, "If you do something to him he won't say anything, but if I do something to him he will have my ass. You've got to do it with me." I said, "What do you propose?" He said, "Let's get him with the Gatorade." As time was winding down, Parcells took his earphones off and we doused him with the Gatorade. Nobody really saw it.
That was the one instance it occurred, in 1985. The next year, we lost our first game against the Dallas Cowboys. In the second game, we were playing the San Diego Chargers and nobody thought we'd win. As it turned out, we did win. We were all very jubilant about winning the game, so I grabbed the bucket of Gatorade and I doused Parcells.

The next week, we won again. I had to douse him again because if you do something one week and it works, you've got to keep doing it. Parcells is very superstitious and some of us were also very superstitious. So as long as we were winning, we had to get Parcells with the Gatorade. That's how the whole thing started. It perpetuated itself during the '86 season. It's one of those things now that everybody does and after all these years, players are still doing it.

Standing Next To Bill Parcells During National Anthem
It was just one of those things that happened. I remember the first time standing there as captain. I was standing there because I had to get instructions from Parcells as to what to call on the coin flip, or what side of the field we were going to defend. If I wasn't by him when the national anthem was being played, he'd call me and I had to stand to his left.

That's the way it happened and I really didn't think about it at the time. In retrospect, there were people who noticed. There are people who have written about it. He's a very superstitious coach and it's almost funny thinking back as to how superstitious he was.

Pro Football Hall Of Fame Induction
The Hall of Fame was never a goal of mine. I saw what it was doing to people around me more so than me. I was pretty good dealing with it. When people care about you, they want the best for you. I think there were so many people who wanted the best for me, when they held that Hall of Fame voting and I didn't make it, there were people who were upset. They would cry, they'd show anger, and so forth. It was like I was the only one who was taking it in stride.

I remember going to the gym to work out. There were people who would avoid me in the gym because they didn't know what to say. It's like having a death in the family and you don't know what to say to someone who is close to the person who died. You avoid them so you don't have to say anything. Many times people said, "Oh, I'm so sorry. You'll get it next year."

After five years, you get tired of hearing it; they get tired of saying it. And, they start to avoid you. Or, you go to a dinner at the

Waldorf Astoria and there's an emcee and he's introducing the athletes or celebrities in the audience. It would always come down to, "This man should be in the Pro Football Hall Of Fame." When you hear that over and over and over, you get tired of hearing it.

I made a decision that I wanted to take my name out of consideration for the Hall so I could live my life and just be a private person. I sat down, wrote a letter, and asked them to remove my name from consideration. It wasn't out of frustration as a lot of people thought. Honors really don't define me. They never have. I wanted to take possession of my life, take it back and just be able to go on and quietly do the things that I wanted to do without any kind of fanfare.

In 2006 when I found out I was being enshrined, it was interesting because I had divorced myself of the whole Hall of Fame situation. Once I wrote the letter and dropped it in the mailbox, I was done with it.

When I was elected, I didn't really have any feeling about it because it didn't mean anything to me. When I make up my mind to do something, my mind is made up. I really didn't feel anything. I had to accept the award. I could've easily have said, "Thanks, but no thanks," but my wife sat me down and told me I couldn't decline the honor because it wasn't about me. It was about my coaches, my family, and my kids. She was right.

Mr. Mara was probably my strongest advocate. He was my big supporter. For me to say, I don't want to deal with this, probably would have been an insult to him. I just decided to move forward and accept the award. During the days leading up to the Hall of Fame ceremony, I didn't really have a speech. I could have just got up and said thank you and then sat down, but I wanted to use that moment as an opportunity to shine the light on the issues of retired players.

Quite frankly, the first thing that I said, and that was probably the only thing that I remember about the speech, is that I implored the NFL and the Player's Association to do a better job in taking care of its own players. Doing that shined a light on the issues of meager pensions for former players.

Being Only Member Of Giants At Midfield For The Super Bowl Coin Toss

That wasn't planned. At least I didn't know anything about it until it happened. Coach Parcells told me to go out there. I started walking out on the field by myself and I felt the Bronco players walking toward me. I was like, oh man, wow, what five, six, seven, eight ... and I was the only player representing the Giants. It was an honor for me. I recognized at that time there were some great players on the team, but I was being singled out to lead the team, represent the Giant organization, and represent all the Giant fans. That was a tremendous honor for me.

New York Giant Harry Carson runs after intercepting Washington Redskin Joe Theismann's pass as Theismann tries to make the tackle. Photograph copyright Associated Press

Chapter 16

Tony Dorsett

> College:
> Pittsburgh
>
> Career History:
> Dallas Cowboys (1977–1987)
> Denver Broncos (1988)
>
> 1994 Inductee Pro Football Hall Of Fame

College Choice
I was a big fan of Lydell Mitchell and Franco Harris who played at Penn State when I was a kid. All I wanted to do was go to Penn State to be like Lydell Mitchell and Franco Harris. That's all I talked about. As a matter of fact, my last game in high school, I had a monster game and in big bold print in the newspaper the next day was Penn State, next stop.

I was what you call the Blue Chip recruit. USC, UCLA, Arizona State, and schools way out west, recruited me. Michigan, Ohio State and all these schools back on the East Coast were recruiting me. I was waiting for Penn State Coach Joe Paterno. I'm like, "Where is he at?" I lost interest in Penn State after a while because I thought that they showed a lack of interest.

Another thing that caused me lose to interest was my Penn State visit was one of the more negative visits that I took. Back then, we had unlimited visitation rights. I was going somewhere almost every weekend. I was also getting frustrated and confused along the way. When I went to Penn State, all of the players I talked to said, "You may come here as a quarterback, but you may leave here as a center."

Penn State had John Cappelletti and he was going into his senior year. He was a contender for the Heisman, which he ended up winning that year. Joe Paterno told me when I finally had my visit,

that he wanted me to be a defensive back my first year. He said when John Cappelletti graduated he would put me at running back. The only thing that kept going through my mind was the fact that all the players said, "Come in as a quarterback, you may end up as a center." My training was to be a running back first.

I figured, and don't take it wrong, I had cockiness and everything, but I had a little swag back then. I said to myself, "If Joe wants me to be a defensive back, I'll be a be damn good defensive back. Then, Joe's not going to want to put me back on offense."

When Notre Dame was recruiting me, Tom Pagna, Coach Ara Parseghian's right-hand man, supposedly told Ara that I was just a skinny little kid from Aliquippa, Pennsylvania who would never make it as a major college running back. You could only imagine what my thoughts were during the week of preparation to play the Fighting Irish. That tells it all right there. That's one of the motivating forces that helped get me ready to play against the Fighting Irish. Against Notre Dame as a freshman, I think I went for over 200 yards rushing and then as a junior, 303 yards rushing. I set a record for the most yards against an opponent and that was Notre Dame. They had great defenses back then.

Adjustment To College At Pittsburgh
There was an adjustment to college. I almost left school because I was pretty much a very introverted young man. It was hard for me to make friends. I hid behind my little dark round sunglasses. I could play on the field, but socially, it was hard for me to make the adjustment.

As a matter of fact, my hometown is only about a 30-minute drive from the university so I spent more time back home. My mom was like, "Boy, what are you doing home?" It just took me a while to get acclimated. Once I did, my Mom was saying, "When are you coming home?"

Socially, it was a big adjustment for me. Pitt was rebuilding at that time and it was just a perfect fit. I was glad that the University of Pittsburgh made a coaching change because I probably wouldn't have gone there if they had not.

Pittsburgh Winning National Championship
We went to bowl games every year and won the National Championship my senior year. That was a script made for Hollywood.

We lost our first two starting quarterbacks my senior year. The second or third game of the season we went down to Atlanta. For Robert Haygood, our starting quarterback, it was his hometown. He got hurt tearing his knee up. We lost him for the year.

Then Matt Cavanaugh came in as the starting quarterback. During training camp those two were fighting for the starting position, the outcome could have gone either way. Matt came in and about three or four games later, Matt got hurt. Fortunately for us, it wasn't for the whole year. We were down to our fifth year quarterback who had never taken a snap.

Our offense was pulling for our defense and our defense was pulling for the offense. Our defense won a couple of games for us. They came up big for us during the absence of Matt Cavanaugh. Tommy Yewcic, who is a congressman now, filled in pretty good for Matt while he was out.

Matt came back later in the year. We ended up undefeated. We went to the Sugar Bowl and beat Georgia. We beat the dog and we won the national championship.

NFL Draft
Tampa Bay just hired coach John McKay from USC, who had coached Ricky Bell there. Ricky Bell was "their prototype running back" at 6'3", 230 pounds, whereas I was 5'11", 183 pounds.

John McKay knew all about Ricky Bell because he coached him at USC. He drafted Ricky Bell with the first pick in the draft. Seattle had the second pick. Somehow the Dallas Cowboys bamboozled them for the pick and I ended up in Dallas. Thank God for that because I found it a lot healthier for me to be running behind an established offensive line with Dallas than Seattle, an expansion team in the NFL the year before.

Roger Staubach

I was blessed to have the opportunity to play behind one of the more prolific quarterbacks at that time in the National Football League, Roger Staubach. He was a role model, the ultimate pro, ultimate family man, and a God-fearing man. We had his leadership. You learn from guys like that on how to become a real pro, how to handle yourself both on and off the football field. I was privileged to have that opportunity. I respect him to this day. I have nothing but admiration for Roger Staubach. I always say, if I wanted somebody to be my role model and my mentor, it would be Mr. Staubach.

Not Being Inserted into Starting Lineup Until 10th Game of Rookie Year

Coach Landry and I went at it indirectly through the media. Tom Landry had a way of humbling people. Coach Landry said he saw a young kid coming in who won the national championship and got all this media attention. To keep me grounded he did not start me until the 10th game of my rookie year.

When I finally went in to have a one-on-one with him, he told me, "We expected you to be a starter by now." I said, "Coach, so did I." I guess he realized he was getting the best of me because I was getting a little lackadaisical.

My attitude changed after I told him, "Coach, I've written this year off." I was pretty much going to go to training camp the next year and start up. He told me, "All you need to do is just pick it up a little bit, change your attitude a little bit, and act like it bothers you when you drop a pass or something like that. Then you'll be a starter."

I went out to practice. I started exhibiting a little bit more effort, and he made me the starter. I felt bad because Preston Pearson was the starter. Preston came in from the Pittsburgh Steelers. I had just been in Pittsburgh a year earlier, winning the national championships. He made me the starter coming back from playing the Steelers in

Pittsburgh, which was a great feeling for me. From there, I guess you could say the rest was history.

First Player To Win National Championship In College & Super Bowl The Next Year

It was like a set-up, because I didn't have anywhere else to go, but down. I won the national championship one year and the Super Bowl Championship the following year. Fortunately for me, it didn't go down. We didn't win another championship, but we went back to the Super Bowl the following year. We were in three other consecutive conference championship games, but unfortunately we weren't able to get over that final hurdle to win another Super Bowl. I enjoyed it. I had a lot of great teammates. I had a lot of great rivalries going and made a lot of great friends during my career in the National Football League.

It was great winning the Super Bowl. I thought, this is what it's all about right here. We already had a Super Bowl win. I thought it was going to be cool, but it just didn't work out like that. We were always in the thick of it. We had some great teams and great players. I enjoyed every one of my years here in Dallas.

Losing To Steelers In Super Bowl

I was mentally prepared, mentally ready to play against the Steelers. Growing up in Western Pennsylvania, the Steelers are what you're all about. I'm still a big Steelers fan. That's my roots. That's what I'm all about. I watched those guys play when I was a kid. Then all of a sudden, I got the opportunity to play against them in "the ultimate game." I was up and ready to go. I was hyped. Trust me, I was hyped and ready. It was just unfortunate; it was one of the better Super Bowl games. I think it was 35-31.

99 Yard Touchdown Run On Monday Night Football

That's one of the more memorable moments of my career. There are a lot of people who remember that run more so than any other run because of the platform that it took place on, Monday Night Football. It was the only ticket in town. Everybody was watching the NFL. You can only tie that record.

We only had 10 men on the field. It was partly my doing because I came in with the play and you can run that play from the two-back or a single-back set. In the single-back it's going to be me. I told

Ron Springs, the other running back, to get out. I said we're going to run a single-back formation.

When Ron went back to the sideline, everybody said, "You're supposed to be on the field." He always said, "There was no way I was running back out on that field." He realized we could never play with ten men on the field. He said, "I wasn't about to get us a penalty, backed up on the one-yard line and have to come back and face Tom Landry." So he stayed on the sideline and I said, "Well, he wouldn't have been able to run that far anyway so it's a good thing he did not come back in."

When I got to about midfield I made a move and I was behind Drew Pearson. There were two defenders ahead of me. I was looking at Drew Pearson's legs from behind. Drew's a little knock-kneed and pigeon-toed. I was looking at his legs and he started tiring and I said you know what, I'm going to make a move right now and see if I can get past Drew and these guys. I actually thought I was going to get pushed out of bounds because I was so close to the sidelines. I was tiring myself. The opponent pushed me, but he didn't shove me hard enough to push me out of bounds. I ended up going all the way for a touchdown.

Photograph copyright Associates Press

Chapter 17

Steve Largent

> College:
> Tulsa
>
> Career History:
> Houston Oilers (1976)
> Seattle Seahawks (1976–1989)
>
> 1995 Inductee Pro Football Hall Of Fame

College Choice
I would have loved to go to Oklahoma University. The football team there was running the wishbone offense at that time. I was a receiver even in high school. There weren't a lot of opportunities for catching many passes at OU with the wishbone offense. They also signed Tinker Owens that year.

My grandfather was a big influence in my life when I was deciding where I would go to college. He had really encouraged me to consider the University of Tulsa. Then when they ended up offering me a scholarship, it was a done deal.

NFL Draft
I was drafted by the Houston Oilers in the 4th round of the NFL draft in 1976. Bum Phillips told me that I was not good enough to play in the Oilers organization. They released me and I packed my bags and headed home looking for work. The Seahawks called me the same week and said, "Hey we want to give you another chance." It turned out they worked out a trade with the Oilers.

I was not a good rookie player. I didn't really know how to study; I didn't know how to prepare myself for practices or for games. It was a real learning experience for me going through the process that I did after being released from one team and getting a second chance in Seattle. I did everything I could to take advantage of the chance I had.

Joining Seattle Seahawks, An Expansion Team

I knew when I went into the Seattle locker room that it was a different situation. Even the veterans in training camp that year had their names written on tape on their helmets. Nobody knew each other; everybody was vying for a position on the team. The real key for me making the team was the fact that Jerry Rhome had come from the University of Tulsa, my alma mater, that same year to become the quarterback and receiver coach. He was the guy that really convinced the Seahawks to get me after the Oilers released me. When I came to Seattle, we were essentially running the old University of Tulsa playbook. We ran the same plays in Tulsa for three years. I knew the game plan in terms of the passing attack with the Seahawks the first day I stepped on the field. That was a real advantage for me.

Jim Zorn

Jim Zorn and I became fast friends and teammates as well. He is my best friend to this day. There was a connection that we had that is unusual for quarterbacks and receivers to have. Our relationship was one that carried over beyond the playing field and locker room. I think that was extremely instrumental in our development as players with the Seahawks. Jim was vying for a starting job as a quarterback and I was doing the same thing as a receiver. We just kind of connected because we were both guys that like to work hard, stay late practicing after the coaches had blown the whistles, and all the other players headed into the locker room. We would still be out there working on routes, catching balls, and just throwing the ball as much as we could. I think that really worked as an advantage for both of us.

Jack Patera

The first season for the Seahawks was also Jack Patera's first year as a head coach. We didn't win very many games. He was willing to do anything, including running fake field goals, punts, and things like that just to try to keep the ball on offense. Actually, during Jack's first several years as head coach, the one aspect of the team that worked well was the offense. Defensively we had more struggles.

Offensively, most of the time, we put a lot of points on the board. It was fun to play on that team because we had a lot of great veteran players that came from other teams. They would tell us stories about the way they did it in Miami, Cleveland, Dallas, or wherever they came from. There was a good nucleus of players, including Sherman Smith and Dave Brown, with whom you could really bond. You knew they were winners even though we didn't win that often in Seattle.

We were two and twelve that first year. I don't think the Tampa Bay Buccaneers won a game. In fact one of the two wins we had was against Tampa. We were not very good, but we were better than Tampa.

Playing Philosophy
My attitude was always, how do we win? It was not how many passes I caught. I worked just as hard during the offseason after my first season, as I worked before my first season in the NFL. It was never about how good could I get. It was about how could we get better as a team. That was always my focus every year I played.

Seattle Seahawks Progression
We were nine and seven in both the third and fourth seasons. That was pretty incredible back then considering that we were playing in the AFC West with the Oakland Raiders, Denver Broncos, San Diego Chargers, and Kansas City Chiefs, all of which were good teams. We were very competitive and felt like we were right on the cusp of becoming a real playoff contender. Unfortunately, that didn't happen because the wheels kind of fell off after the fourth year.

Transition At Quarterback From Jim Zorn To David Krieg
In the middle of the 1982 season, Jack Patera was fired. In 1983, Jim Zorn's position as our starting quarterback really began to be challenged. During the 1981 or 1982 season, Jim broke his ankle. Jim was never the same after he broke his ankle; he wasn't as mobile as he had been the previous five to seven years. Jim's decreased mobility really hurt us as a team and him as a player. The Seahawks began eyeing other quarterbacks. Dave Krieg came in about 1982 or 1983, and started contending for the starting position, which he eventually took over by the end of 1983.

Chuck Knox

Chuck Knox came in in 1983 as head coach and really turned the team around. He got a few veteran players from other teams and he really inspired the young guys and me. We knew this was a guy that knew how to win and get us into the playoffs. We all thought he was going to take us there. We didn't know it was going to be in his first year. He drafted Curt Warner from Penn State, in the first round. Curt came in and had an outstanding year. He ran the ball great, rushing for twelve or thirteen hundred yards. We played great football. After a couple of dismal years it was fun being a playoff contender that first year under Chuck Knox.

Chuck had experience. I think it's really important for a team to believe in their coach. The fact that Chuck had coached teams that were championship level teams meant he knew what needed to be done. He implemented what needed to be done immediately. Everyone had a lot of confidence in him, his coaching ability, and his coaching staff. That meant a lot to our team and was what we were missing before Chuck got there.

1982 & 1987 NFL Lockouts

The NFL owners locked out the players. My philosophy was that I signed a contract with the Seattle Seahawks not with the players association. My first obligation was to play.

In 1982 I felt obligated to play, but there was no opportunity. In 1987, there was an opportunity to play because there were games with replacement players. I went to play in the first game when they had replacement players and the ownership actually came to me and said, "Steve we don't want you to come in. We want you to stay out and let this process work out because we don't want to disrupt the positive momentum we have as a team right now." I listened to them, and I said, "Okay. I'm not going to do that." Toward the end of the strike, they said there was a deal; then they said there wasn't a deal. The owner said he erected a superficial time-line that if you weren't in by this certain time, you couldn't play in the game the following week. I reported for the last game for the replacement players in 1987. I played that game in Detroit.

I think all of us were frustrated with the deliberations, or lack of resolution, to the situation. In my situation in 1987, that was about my twelfth year in the league. I knew I didn't have many years left; in fact I was playing on borrowed time. The fact that we were under a union that was striking, was penalizing me in the opportunity to play in what I viewed the twilight of my career.

My teammates reported, literally two days after I did. They had come in after the deadline so they couldn't play in the game that Sunday. Since I had reported two days earlier, I was able to play in the game on Sunday. When I played in the Sunday game, the overwhelming majority of the guys didn't hold it against me. There were a few players, including prominent ones, who held it against me. They even continued to hold that grudge against me until a few years ago.

Most Memorable Tackle
In 1988, we were playing the Broncos in Denver and I ran a twelve-yard post route. Dave Krieg hung the ball and Mike Harden got to me just before the ball did. He hit me with a forearm to my head. He bent me over backwards and I was out before I hit the ground. I don't even remember hitting the ground. In fact, the ball came down, hit me on the chest, and rolled off. I think the league fined him $5,000, which was a lot of money back then. Then we played the Broncos in Seattle in December in the next to last game of the year, which was an ESPN game. Harden made an interception in the end zone and came running out of the end zone. I was on the other side of the field. I just drew a beeline right for his chest and I made a great tackle and the rest is history. I will never forget that tackle.

Lester Hayes & Mike Haynes
Lester Hayes and Mike Haynes were both equally good cornerbacks. Mike is in the Hall of Fame and Lester is not. They were both very good. Lester Hayes played linebacker at Texas A&M. He was a big, strong cornerback, but he could run too. They were both very difficult to play against. I played against Lester before Mike. Mike was with the New England Patriots before going to the Raiders.

Lester loved to wear that Stickum. Every time I played against him I would end up being covered in Stickum. He would have it on his hands, wrists, shoes, and socks. They played bump and run coverage and he got it all over you. I would get grass and all that other kinds of stuff sticking to me. It was gross. Lester felt like he could catch the ball better on interceptions if he wore it. Fred Biletnikoff used it, so Lester was going to use it too.

Pro Football Hall Of Fame Induction

Being inducted was like a dream. I had never really thought of myself as a Hall of Fame player. I had never let myself imagine that big of a dream for myself. It was extremely fun, extremely gratifying, and rewarding. I've always looked at it as an honor that I share with my teammates, coaches, and the organization that helped get me there.

Physical Traits As A Wide Receiver

I was average sized and had average speed. They used to say I could play well in a phone booth, meaning I didn't have the breakaway speed of a James Lofton or John Jefferson. If I needed to catch a seven-yard pass or fifteen-yard pass, I could get open and catch the ball if the quarterback got it there. That's kind of the role I played in Seattle. It's really surprising that the passing game is totally different today than it was when I played. I averaged over sixteen yards a catch. At the time, I held the records for the most yards and most catches in a career. The sixteen yards per catch that I had is pretty amazing when you consider that I was known as the too small, too slow guy.

What I found is that the guys who were really, really fast didn't really like going over the middle. I was just one of those guys who wasn't very fast, but didn't mind going over the middle. I didn't love it. Nobody loves getting their brains beat out, but I could make a living there, and I did. There is a place for every style, fashion, and form of a NFL receiver. I had one style and I tried to maximize it.

I say this to young people, including my four kids, all the time: "Don't let other people limit your desire or your ability. Just make the most of what you've got. You'll surprise yourself and surprise a whole heck of a lot of other people as well."

Photograph copyright Associated Press

Chapter 18

Earl Campbell

> College:
> Texas
>
> Career History:
> Houston Oilers (1978–1984)
> New Orleans Saints (1984–1985)
>
> 1991 Inductee Pro Football Hall Of Fame

College Choice
I felt like Texas, with Darrell Royal as head coach, was the best school for me, not Oklahoma. Those were the two schools that were really dominating everything when I was coming up. So many people were going to Oklahoma. It wasn't that I was afraid of it. I just thought that being from the state of Texas, it was best to have players from the state of Texas there. It worked out.

Darrell Royal had a scout named Ken Dabbs. Ken Dabbs spent more time with me than Darrell Royal, because he was the recruiting coordinator. Once I got a chance to meet Coach Royal, we hit it off right away. Coach Dabbs started coming to my high school during my sophomore year, recruiting guys. He lost those guys, but I believe that I was the first one he recruited to come to UT that he was after. Then Coach Royal and I got involved.

Darrell Royal
He was a great man, no-nonsense. He wanted the best players and wanted to get the best out of you. It was about football, but it was also about being a student and getting you ready for life after sports.

Coach Royal suddenly decided to retire after the 1976 season. It was a shock then. As I got older, I learned that after you've stayed in the game so long and won national championships and all that, there's nothing left to do. I've heard that he couldn't control some of the players and couldn't sign the best players like he previously did. I believe that he decided I came in winning; I'm going out a winner. Nothing's wrong with having another interest in life.

Fred Akers

I was sure Darrell Campbell was going to replace Coach Royal as head coach because he was the defensive coordinator under Coach Royal for many years. He was right under Coach Royal, so I felt as though he was going to take over. During my freshman year, Fred Akers was the running back coach. He had been working for Darrell Royal for twenty some years. When he got the job it just made sense, because we all knew Fred Akers.

Looking back on it, the best thing that happened in my whole career was when Coach Akers came in and changed everything up right away. I believe that's why I was able to win the Heisman Trophy. Even though we lost against Notre Dame in the national championship, we competed. Coach Akers is the coach with the most wins in the history of the university.

All the guys knew him because he was there with Coach Royal. He was a great guy and a dynamic coach. We always used to get on him because he was just very neat all the time. You'd see him at practice and he looked like he was a GQ model. On game days he always had his suit on. He was an unbelievable guy and a very, very good coach.

I will continue to say the best thing that happened to me in my football career was when he came and changed the offense from the wishbone to the single backup. I won the Heisman Trophy and competed for the national championship. As a gentleman told me a few years ago, "Fans weren't wondering how many games Texas was going to win back then. We were wondering how many points we were going to beat them by."

1978 Championship Game Against Notre Dame
It was great. We were just getting into redshirting players. Not to make any excuses, but Notre Dame had been redshirting players for years. We had fourth year guys playing against fifth year guys from Notre Dame. One of the fifth year guys for Notre Dame was Ross Browner. They had a very good football team. Unfortunately we fell short, they won, and life goes on.

Joe Montana
I really didn't realize who Joe Montana was until I got into pro football and he was playing for the San Francisco 49ers. O. J. Simpson was on the 49ers. We were playing the 49ers in the Astrodome and I was concerned about watching O. J. Simpson as a runner. I saw Joe Montana and I said, "Oh, that's the quarterback from Notre Dame, that beat us."

Winning Heisman Trophy
Winning the Heisman Trophy was unbelievable. I never knew what the Heisman Trophy was until a guy named Tony Dorsett won the Heisman. I was working a construction job during the summer before my senior year and a guy on the construction job had a newspaper. He was reading it and talking about Tony Dorsett the Heisman Trophy winner joining the Dallas Cowboys.

That is when I made the decision that I wanted to try and win that trophy. I went and told the Texas trainer, Frank Medina, my decision. He said, "If you want to do that, you come over here and work out." That season our team was on a roll and I won the Heisman Trophy. Dreams can come true.

NFL Draft
I really didn't know I was going to be the first pick in the draft. My roommate was a guy named Alfred Jackson. He played split end on our team, and he went to the Atlanta Falcons in the draft. I was a speech communication major. The day of the draft I had a test. Alfred said, "Hey, what are you doing, Earl?" I said, "I've got tests today. I'm going to school." He said, "Man, are you crazy?" I said, "No, Albert. I've got this test. I'm going to school. I'll be back in a while."

I got over on campus and was messing around with some guys. I didn't make it home until 6:00 p.m. Alfred said, "Man, you've got to be the luckiest guy in the world. This guy named Bum Phillips has been calling you." I said, "What did he want?" He said, "That's gonna be your coach, that guy wearing a cowboy hat down there in Houston, Bum Phillips." That's how I found out I that was the number one draft choice.

Bum Phillips

Bum Phillips never knew my name was Earl Campbell up until this day. He knew me as "EC." Back then, it was popular that you'd get the uniform number you had in college if you were the Heisman Trophy winner or one of the big-time running backs. I wore number 20 in college. He said, "Hey, you want number 20?" I said, "It doesn't matter to me. I don't think a jersey gets you into the end zone." He said, "I don't have number 20, but I'll get it if you want it." I said, "No, it doesn't make any difference."

We were in the Oilers locker room and he reached in a laundry bag, got a jersey, threw it, and hit me in the face. He said, "Have you thought about this number?" I said, "Great with me." That's how I ended up with number 34.

My relationship with Bum was like a marriage from heaven. Bum and I were like father and son.

All I wanted to do was prove that I wasn't going to be a failure as a Heisman Trophy winner. Back then most of the Heisman trophy winners didn't produce in the NFL. The way Tony Dorsett produced in Dallas, I wanted to be like that in Houston. I knew I could play football. I knew God gave me that gift. Bum Phillips was about being part of a family. I think Bum Phillips cut some good guys that didn't want to work as part of the team. He wanted us working as a team. There was no "I" with him, and that was fine. I believe our football team was a team of overachievers because of his belief.

Bum was the total opposite of any coach. He was just a great, great guy. I really miss him. He knew a lot about life, too. He was a cowboy who loved country music and had ranches with cutting horses. Bum and Mel Blount of the Pittsburgh Steelers were really tight because they would compete with those horses. Mel would go to his ranch a lot. Mel was always in our locker room. We would play against each other hard. Everybody loved Bum, because it was more than just about football, it was being a good human being.

Ranching
I used to work on a ranch when I was growing up. It used to be in my mother's family when she was a little girl. I went back and bought it during my rookie year. The owner told my mom he would only sell it to me for this price. I bought it in 1978, and have owned it since.

Work Ethic
I would have to say my mother taught me the work ethic that I have today. Darrell Royal messed with it a little bit, put his blessing on it; Fred Akers put his blessing on it; Bum Phillips put his blessing on it; but the good Lord and my mother taught me how to do all that.

My mother was my toughest critic, as far as making sure I was trying to do the right thing. Of course, I have six brothers and four sisters. As she says, "Earl is just one of my kids, number seven in the family."

Nickname "The Tyler Rose"
Tyler, Texas is known as the Rose Capital of the World. I started working on ranches, hauling hay and all that stuff. That's what I would do as my second job. My first job was working in the rose field. My family owned a rose field business and we worked in the rose fields for other people. One day this guy named Rick Ingraham, who was our left guard for Texas, heard me doing an interview. He said, "Way to go, Tyler Rose." Rick's mother was from there, and that's how he knew. That was my freshman year, and that's how I got that nickname. It stuck with me, "The Tyler Rose."

Competing Against Tony Dorsett
I competed against a guy in Texas named Tony Dorsett. I would get the pilot on the airplane to call Dallas and see how many yards Tony Dorsett gained. I always wanted to outdo him. On Mondays I would try to find out what Eric Dickerson and Walter Payton did. I think in my day, Walter was the top out of all the running backs. Of course,

the master was Jim Brown. The more I played, the more people said I was like Jim Brown, but Tony Dorsett and Walter Payton were the two guys I really competed against.

Walter Payton
Walter Payton could kick those legs and put a move on you, and he could run over you as well. He was an all-around running back. My deal was I couldn't catch the football very well. I didn't like that. I wanted to run with it. Different running backs will do different things.

Dallas Cowboys America's Team
The Dallas Cowboys used to play the Washington Redskins every Thanksgiving. The first year Dallas decided to play somebody else, it was the Houston Oilers. During his pep talk before the game, Bum Phillips said, "Hey, let's go play, guys. Hell, let's go play America's team. They may be America's team, but we are Texas' team." We beat them on that Thanksgiving Day.

That was a time in Texas when the Cowboys were hot; the Oilers were hot. Everything was just great: Nolan Ryan was pitching for the Houston Astros; Hakeem Olajuwon was down there in Houston. That was a great time to be in Texas.

Common Opinion Bum Phillips Ran Earl Campbell Into The Ground
I feel if I didn't run the football twenty-five, thirty times a game ... right in the middle of the fourth quarter was when I woke up and really wanted to play football. I needed that football in my hand that many times to do what I had to do. You pay a price for everything. To get something out of life, you pay a price for it. I paid a price for it, but I did it my way.

Toughest Defense
There isn't any doubt; it was Joe Greene, L.C. Greenwood, and the Pittsburgh Steelers. You get through Joe and you had to deal with L.C. You get through L.C., you had to deal with Dwight White. They were just good all-around.

Steve McMichael
We used to call Steve McMichael Bamm-Bamm in college. He had his hair sticking up like Bamm-Bamm on that cartoon. People in Chicago

say Steve McMichael to me and I say, "Who?" They say, "Your teammate." I say, "Oh, y'all are talking about Bamm-Bamm." When he tackled me, I would say, "Bamm-Bamm, take it easy."

Decision To Retire

I was playing one Sunday with the Saints in New Orleans, and I noticed I couldn't get in there and fight the opponents like I used to. In preseason, you've only got three to four hours after the game to mess around and go do what you want to. Then one Saturday night during pre-season Ricky Jackson and a bunch of guys were saying to me, "Come on, Earl, come on, go out." I said, "No, man. I can't." When I wanted to go to the restroom, I was crawling on the floor because my feet had swelled up so much and were so banged up. I just said to myself, "Earl, this is enough of this." I called my wife and Bum Phillips and said, "Hey, this is the way I want to go." Bum said, "You've gotta do what you've gotta do," and so I did.

Pro Football Hall Of Fame Induction

I don't know how it feels to be President Obama, but that's the way I would say that it feels getting into the Hall of Fame. That's the highest honor you can get as a pro football player. I am very proud that I played well against the people I played against. I am also proud that my peers thought enough of me and felt like I was good enough to belong in the Hall of Fame.

Earl Campbell Statute Outside Darrell K. Royal-Texas Memorial Stadium

That was a great honor. My mom is no longer here, but I'm so happy she had a chance to be at the ceremony. That's something that represents your life and your accomplishments. Not only the state of Texas, but also the University of Texas, felt like I deserved it. I felt honored to be alongside the Ricky Williams statute.

Photograph copyright Associated Press

Chapter 19

Tony Dungy

> College:
> Minnesota
>
> Career History:
> As Player:
> Pittsburgh Steelers (1977–1978) San Francisco 49ers (1979) New York Giants (1980)
>
> As Coach:
> Pittsburgh Steelers (1981–1983)
> Defensive backs coach
> Pittsburgh Steelers (1984–1988)
> Defensive coordinator
> Kansas City Chiefs (1989–1991)
> Defensive backs coach
> Minnesota Vikings (1992–1995)
> Defensive coordinator
> Tampa Bay Buccaneers (1996–2001)
> Head coach
> Indianapolis Colts (2002–2008)
> Head coach
>
> 2016 Inductee Pro Football Hall Of Fame

College Choice
I grew up in the heyday of Michigan State football during which they played to a 10-10 tie with Notre Dame. I always wanted to be a Spartan. During my senior year in high school, Duffy Daugherty retired and that took a little luster off things. Michigan State was looking for a coach and Duffy's number one assistant, Cal Stoll, had recruited some monster players for the Spartans. Coach Stoll got the job with the University of Minnesota. Coach Stoll knew my high

school coach and one thing led to another. I took a visit to Minneapolis and loved it. It was a great opportunity for me.

I met Bobby Bell on my recruiting trip up there. They had an African-American quarterback by the name of Sandy Stephens, who led them to the national championship. He was the first African American quarterback to play on a national championship team. Obviously that meant a lot to me and it made a big impression on me. They played some really good football in the early '60s. It had been a while and we kind of set out to rekindle some of that flame. It was a fun, fun time.

NFL Draft
I thought I was going to get drafted. I worked out for a lot of people before the draft, including a lot of NFL quarterback coaches. I felt that I would get a chance to play. Marv Levy was actually the coach of the Montreal Alouettes in the Canadian league at that time. They had my rights there and they wanted me to sign with them before the draft. I said, "No I'm going to wait and just see what my options are." I didn't get drafted and that was a huge disappointment. I just thought my career had really come to an end. I was thinking of taking up Coach Levy on his offer and going to Canada.

I got a call from Tom Moore who was my quarterback coach my first three years in Minnesota. He had taken a job with the Steelers. They wanted to sign me as a free agent and switch me over to defense. That was something I had not even thought about, the option to play another position. When I got that call something just told me I wanted to play with the best and I wanted to see if I could make it in the National Football League. I think it was God's way of kind of delivering me into the coaching profession. I went to Pittsburgh and it was the best thing that happened to me on a number of fronts. I learned a lot about football, I had the opportunity to be around Coach Noll, to be around some great Hall of Fame players, and win a Super Bowl. It was the best of all worlds.

Tom Moore
Tom Moore was tremendous. We ran the exact same offense the Indianapolis Colts ran with Peyton Manning, but we did it 30 years before. It was a no huddle, up-tempo offensive. The quarterback

controlled everything at the line of scrimmage. I loved playing for him. We set some Big Ten passing records back in the '70s. It was fun but the big thing for me was having to control things, take things that you learn in the meeting room from watching the video, and put it into practice out on the field. It was a lot of fun. I enjoyed that.

He ended up going to the Steelers to coach their receivers. When I got there, he kind of paved the way for me. I was playing defense but I loved working for Coach Moore. Years later I ended up having him on my staff as our Offensive Coordinator in Indianapolis.

Chuck Noll
Chuck Noll was absolutely the best. He was a teacher. He helped you play better and learn not only about the game, but also about yourself as a person. I remember our first meeting because he said two things that I will remember the rest of my life. The first thing he said was that the National Football League was business; it was a profession, but you couldn't make football your life. For those of you who make football your entire life, you'll leave the game disappointed. You have to be well rounded. He wanted you to look at other things and get prepared for your next career. You can't pour everything into football.

Then the second thing that he said was, champions in this league don't do extraordinary things, champions do the ordinary things better than everyone else. That's what we're going to work on. We're going to be fundamentally sound and we're going to out technique people. We're not going to out think people and fool people. That became my philosophy. It was very successful there, and I put that into practice as a player.

Then, I got a chance to work on his coaching staff for eight years. I learned why he said those things and how to get that message across to people. He was just the best mentor and tutor that a person could have in football.

Coach Noll always talked about preparing yourself for your life after football, away from the job. He taught me that. He had a lot of things that he enjoyed doing. I watched him as a player and then when I was on his staff, the things that he did away from the game.

We used to have seven weeks off in the summer and we would never hear from him. There wouldn't be a call to check in or any of that. He was gone doing different things.

He gave us one week a month off during the off-season and that was a practice that I tried to continue with my coaches as well. Those guys work so hard during the season, when they're in the off-season, they should get away from it and find other things to do. When he decided to retire we knew that we wouldn't see him involved in football again.

Being Named Youngest Assistant Coach & Also Youngest Coordinator In NFL History

It's funny because I played three years in the National Football League and at 24 years old, I was basically done. I had been traded a couple of times and cut once. I wasn't sure what I was going to do. Coach Noll said, "I would love for you to be on our coaching staff. I think you have a good head for the game. You would be an asset to us, and you would benefit." I was 25 years old when I started with him. Three years later, assistant coaches had moved up to the ladder and we lost some coaches to promotions.

Coach Noll said, "You know more about the defense than anybody else in the country. You're going to be the coordinator and you're going to run it." I was 28 years old with not much experience. That was the way Coach Noll did things. He didn't worry about what other people thought. He had faith in his people. I owe him a lot for making that move when I was so young.

Waiting For Chance To Be Named A Head Coach In NFL

I was still very young, so I wasn't worried about it that much. People started talking after Pittsburgh had some success in the late '80s, that maybe I was going to be the first African American head coach in the NFL. I was still 30, 31, 32 years old so I knew I had quite a long time to go. The one time that I did get disappointed, was in 1993. I was the defensive coordinator with the Minnesota Vikings. We had the number one defense in football that year, leading the league in fewest yards allowed and in most takeaways. We played great. There were seven job openings and I didn't even get an interview. That's when I thought man how many times are you going to have the number one defense and have this many openings? If it doesn't happen this year it may never happen.

I was really fortunate the chaplain with the Vikings, Tom Lamphere, a good friend of mine said, "You can't worry about those kind of things. You just have to do your job the best you can and let God control everything else." That kind of took my mind off of it. I thought, let me just do my job and not worry about anything else or about what's going to happen. Two years later I got the job as head coach with the Buccaneers, and it was the perfect timing for me.

John Randle's Trash Talking
I told John Randle, "If you spent as much time on the game plan as you spent on finding out about the other team's offensive guards and their life history, we would be a lot better." John loved trash talking. He was a smart player and felt trash talking would give him an advantage. He worked on our stuff and our game plan inside and out. He would spend hours finding out little details about the opponents that he could just spring on them at the right time. He was a great trash talker.

He tried to tell everyone how to do it, but nobody could spend that much time finding out those little details and nobody was that bold to say some of the things about people's parents, girlfriends, where they went to school, and maybe their transcript or police record. He would research everything on guys.

Being Named Head Coach Of The Tampa Bay Buccaneers
By that time I was 40 years old. I was fired up about being named a head coach. The Bucs had had a losing culture. They had 13 straight losing seasons and everyone told me don't go there, it's not a job you can succeed in. We had some tremendously talented players. It was a challenge for me to change the attitude and get guys to think like winners, and believe as Coach Noll said, "Ordinary things would make a difference." I talked about being on time and being places when we say we are going to be there. If we are scheduled to have an appearance, to be there not on time, but be there ahead of time. I wanted them to represent the team and the city well. We talked about those things constantly. When that got going, our play on the field picked up.

Key To Buccaneers Success

It was getting guys who could play and had talent. Then getting them to buy into the system, believe in it, and to support each other. So much of it was really, really good fortune and again, I think God's planning and timing. When I was with the Vikings, we had an idea of the type of players we wanted. When I was with the Vikings and John Lynch was coming out of college, I remembered saying, "Boy he would be perfect for us." Tampa Bay beat us to the punch in drafting him. In 1995, my last year with the Vikings, we had a chance to draft Warren Sapp but we didn't. I was disappointed Tampa took him with the very next pick. Now I started focusing on Derrick Brooks and what do we have to do. Maybe we can get him in the second round in 1995. Tampa traded up and got ahead of us, and took him. I said, "Here are two great players and now I'm going to play against them the rest of my life. They will torment me forever."

The next year I was the head coach in Tampa and all of those guys were sitting there waiting for us. I remember having the conversation early on when I first got the job, hey you guys are going to be the key to this defense, the under tackle, weak side linebacker, and strong safety, the three most critical spots. You've got to carry the load; you have to be the leaders for us. We had another middle linebacker, Hardy Nickerson, who had played for me in Pittsburgh. He was there and understood how we did things.

Getting those guys to buy into it, have the determination to be the best, and to support each other was great. We had a lot of communication with our scouting department. What we were looking for in players were guys who didn't need to be the biggest. We liked speed, mental toughness, physical toughness, and explosiveness. If we could get those things in a player, it didn't matter whether you were from a big school or small school. If you were undersized it didn't matter. If you didn't run the 40-yard dash as fast as people thought you should, it didn't matter. If you were productive and tough, we could use you. Then we got Donnie Abraham, Ronde Barber, and a number of players who were under the radar, but were exactly what we needed. That defense became a tremendous unit.

We built our team where we were going to have a strong defense and we could also run the ball. By running the ball we shortened the game.

We played low scoring games and a style that people weren't used to or familiar with, and it was to our advantage. We built our offense around the running game with Mike Alstott and Warrick Dunn. We were able to control the clock and win a lot of those low scoring games. It was a different style. We called it "Buc Ball." It wasn't throwing the ball all over the field and scoring points. It was playing a physical style, and it became our trademark. It was a lot of fun for the guys.

Being Fired By The Buccaneers And Being Hired As Head Coach With Colts

Our owners got a little frustrated when we got close and didn't win it all. We were making the playoffs but weren't winning it all. We lost the NFC Championship game in St. Louis 11-6, and our owners were very frustrated. The owners said, "If we just scored a couple of touchdowns we would have been in the Super Bowl. We want to make changes." We had to get people to buy into it and stay in tune with what we believed. That was a challenge. It was different and wasn't what people were used to. Maybe it wasn't going to sell tickets, but we felt we could win that way.

What happened was we raised the bar and the expectations; however, it wasn't enough to be a winning team. It wasn't enough to go to the playoffs. It was the Super Bowl that everyone was focused on. Jon Gruden came in as Head Coach with his group and they did a great job. They actually changed the offense around and got a little more explosive. They won the year after I was fired. It was difficult seeing a lot of our players and the guys that I coached in the Super Bowl. By that time I was in Indianapolis as head coach, and looking forward to that challenge. We were a little different team in Indianapolis.

Indianapolis had a great offense when I got there. The challenge was to get the defense up to speed. We had more of a challenge because of the salary cap. We had so many high-priced offensive players, we couldn't pay a lot of the defensive players. So, we had to do it with young talent. It was a fun challenge to put that together and get guys who could protect the lead and rush the passer. We played a different style in Indy then we did in Tampa, but we adjusted.

Tom Moore

Tom was with the Colts when I was hired. He had coached me 25 years prior. I knew his style and it was very compatible to what I wanted to do. I knew the offense was in good hands. We had to get the defense up to speed and there was a lot to concentrate on that side of the ball. We got some players in Dwight Freeney and Gary Brackett and got some impact players like Robert Mathis on defense. We got to the point where we were challenging to win championships every year and it was fun. We put together a run of 12 win seasons that was really, really enjoyable. It was exciting football and we finally got that Super Bowl championship over your Bears in 2006.

2006 NFL Playoffs

The first game that we played was against the Chiefs in the playoffs. The Chiefs Head Coach Herm Edwards and I we were on the Hula Bowl team together. We had been friends for years and coached together. Then, I was coaching against him. We were able to beat them and then we came to the Super Bowl against Lovie Smith, the Bears head coach. I know how Super Bowls are, if you win you're the hero and you're going to be highly praised; if you lose everybody is going to point the finger at you. I guess it was better they pointed at Lovie then pointed at me. That part of it wasn't fun.

Tampa 2/Cover 2 Defense

I absolutely did not invent it. I learned it when I went to Pittsburgh in 1977. Bud Carson actually brought it to the NFL in the early '70s. Bud and Coach Noll perfected it. I laugh because I tell people that the playbook I put in Tampa Bay in 1996, was exactly the same as the 1976 playbook in Pittsburgh. It was plagiarism all the way. We didn't change much, and it still worked 20 years later.

Christianity

I am a strong member of Fellowship of Christian Athletes and I wanted my players to see that yes, I was an athlete, I was a coach, but I was always going to be a Christian first. I was going to treat them that way and we could be successful doing it that way. I had some great role models like Coach Noll, Tom Landry, and Joe Gibbs. I was watching them when I was a young coach. They were winning Super Bowls and winning the right ways. It was a tremendous reassurance to me that you could be a man of faith and have that in the forefront, while still doing your job in an excellent way.

Decision To Retire
It was just a matter of what was the right time. I started coaching very young, at 25. By the time we got to 2007 and 2008, even though I was still relatively young at 51 or 52, I had been coaching 25 years already. Most of my married life I had been a coach. My kids grew up around the game, and they loved it. But, I felt like I needed to branch out and do some other things. In 2009, I felt it was the right time and it was. It was perfect timing for me.

No Huddle Offense
The no huddle offense is a great tool, but you have to have faith in your quarterback. You have to have quarterbacks who want to put the time in to learn and they've got to be as well versed as your coaches. If you have a quarterback like Peyton Manning who loves it, who wants the responsibility, it can be a big advantage.

Peyton Manning
He was just so driven. He wanted to not only be the best, but he wanted his team to excel and he put the hard work into it. He's very, very fortunate because in Indianapolis, he played in one system his whole time there. He never had to switch or learn a new system. The scouting was so good that we got players who fit the system. We had Marshall Faulk, Edgerrin James, and Joseph Addai as running backs and receivers like Marvin Harrison, Reggie Wayne, and Dallas Clark who just fit the system so well, and for 6-7 years at a time. It just allowed the timing to grow. It was just a perfect storm of a very, very talented player in Peyton, a lot of other talented players who fit the system, and that system basically staying for 13 years.

Pro Football Hall Of Fame Induction
That was one of those that you don't expect; you don't even think about. As a kid I dreamed about making it to the NFL or about a Super Bowl, but never dreamed of being in the Hall of Fame. That Thursday night before it was announced, there was a reception with all of the finalists. There were 15 other guys in the room and I was thinking, gee I would vote for this guy, I would vote for that guy, I would vote for that guy. You don't see any way people are going to

vote for you. I just didn't think it was going to happen and when I got the knock on the door it was quite a surprise.

Indianapolis Colts coach Tony Dungy is hoisted after the Colts defeated the Chicago Bears 29-17 in Super Bowl XLI at Dolphin Stadium in Miami, Sunday, Feb. 4, 2007. Photograph copyright Associated Press

Chapter 20

Lee Roy Selmon

> College:
> Oklahoma
>
> Career History:
> Tampa Bay Buccaneers (1976–1984)
>
> 1995 Inductee Pro Football Hall Of Fame

Playing In College At Oklahoma With Brothers
It was an awful lot of fun. I look back on it and have a greater appreciation for the opportunity to play with my brothers, Lucious and Dewey. Those were some really, really, really good times for that reason. We look back on it and reminisce.

NFL Draft
What was most exciting for me about the draft that year was not the point of being selected where I was, but that my brother Dewey was also selected by Tampa Bay. We got to play six more years together here in Florida. I can say the good Lord knows exactly what you need, because I certainly needed him here. We broke into the league together and I think that's the reason why I was able to hang around for as long as I did. As rookies, you're just glad to have an opportunity for your dream to come true. For us, it was to play in the National Football League.

Joining First Year Expansion Team In Tampa
There was some tough treading along the way, but people realized we were a young team and an expansion program with a lot of young players just like myself, trying to learn how to play in the National Football League. We had no idea the level of competition and all that we needed to do to compete and be successful. The first year and part of the second year was what that was all about. I think that

John McKay did an outstanding job of positioning us to where, even though we were losing games, we could still hold a positive outlook, go out and practice hard, and just keep trying to get better.

Best Selmon Football Player
There's never any argument there. I've always said that my brother Lucious was the best, Dewey was second, and I was last. That's in order of age. That started a long time ago and it's still that way.

Rule Changes To Make The Game Safer
I understand the intent of the rules and trying to make it a little bit safer for the players and everything, particularly now that we know what some of the long-term effects are as we get older. With the physical nature of the game, I doubt if there are any rules that are going to change that. It's moving so fast. Even if a player is trying to avoid a helmet-to-helmet hit, or if both players are intent on trying to avoid it, they end up in the same spot anyway. How can you tell if that was intentional or if they were trying to avoid it; it just happened. I think it's tough, but I do like that they are at least looking at it, and trying to determine if there's anything that can be done to maybe reduce that particular risk a little bit. I think that it's worthwhile in the long run.

I think the nature of the game and what's being found out about it, should be a part of the conversation. We certainly need to figure out what we can do to keep the players as healthy as possible. You only get one head and one brain. If you can protect it better, than I think you should.

Evaluating Players Performance Thru Statistics
I think that there are many ways to contribute to teams. This league is so competitive and so tough to where if they want to take you out and make you ineffective in a game, they have ways of double-teaming you, slowing you down, and those types of things. To me, when those things happen, and you get that kind of attention, the players know which guy they have to get out and who they have to stop in order to be successful. So, while that is one part of the statistics on players, I generally like to look at what impact a player had overall for his team when he is on the field playing.

Photograph copyright Associated Press

Chapter 21

James Lofton

> College:
> Stanford
>
> Career History:
> Green Bay Packers (1978–1986)
> Los Angeles Raiders (1987–1988)
> Buffalo Bills (1989–1992)
> Los Angeles Rams (1993)
> Philadelphia Eagles (1993)
>
> Coaching History:
> San Diego Chargers (2002–2007)
> Oakland Raiders (2008)
>
> 2003 Inductee Pro Football Hall Of Fame

<u>Bill Walsh</u>
Bill Walsh had been an assistant coach with the San Diego Chargers the year before, being named the head coach at Stanford. Prior to that, he was with the Cincinnati Bengals. You've got to remember, the world was a lot bigger then, and by bigger, I mean you didn't have the Internet or cable television. You weren't able to track people and say, "Okay, we watched a lot of Bengal highlights." On the West Coast, we never saw Bengal highlights. He was an unknown to our city.

The very first meeting he had with the team was in the Maples Pavilion, which is where the basketball team plays. All the guys were sitting around and he started talking to us. He said he wanted us to call him "Bill," that he didn't want us to call him "Coach." He just had this really warm personality, and he started talking about dress codes. He said, "We're not going to have a big dress code when we travel. The only thing … those bib overalls, if you wear those, make sure you wear a shirt under them." Everybody just started cracking up laughing. He just had a great sense of humor.

We learned more about him as the season went along. Everything he accomplished after he left Stanford during his 10 years with the 49ers, just added to his legend. He was Coach of the Year twice and won three Super Bowls with the 49ers. It made those two years that he spent at Stanford even more impactful.

Position Change From High School Quarterback
I got tried at quarterback a little bit at Stanford. Steve Dils, who came to Stanford at the same time as me, was probably in a more sophisticated passing offense in high school than I was. In high school, I threw five to ten times a game. I just rolled out and ran the ball a bunch.

I also played defensive back for a little while at Stanford. George Seifert, who later on was the head coach of the 49ers, was a defensive backs coach at Stanford. I played for him for just about a week, and then I got stuck back on offense. I played a lot of special teams, covering kicks and punts. I had a lot of fun the first few years before I got to be a starter my senior year.

Hall Of Fame Coaches
I had some pretty good coaches who are in the Pro Football Hall Of Fame rub off on me. Jack Christiansen, who played for the Detroit Lions and was one of the greatest punt returners of all time and also a defensive back, was head coach at Stanford. Bill Walsh was another one of my coaches at Stanford. In the NFL, Bart Starr and Forrest Gregg coached me when I was in Green Bay, and Marv Levy coached me in Buffalo. Then there was Art Shell for a quick moment during training camp with the Raiders.

I had a lot of great coaches, who were really influential men. You've also got to throw in there I played a year with Tom Flores, whom a lot of people think should be in the Pro Football Hall of Fame, and also Mike Shanahan. I was really fortunate to play for some good coaches.

NFL Draft
It was so much fun. It was just exciting to get to go to the pros. I didn't start my junior year. Between my junior and senior years, the NFL had reduced the draft from 12 to eight rounds. So going into my senior year I thought, "Man, they cut the draft. I probably won't get drafted. I can make it as a free agent or something like that." It was really surprising that I had what they would now call a "breakout" senior year and was able to move up as much as I did in the draft.

Transition To NFL
It was kind of neat for me because I was going to a team that obviously needed me. The Packers drafted me high with the sixth pick, and I was able to come in and be a starter right away. I didn't have to wait a half a season or a season and a half to work my way into the starting lineup. I was penciled in as a starter from day one and made the Pro Bowl that year. I was the NFC Offensive Rookie of the Year. It was a big transition, but I guess I didn't know any better not to think that I couldn't do it.

Packers Offense
Offenses were pretty much run first and run second all around the NFL at the time. I think the leading receiver before I got to Green Bay had caught 23 passes the prior season. If you look at the numbers they were probably 75% run, 25% pass. Nowadays in the NFL, teams are about 65% pass, and 35% run. So it has really switched around a lot. We were heavily into running the football when I got there.

Bart Starr As Head Coach
I got the opportunity to coach years after I finished playing. There is a tremendous amount you need to learn to manage people. I look at Bart and his coaching career, and obviously, he wishes that he could have had a lot more seasoning, maybe two years more before starting as a head coach. I think because of his leadership capabilities, he was destined to be a head coach.

I heard somebody say about Vince Lombardi, "You either loved him, feared him, respected him, or hated him." Some people said, "He encompasses all four of those." Somebody said, "What about the hate?" He said, "Well, it's such a thin line between love and hate.

There are some days when you love him, and there are some days when you hate him for the way he is yelling at you." But, he had a certain fear about him and a certain respect.

I remember Bart telling us that respect is something that you earn it is not given away. He also said he had to earn our respect just as much as we had to earn his respect. I think that anybody who played for him really loved him and really respected him.

John Jefferson Joining The Packers
It was exciting when John Jefferson joined the Packers. John had such a great start to his career, the first three years that he played with San Diego. With the addition on our team, it really gave us a leg up on throwing the football, and it was a transition period. The Chargers, under Don Coryell, were really throwing the ball unlike a lot of teams had before, and we started to throw the ball a little more once we got John Jefferson. It was certainly exciting. He was a very enthusiastic player and added a lot of spice to the team at the time.

Packers and Bears
There was always a big rivalry between the Bears and the Packers. Players today tend to change teams a lot, and I think some of those rivalries get diluted a little bit. But we had a healthy rivalry against them and a real good respect for the Chicago Bears. I'm pretty sure that Forrest Gregg and Mike Ditka respected each other, too.

Memorable Bears-Packers Games
Probably every one of the Bears-Packers games was memorable. Even the ones played today are fun to watch. I'm looking forward to Jay Cutler going up against Aaron Rodgers, watching Urlacher play, and then watching Clay Matthews play. It hasn't lost any of its appeal over the years.

Raiders Wide Open Offense
Yes, they love the deep passing game. When I got there, we had great running backs in Marcus Allen and later Bo Jackson. Al Davis was always about trying to get the best talent there and get that best mixture so that he could win championships.

Differences In Coaching Between Marv Levy And Bill Walsh
Bill Walsh was kind of a … he was called "The Genius," obviously because of the West Coast Offense that he implemented, so from that standpoint, they were different. Marv Levy had coached for a while, and he said one of the things that he had learned is you hire the people and you let them do their thing. Marv hired Ted Marchibroda, as offensive coordinator, and let Ted do this thing. One of the things that Ted did was have us run the no-huddle offense in Buffalo. It was such a fast pace, that it made it hard for teams to keep up with us. That was really innovative at the time. We won a lot of ball games because of that system, but also because Ted was able to look at the talent that we had and say, "Okay, this is the best way to utilize it."

Playing In Super Bowls
I actually played in three Super Bowls. I played in 25, 26, and 27. I wasn't there when they played in Super Bowl 28. But there was so much winning that goes on in between. There was a stretch where over three years at home, if you add the regular season games, eight of those, we had a couple of playoff games, two more of those, I want to say we were 27 and 3 at home, so that never tires.

We had great players offensively and defensively. It was interesting because we would find unique ways to win, whether it was on offense, defense, or special teams. We had great special teams players, Mark Pike and Steve Tasker. The combination of great players, just getting to win on a regular basis, and going into the game believing you're going to win, helped us win. I think it was the 1990 season and we were playing in the Super Bowl. We were favored in every game that we played that year, whether it was at home or on the road.

Having Jim Kelly As A Quarterback
Jim Kelly was a strong athlete. He was certainly in his prime. He was really confident in his ability, and he would find a way to win ball games, whether it was by big scores or a comeback win. He was extremely competitive with Frank Reich, who was our backup quarterback. He and Jim Kelly had a standing gag bit that Friday's lunch would be bought based on whether or not Jim Kelly completed 100% of his passes in practice, so there was a lot of pressure on the

receivers to not drop a pass because $7 worth of lunch was being bet on that practice.

There was one game against the Oilers where the Oilers' fans, and probably a lot of Bills fans too, thought we lost the game, but we hung in there. We had some fortunate things that happened. Our defense played great in the second half, got the ball back for us, and we were able to pull out a win.

A Career That Lasted 16 Seasons
I never thought about how long I was going to play when I first started playing. I didn't understand how physical the game could be or that you could get cut down by an injury and your career could be over. I didn't think about playing 10 years or playing until I was 30. I just got on a path. I really enjoyed working out there in off-season, so that always made it easy for me to come in to training camp in shape. I was just really fortunate to be in the right place at the right time, I think.

Coaching
Coaching gives you the opportunity to see if you can accomplish something, the competitiveness of the game. Coaching at Stanford would have been a great job. It would have been great to get to go back to the place where you went to school. It's like a way of paying them back, saying, "I really enjoyed my time here." That ship has sailed. They've had a great run with Jim Harbaugh lately, and now, Coach David Shaw is doing an outstanding job there. Coaching college football is a big time commitment. I think the coaches earn every penny that they make.

Broadcasting
It was something that I wanted to do. I broadcasted, I think, for eight years after I retired as a player, then I did eight years as a coach. Now I'm back broadcasting. It's been something that I've enjoyed. They say if you can't do it, if you can't coach it, you might as well talk about it.

Analyzing The Players Actions In Today's Games
I think we just want to know, because we have high definition television and you get great shots all over the place, you want to know what's going on, and you want to almost know it instantly. That's

what Twitter has done to us. You have athletes who are commenting before the reporters get to them in the locker room. There is a lot of information out there, and I think people just thirst for it.

Being Inducted Into The Pro Football Hall Of Fame

I had been on the ballot, but I didn't think of it as a slam-dunk or anything like that. I was aware of it, and I had been a finalist for a couple of years, so I was very grateful when it finally happened. I think the longer that you're in it, the more the importance grows. You realize you are among a select few, especially when you see guys who don't get in who you look at and go, "Boy, he was really a good player that I played against, and hasn't gotten a chance to get in yet."

Favorite Career Moments

Getting to play for a number of teams was really significant. Getting to be a broadcaster in this league has been a lot of fun. I work with Dial Global Sports, who used to be Westwood One Radio. I also worked at CNN and for NBC before they lost football the first time around. Even doing college football has been fun.

But there are some things that are ironic. I won the first NFL game that I played in. I won the last NFL game that I played in. I won the first NFL game that I coached, and I won the last game that I coached. Every game that I broadcasted has been on the winning side. You could call that too. You can say yes, I like that team so they won.

Photograph copyright Associated Press

Chapter 22

Warren Moon

> College:
> West Los Angeles Junior College
> Washington
>
> Career History:
> Edmonton Eskimos (1978–1983)
> Houston Oilers (1984–1993)
> Minnesota Vikings (1994–1996)
> Seattle Seahawks (1997–1998)
> Kansas City Chiefs (1999–2000)
>
> 2006 Inductee Pro Football Hall Of Fame

<u>College Choice</u>
Major colleges didn't want to recruit me as a quarterback. They wanted me to change positions to wide receiver or defensive back. Schools that ran the option recruited me as a quarterback, but I was a passer and I wanted to go to a school that threw the football. I decided to go to a junior college because I didn't get the type of offers that I wanted coming out of high school. I went there for a year, got a little more exposure, had another really good season, and finally started to get recruited as a quarterback.

I had actually committed to Arizona State whose coach was Frank Kush. All of a sudden they signed the two top high school quarterbacks in the nation that year, Dennis Sproul and Bruce Hardy. Once they signed those two kids they told me they were going to change my position. I decommitted from Arizona State.

After looking at my other options, I decided to go to a junior college. It was mainly because I believed in myself as a quarterback and I believed that I could throw the football with anybody. My high school coach was going to the junior college as the offensive coordinator. I followed him and we just continued what we had done in high school. It was just a matter of somebody giving me that opportunity.

I would have never even considered Washington or any other school if I wasn't going to play quarterback and if I wasn't going to be given the opportunity to play. It was a matter of just going where I thought I had the best chance to play was. That's what I looked for. USC was the team that I had grown up admiring and watching all their players throughout the years. Vince Evans was the USC quarterback at the time and he was going into his senior year. I would've had to redshirt if I went there and I had already went to a junior college for a year, so I didn't want to waste another year redshirting. I decided to go where I had a better opportunity to start during my first year. So I went to the University of Washington.

Transition To University of Washington
The transition to Washington was easy in some ways as far as playing football, but we weren't very good. Don James had just come in as head coach. I was part of his first recruiting class. The team was 2-9 before I got there. I knew it was going to be a rebuilding process.

We had a very tough schedule that year. We didn't get off to the greatest of starts. I got a lot of criticism being the starting quarterback. I was 18 years old and in a new city for the first time. I was also the first African American to ever start at the University of Washington. I endured very tough times early in my career. Things turned out very well once we got the type of talent that we needed and we all grew together.

Washington Offense
Robin Earl was a really big running back, 6'5" and 240-45 pounds. We ran a ball control offense, tried to eat as much time off the clock as we could, and keep our defense off the field. I didn't get to throw the ball as much as I wanted to, but I guess that was our best way of winning because we didn't have a lot of speed on the outside.

Don was more of a ball control type coach who tried to keep the score close. We had a pretty good year. We finished 6 and 5 and we were one win away from going to the Rose Bowl. We were very competitive and it was a good start for the players and the new regime.

Senior Year Playing In Rose Bowl
We beat the Mighty Wolverines in the Rose Bowl. We were rated number three in the country at that time. We were 17-point underdogs in the Rose Bowl. Nobody gave us a chance, but we had tremendous confidence in ourselves. We went into that game and let everything flow. I ended up having a pretty good game and was the MVP of the game. It was one of the great days for me in my sports career. I was able to come back to Pasadena, where I lived, which is right outside of Los Angeles, and be able to play in front of my friends and family in the Rose Bowl. As a kid I had always admired the Rose Bowl, watching it and going to the Rose Parade. I was now getting a chance to play in it as a college senior.

NFL Draft
I had the same problems coming out of college that I had coming out of high school. Everybody wanted to change my position. I knew it was a time when African Americans weren't looked highly upon as quarterbacks. There were a lot of stereotypes about us playing the position and I got caught up in that. I wasn't going to let it deter me. Again I was going to go where I would get the best opportunity. Just like I went to a junior college, I decided to go to Canada because they were going to give me a chance to play quarterback. Even though I wasn't going to be able to fulfill my dream, which as a young kid was to play in the NFL, I never lost sight of that dream even though I had to go a different direction to do it.

African American Quarterbacks In NFL
I don't think there were any black quarterbacks in the league when I came back from Canada. In 1978, the Tampa Bay Buccaneers drafted Doug Williams but that was because the Buccaneers coach, John McKay, had always had African American quarterbacks at USC. He had Jimmy Jones and a couple other guys play quarterback for him at USC. So, drafting an African American quarterback for him wasn't anything different.

Who knows where Doug Williams would have been picked in the draft if John McKay hadn't drafted him in the first round. Doug Williams and Vince Evans were in the league, but Vince wasn't playing very much. Doug was dong a pretty good job with Tampa. By the time I came into the league in 1984, they were out of league because of problems they were having getting resigned, so they went to the USFL.

Many African American quarterbacks were changed to different positions. Sometimes your athletic ability penalizes you as a quarterback because they want to put you at a more skilled position, whether it's wide receiver or defensive back. I just never felt like I was that good enough of an athlete to play another position. I was a good athlete for quarterback, but I wasn't a great enough athlete to make the transition to wide receiver or defensive back. Maybe other guys were better athletes than I was and were able to make the transition.

Playing For Edmonton Eskimos
I loved it. It was a great opportunity for me. It was a veteran football team. I didn't have to come in there and be a leader or anything. I could go there and just learn. I got a chance to develop my game. We won a lot. We won five championships while I was up there. It was a great environment for playing football. Even though I was in another country, learning another culture, and a long way from home, because we were winning and I was having fun doing something that I love, playing football, it made it bearable. No question about it.

I became friends with guys on the Edmonton Oilers including Wayne Gretzky, Paul Coffey, Kevin Lowe, Jari Kurri, and Grant Fuhr. They had a great hockey team. At one point we won five straight championships in football and then they won four or five Stanley Cups. During that 10-year period there were nine championships in the city, so they kind of renamed Edmonton the "City of Championships". It was a very good sports town and a great fan base. It was a good time to be living in Edmonton, Alberta.

Decision To Sign With Houston Oilers
I had plenty of teams looking at me. There were scouts in our press box all the time. I was always made aware of the teams' scouts that were going to be watching me. I got a lot of exposure when the NFL

went on strike in 1982, since our games were televised in the U.S. You knew when you had a chance to play on U.S. television; you wanted to play a little bit better. It was kind of a motivator. It was just a matter of my contract getting to a point where I could get out of it, or it running out. Then was I going to decide whether to go to the NFL or not because I really was enjoying playing in Canada.

My dream was always to play in the NFL. I had accomplished so much in Canada over those first five years that there wasn't a whole lot left for me to do up there. That's when I started saying, "Hey, maybe it's time for me to go to the NFL." I wanted to get the right opportunity in the NFL and see exactly how good I was as a quarterback. I think the only way you can judge yourself is to play against the best, and there's no question the best were in the National Football League.

It came down to the Houston Oilers and Seattle Seahawks, which is where I was living in the off-season. I went to school at the University of Washington, so it was a natural progression for me. Chuck Knox was the Seahawks coach at that time. They had a very good football team. They had gone to the AFC championship game and lost, but Dave Krieg was their quarterback at the time, so the Seahawks were making a big push for me. It kind of puzzled me that they even wanted me as their quarterback because they had a really good football team.

Houston was more of a draw for me, because it was an up and coming franchise. It was a team I could build with as opposed to going to Seattle, a team that was already good. I really liked the challenge of going somewhere and making a bad team good. Also, my head coach from Canada, Hugh Campbell, was named the head coach of Houston. I went to a team that had a coach who was familiar with me and I was familiar with him. I thought maybe we could have some of the same success we had in Edmonton in Houston.

Joining Oilers
The Oilers didn't have great talent when I got there. They were coming off a 2-14 season and we had to rebuild our personnel. We had a very young offensive line, with some really good offensive

linemen for the future. Bruce Matthews, Mike Munchak, and Dean Steinkuhler, who was the number two overall pick in the draft, were on the offensive line when I first came in. We were building upfront with young guys. Later on, we got more outside talent with Ernest Givins and guys like that, which really made our passing game start to take off. Once the talent was around me, we could utilize my strength, which was throwing the football. Then we started really making some noise offensively.

Jerry Glanville

Jerry was a very energetic coach. He was known at the Man in Black, or whatever he wanted to call himself. We had some really hard-hitting defenses. The Astrodome became known as the House of Pain on the defensive side of the ball. There was a lot of enthusiasm built into our football team when Jerry took over as coach. We started to run more of the spread offense, more of the four-wide receiver type thing called the Red Gun. Later on we changed it to the Run and Shoot.

He was a very big personality who liked a lot of attention. We'd butt heads sometimes. I think it was because as a quarterback, I got a lot of attention and I'm not sure if he always liked that. I respected him because he was my head coach and he called the shots, but there were a lot of things that he did as a coach that I didn't necessarily agree with.

1992 Oilers vs. Bills Playoff Game "The Comeback"

It wasn't a very good day. It started out to be a very good day. We jumped ahead, something that we wanted to do early to try and get the crowd out of the game and take the momentum away from the Bills, especially being on the road and being in Buffalo. We were able to do that. We had a commanding lead at half time, I think 28-3, and then we jumped ahead 35-3 in the third quarter. Then that's when the dam broke and we gave them the opportunity to get back into the game with two quick scores. Then after an on-side kick, they got the ball back again and the momentum in the ballgame just changed from there. We just didn't put them away when we had them down. We have nobody to blame but ourselves.

Being the quarterback of that football team, I put a lot of blame on myself for not being able to make the plays down the stretch to make the game ours. That's something that I'll always look back on and say, "We let that one get away," because I really thought that team was good enough to make it to the Super Bowl that year.

Being Traded To Minnesota Vikings

I was a little bit surprised, but not after it was explained to me. I had gone to six straight Pro Bowls. We had just come off of a 12-4 season. I was being traded mainly because the salary cap had come into play and our backup quarterback, Cody Carlson, had just been signed to a pretty good deal the year before. They couldn't keep us both because of the salaries, so they looked at me being 38 years old and him a younger guy, they had been developing for the future. They decided to make the change because they didn't know how long I was going to continue to play at that level at that age.

They thought Cody was ready to take over as starter. I understood where they were coming from. I also knew how I felt as a player and where I was physically. I told Floyd Reese, our general manager at that time, "I think you're making a mistake, but you've got to do what you feel is best for the organization."

I went ahead and accepted the trade to the Minnesota Vikings. I thought the Vikings were a team that could be pretty good if they didn't lose some guys on defense to free agency. All they were really lacking was on the offensive side. I went there and we had a couple playoff appearances, but we never were able to really get over the hump.

Favorite Moment In Professional Football

The day that I signed my first NFL contract because I had to take such a long road to get there. My dream was to play in the NFL all the way back to when I was a young kid. No matter what I had to do along the way, whether it was going to high school, junior college, or going to Canada and play after my college career was over, I finally got to the NFL when I was about 28. I think my most memorable day was when I was able to sit down and actually sign that contract as the richest player in the NFL at that particular time, believe it or not. After all I had gone through, that's where I ended up. That was one of the most memorable days for me, being able to sign that first NFL contract.

Opening Opportunities For African American Quarterbacks

I think my success coupled with Doug Williams's success winning the Super Bowl in 1988, and Randall Cunningham's success, helped the next generation of African American quarterbacks get more opportunities to be drafted. We all played at about the same time and we were three African American quarterbacks playing at a very high level. One of us won a Super Bowl, one was an MVP of the league, and I had a very consistent career, playing at a very high level over a long period of time.

Not only did I play a role in it, so did those other two guys that I talked about. That's something I think we'll all be very proud of for a long time. We were able to make a difference in people's minds in the NFL and open up the gates for other young quarterbacks like Donovan McNabb, Daunte Culpepper, and Michael Vick. They now have an opportunity to play at a very high level and are drafted high in the draft.

Pro Football Hall Of Fame Induction

I knew compared to who was already in the Hall Of Fame, that I had a chance to make it in there one day. I wasn't really sure because it's not in your control. Other people are voting on you. I knew I had a pretty good resume. I knew I didn't have a championship under my belt, but I also knew that there were other quarterbacks in the Hall of Fame that didn't have championships under their belt either. When I got the call in my first year of eligibility that surprised me a little bit, but I took it.

Favorite Receiver

My favorite receiver was probably Cris Carter, who finally made it to the Hall of Fame. I got a chance to play with him for three years in Minnesota. He set an NFL record for most receptions the first year I was there with him. The record was broken the next year by one reception. Over a two-year period, he caught 244 balls from me. We had a very good rapport early on, even though we didn't know each other that well. That was because we both practiced really hard and we gave each other a great picture in practice. Once we got to the game, it was like second nature. It's like we had been playing with each other for years.

Toughest Defense

I would say that maybe the Philadelphia Eagles had the toughest defense. One year when I was with Houston, the Eagles had a very physical defense. Reggie White, Jerome Brown, and Seth Joiner were with the Eagles. They had a really, really physical defense and they got after our Run and Shoot offense pretty well. They intimidated our receivers and knocked them around. They were one team that I had difficulty with in the one game we played against them that year. In our division, Cleveland always gave us a lot of problems in the AFC Central because we played them so much and we knew each other so well.

Buddy Ryan & Kevin Gilbride Fight During Oilers/Jets Game

During the game, Buddy Ryan took a swipe at Kevin Gilbride. Their issues started way back during training camp when Buddy took over as the defensive coordinator. Buddy wasn't a big proponent of our offense. He felt his defense could dominate and stop our offense, so it became a them against us thing in training camp. It probably shouldn't have been. Jack Pardee, the head coach, probably should have nipped it in the bud at some point. Buddy and Kevin competed too hard in practice.

It finally came to a head that game when Kevin called a play and the ball was intercepted. Cody Carlson was our quarterback at that time. Buddy felt that we should have run the football and run the clock out at the end of the first half. Kevin called a pass and it was picked off. Buddy's defense had to go back out on the field, so Buddy was pretty upset about that. That's when they got into the argument and that's when Buddy took a swipe at him.

Playing For Seattle Seahawks Toward End Of Career

Seattle was of the places where I thought I was going to go coming out of Canada. I'm glad I got a chance to at least play up there for a couple of years, even though I was 41 when I got there. I really enjoyed my couple of years playing there. I led the league in passing my first year there. I was MVP of the Pro Bowl that year, too. It was a fun year for me. I got a chance to play in front of all of those fans that I played in front of in college. I really thought my career was over after playing for Seattle, but I got a call from the Kansas City Chiefs to come play for them. I decided, "Hey, I can still play physically, so maybe there's an opportunity there." So, I went to Kansas City.

Favorite Player Growing Up
Wow, there are too many to name. I was a big Rams fan because I grew1 up in L.A. and Roman Gabriel was one of my favorite quarterbacks. I also loved Roger Staubach because I used to watch the Dallas Cowboys all the time because they were on TV, it seemed, every weekend. I just loved the way he played the game. Believe it or not, O.J. Simpson was one of my favorite players as well when he was in college.

Photograph copyright Associated Press

Chapter 23

Dan Hampton

> College:
> Arkansas
>
> Career History:
> Chicago Bears (1979–1990)
>
> 2002 Inductee Pro Football Hall Of Fame

College Choice

Frank Broyles was an iconic figure. This was back when the Arkansas Razorbacks were the only game in town. Anything to do with the Razorbacks was bigger than life. When Frank Broyles showed up at my little modest home, my mom and him sat on the couch. It was a big deal for us. Frank Broyles was bigger than the governor of the state of Arkansas at that time.

I got to play at a time in the late '70s, when Jimmy Johnson was our defensive coordinator under Frank Broyles, and then we got Lou Holtz as head coach. We won the Orange Bowl. It was a great time to be a Razorback football player.

Under Lou Holtz, Monty Kiffin was our defensive coordinator. Obviously, Monty Kiffin has made a name for himself in both college and pro-football over the last 25-30 years. I used to tell people, "If I would have had coaching worth a damn, I could've done something." I was the most fortunate guy in the world. I had Hall of Fame coaches up and down the aisle during my career. I can't say which one meant the most because they were all huge, and in their own special way, they were amazing to play for. Lou Holtz made young people understand that you're not just an 18-year-old kid; you've got your whole life ahead of you. You need to start thinking about bigger things than the team and winning, like building your career and all of those things. Jimmy Johnson taught the little techniques that kept me in the NFL long after I couldn't run and play the way that I once did. Each and every one was special to me.

Lou Holtz
Lou Holtz had all those great one-liners, like the one he used when he was asked how he decided who would start. He said, "I told them that we're playing the number one team in America. They have five All-Americans and everybody that's played them has been beaten 50-0. The last 11 out of the locker room have to play." He said some crazy things. Lou showed up after quitting as head coach of the New York Jets. As a football player, you never quit and you never say die. Here's a guy who had things that didn't work. We knew that he had credentials, though. It didn't take long, after a day or two of being around him, to know that he had a plan. He knew what he wanted and what we were going to doing. From the get go, we were all on board.

When I heard the rumor that he was hired, I wasn't that impressed. I think a lot of people realized that Jimmy Johnson wanted the head job, but Frank Broyles didn't think he was ready. Frank said, "I'm not going to hire you. I don't promote assistants." Jimmy proved that little scenario incorrect. He went on to Oklahoma State, Pittsburgh, University of Miami where he won a National Championship, and then Dallas where he won two Super Bowls. We were all hoping that Jimmy would get the job. Jimmy had played for the Razorbacks 12 to 15 years earlier. He was a hog. Barry Switzer and Jerry Jones were the offensive guards and Jimmy was a nose tackle on the 1963 Arkansas National Championship Team. At first, we were a little reluctant to embrace Lou Holtz, but it didn't take long for him to win us over. He had a hell of a soft stitch.

We came within one play of winning the National Championship. Losing to Texas was the only loss we sustained. We were leading up until the last seconds of the game when Earl Campbell caught a screen pass and went 28 yards. He had never caught a pass before that and didn't after that. We weren't prepared. It was a great treat to play for Lou Holtz.

Steven McMichael reminds me, almost on a daily basis, that we never beat Texas. We won the Southwest Conference twice and beat everybody else, but we never beat Texas. A lot of people want to know why the Chicago Bears defense, the one that Buddy Ryan coached, we built, and a lot of people say was the greatest defense of all time, was so good. In baseball they have the old creed, good up the middle. I was the 1978 Defensive Player of the Year in the Southwest Conference. Steve McMichael was the 1979 Defensive Player of the Year in the Southwest Conference. Mike Singletary was the 1980 Defensive Player of the Year in the Southwest Conference.

We really felt that was the best conference and the best brand of football in America. We were obviously pretty good players in that conference. I think that was instrumental in what we were trying to build in Chicago. For a decade, I think that we were rated the best defense in the NFL.

Brad Shearer was the player of the year the year prior to me. Brad came with a load of knee problems. He had had two or three surgeries in Texas. He had three or four while he was with the Bears. His career was always cut short by October. I always said that Brad never brought a coat to Chicago because by October, he was always back in Austin. I'm making light of it; I hated it. Brad was a great college football player. He was the Outland Trophy winner and the Player of the Year in the Southwest Conference. You can't scowl at that.

Realizing He Could Play In The NFL At A High Level
It was interesting. You never know where you're going to end up. I was one of the last guys recruited at Arkansas, and after a year or so, I figured out that I could play! I'll never forget Jimmy Johnson talking about the pro-scouts coming to see some of the upper classmen, but they wanted to see me, the skinny kid who was a sophomore. It was all predicated on hard work, and I worked really hard. People have told me over the years that Lou Holtz said I worked harder than any kid he ever had. In a way, I had to. My father died when I was in 8th grade. My mom went to work, but it wasn't much. Football was my vehicle to do something and achieve something. So, I worked real hard, had a lot of great teammates, and had a lot of great help and great coaching.

When I went to Chicago, I didn't know anything about the NFL. I didn't realize that the pass rush was the ticket. In college, I was playing the run because everybody ran the ball. I didn't have much in the way of pass rush moves, arsenal, or whatever you want to call it, early on. I'll never forget when Ted Albrecht, our offensive tackle said, "Hey, you need to watch Lee Roy Selmon. He's the best in the business." I watched a film of him before we played the Tampa Bay Buccaneers, and I think I got two or three sacks that Sunday. I was the Defensive Player of the Week in the NFC. It all kind of crystalized right in my head how to rush the passer. At that point I thought I could be pretty good.

In 1982, Pro Football Weekly voted me the Defensive Player of the Year. It was an abbreviated strike year with only nine games. Don Pierson, our beloved football writer in Chicago, didn't vote for me, but everybody else did. By that time I had kind of figured it out. I had a bunch of great players around me like Steve McMichael, Mike Singletary, Mike Hartenstine, Richard Dent, and Otis Wilson. I could make a list.

I really, really felt like I had a chance to be a great player. During my second or third year I was having dinner with Ed O'Bradovich and he said, "Hamp, I played with some Hall of Famers. You can be a Hall of Famer." I kind of laughed and said, "Yeah, yeah, yeah. When that day happens, I will call you and you can induct me." It was kind of a running joke over the years.

I think that from the 1983 season on, I would have to go to the hospital and have knee scopes every off-season. I was under doctors' orders for no lifting and no running for two to five months sometimes. Other times, I would be on crutches for a couple of months. It was one of those deals where there was always an obstacle that I would have to overcome. I'll be the first one to tell you that in 1989, I wasn't the same player I was in 1984 or 1982. With age, I had kind of figured it out. I knew what to do and learned to live on the margins. I wouldn't make a bad step and on any pass rush I wouldn't flop and flounder around like a lot of kids today. There was no wasted motion and I was still pretty effective.

Going into the Hall of Fame, did I ever think that I would? Did I ever think in a definitive way? No. Did I ever hope to? Did I aspire to achieve that? Hell yeah. Like I said, would it have happened in Tampa? Would it have happened in Seattle? I don't know. But in Chicago, I got lucky and I got to play with what people say was the greatest defense of all time.

Reason Don Pierson Didn't Vote For Me As Defensive Player Of the Year

I think he was infatuated with who knows, Lawrence Taylor or somebody. Everybody has his own perception. A defensive tackle player of the year ... you know, back 30 years ago, nobody paid much attention to defensive tackles like they do now. All I can tell you is that I'm flattered that people today really have a better understanding of the game. They understand what a dominant, what I used to call a wrecker, a guy that could collapse the pocket, how much their value is in the NFL. To get the answer, you'd have to ask Don. I'll just tell you this, I've seen him many times over the years and I've never really gotten a great answer, so I don't know.

Enduring Legacy Of 1985 Chicago Bears

I've got two businesses in Chicago. A lot of the guys that played on that team have different things that they do, the residuals, the benefit of playing on that team. Nobody really makes a living by being one of the members of that team, but it is kind of cool. We still have a certain level of notoriety because of our association with the team.

Look at what Mike Ditka has been able to do. I know that he coached in New Orleans for a while, but I ask you to find me a coach that is probably more well known in Asia or Africa than Mike Ditka, and why? Did he coach somebody a year ago or 10 years ago? No. It was what he did with the Chicago Bears organization back in the '80s, and I have to say it was kind of like being validated. You get to be prom king for a long time.

A lot of people in the media want to ridicule it. The media doesn't propel this or basically propagate it. It's the people of Chicago. They just absolutely loved that team at that time. It was a great time to play for the Bears. People say, "That's our team." If I could build a team, that's the kind of team I would build. Nobody is fighting that, but we're just tickled pink that we were able to be a part of it.

Changing Positions

When I went to practice long ago, I was an offensive lineman. Jimmy Johnson said, "No. I want him on defense," and so I moved to defense. I understand the old motto and the old creed, the more you can do to help the team, well, that's the whole thing. I was drafted as a tackle and Al Harris was an end. Al hurt his knee and Tommy Hart, the old defensive end, hurt his knee. I was moved to defensive end, and boom, I did pretty well. They kept saying, as soon as Alan Page retires, we're moving that ass inside. I would shake my head and say "No way, no way. I like it out here because there's a hell of a lot of beatings going on inside. You got people falling around your legs and you're getting double-teamed." I liked being outside with a lot of one-on-ones."

In the light of day, you've got to just say, "I was the logical one to play that position, and so I did." I really fit it and I was a pretty good end. I made the All-Pro and Pro Bowls, but I was a better defensive tackle. I was pretty dominant inside. It was good for our defense. Everybody, in a vicarious way, was able to benefit from it. That was great.

Then, in 1985 they drafted William "The Fridge" Perry. After a while they wanted Fridge to play and McMichael couldn't play end, but I could. I was the logical guy to go back outside, so I went back out to end. Then after a few years, Fridge had knee trouble and got too heavy. By the end of the 1988 season they moved me back inside and that's where I finished my career.

At the end of the day, it was where could I help, and what could I do to help. Most of the guys on the defense all had that same attitude.

Not Being In the Super Bowl Shuffle

Willie Gault came to me and said, "You've got to be in it. You're the only one who can play an instrument." I said, "Don't let that stop you," and it didn't. The shuffle crew was going to the Super Bowl. I didn't mind them saying it, but I couldn't say it because we had never been to the Super Bowl. A lot of those guys were still in their second, third, and fifth years. I think I was in my seventh or eighth year. I didn't want to jinx it. I'm superstitious. They wrote a part in it for

McMichael and he said to me, "Why didn't you take it?" I said, "You idiot, your more superstitious than I am. What do you mean, you're thinking about it?" He said, "You're right. I ain't doing it." We would mock the guys that did it, but I'm really happy they did. Every time I see Fridge I say, "You're looking at the Fridge, I'm the rookie …I may be …" It was a great source of entertainment for us. We'd tease them and it was amusing to us, but it wasn't right for me and it wasn't right for McMichael.

It had a great little tune. It was catchy with clever little words, and it made some money. Yeah, the guy was a damn thief and took off with the cash … I don't know. All I'm saying is, almost 25 years later we're the only ones that ever had a soundtrack to our season. What's wrong with that?

I will do an appearance at Jewel or a car dealership, and somebody will start singing some of those words. I am telling you, it's an amazing little piece of Americana.

Two weekends ago, my buddy texted me letting me know he was at a wedding in Minnesota, and they were playing the Super Bowl Shuffle. I was like, get out of here. Oh my God, let it go. But, who am I to fight it?

<u>Transition From Neill Armstrong To Mike Ditka As Head Coach</u>
So much of the time, when you're in the middle of it and almost in a selfish way, you don't worry about everybody else. In subsequent years, I've looked back and I felt bad for Neill Armstrong and some of the other guys on the offensive staff. They were good people, but it was just not working. Our offense was in disarray.

One reason that Buddy Ryan and his assistants kept their jobs was there was progress. I think that back then, there were 26 to 28 teams in the league. We started out the season 23rd or 25th, and by the end of the year we were 3rd or 4th. The offense was turning the ball over. I feel bad now, but at the time I was pragmatic. I was like, who gives us a better chance of winning. We're not winning now; these guys aren't doing what they have to do for us to win. It didn't bother me at the time. Like I said, years later I felt bad, but I wanted to win.

I had never won anything and I couldn't live with losing. When I started in high school, the team was horrible. By the time I was a senior, we had gotten into the playoffs. In college, initially we weren't very good but by the end, hell, we were in the top 10 in the nation. I just couldn't stand losing.

When Ditka came in, he made some comments that made an awful lot of sense. He said, "I've been in the Super Bowl as a player. I've been in the Super Bowl as an assistant coach, and I know what is required. We got a lot of guys that give us a chance to be there, but we've got to make some changes. We are going to have to work awful hard." I thought, that's no problem; let's work. I've always been an optimist. I've always been a pragmatist and it just seemed like a natural thing to do. I had been through a change in college and it was for the better. We became a better team and there was every indication that we would become better. It didn't take long.

I'll tell you this; everybody asks me what I miss about playing. I miss being in the room the Saturday night before a game when Ditka would ask the waitresses to leave and close the door. That's what I loved.

It didn't take long for me to understand. The first two games we got beat in overtime, Ditka went nuts, punched a trunk, and broke his hand. Everybody laughed and mocked it. I loved it. I was like, this guy … he wants to win. Nobody had ever punched a trunk before. We had lost a hell of a lot of games and nobody …. I'm just saying that I welcomed it because I wanted to win. I couldn't live with losing, and to me Ditka was the better chance to win.

Losing To the Miami Dolphins & Not Going Undefeated In 1985

Over the years, we have all become so sickened by the Miami Dolphins and their nostalgia overload about their perfect season. In a way I'm glad we didn't go undefeated because everybody would really hate us the same way. Have you've seen those movies where the rock stars don't know what town they're in, but they just keep going and they keep on? That was kind of the way it was. We had things that did not work out for us in Miami, but you know the one thing about it is the Dolphins weren't some expansion team. Their quarterback is in the Hall of Fame. They didn't get there by being dumbasses; they knew what they were doing. You know what? We played dumb and did a lot of stupid stuff as far as our preparation, our game plan, and our actual performance. Sometimes you don't deserve it and we didn't deserve to win.

Numerous Surgeries
I think I'm probably the clubhouse leader right now in the amount of surgeries I've had. On each knee and then replacements, I'm at a smooth 15. I have had a bunch of other operations on my fingers and this and that. It's an unfortunate moniker being the surgery king.

I remember about 1985 or 1986, the doctor said, "You need to quit." I looked at him and I could tell he thought I was nuts but I said, "No way. No way. I love it." I loved being on a team and on Saturday night finding out what we were going to do, and the next day going out and doing it. I mean there are a lot of great things in my life today. I have my wife, my kids, and I get to play golf. That place and time, can never be recaptured. It was a great ride.

Chicago Bears Dan Hampton leaps over a Minnesota Viking player to corner quarterback Tommy Kramer. Photograph copyright Associated Press

Chapter 24

Dwight Stephenson

> College:
> Alabama
>
> Career History:
> Miami Dolphins (1980–1987)
>
> 1998 Inductee Pro Football Hall Of Fame

<u>Pro Football Hall Of Fame Induction</u>
Being inducted into the Pro Football Hall of Fame is an accomplishment that I never ever considered possible. It is awesome to be in that club with the great guys whom are already in there. I am happy to be in the club.

Being inducted into the Hall of Fame was truly an honor. It was something that I didn't even think was possible. I look at and compare myself to some of the guys already in the Hall of Fame, and I realize some guys had a lot longer career. They deserve to be in the Pro Football Hall of Fame. I am in there even though my career was not 15 years long. I was in the league nine years; eight as a player and one year was on injured reserve. Compared to some guys' careers, my career is not that long. It is one of those honors that I am not going to give up. I am very, very happy to be there. Because I did it only playing for eight years, I am even more proud.

<u>Only Playing For Two Head Coaches In College & NFL</u>
I didn't really realize how fortunate I was at the time. Playing for one coach, Bear Bryant, probably the greatest coach ever in college football. He taught me things that I still carry with me today.

I left there and went to Miami where I played for probably the greatest coach to ever coach in the NFL, Coach Don Shula. I knew I was around some guys that were the best at what they did, but I probably didn't appreciate everything the way I should have. I really enjoyed it. If I had to do it all over again, I think I would probably just appreciate it that much more. I enjoyed playing at the University of Alabama and playing for Coach Bear Bryant. It was a great experience.

College Choice
I had some really great high school teammates, that could have gone anywhere in the country. Scouts from Alabama and a lot of other schools came to our high school, because there were two great football players there: Woodrow Wilson and Simon Gupton.

We all went to grade school and high school together. They had the opportunity to go pretty much anywhere they wanted to go in the country. The University of Alabama came to our high school to recruit those two guys. Coach Mike Smith, my high school coach, who is a great coach in his own right said, "We got Dwight Stephenson here and I think he can play at the University of Alabama." Anyway, they looked at me and said, "Okay, yeah, we'll take him too." I think they really thought they were going to get those other two guys and that I was coming along. Those other two guys had a deal they were going to go to school together. They went to North Carolina State. We all signed on the same day. I decided to go to the University of Alabama. After I had already made my commitment, the other two guys decided to go to North Carolina State.

It worked out well for everybody. I went to the University of Alabama and had a great time. Then they went to NC State, and both of them made All Conference. They did well there. We are still great friends today.

Bear Bryant Said Dwight Stephenson Best Player He Ever Coached
When people say that, I tell them, "No, no he didn't say I was the greatest player or the best player that he ever coached." What he said was, "I was the best Center that he ever coached." That alone means a whole lot to me, right there. There are some great players that played for him at the University of Alabama. Joe Namath, John Hannah,

Terry Jones, and Tony Nathan were some great, great football players. I am happy to be mentioned with them.

Importance Of Center Position

The Center is very, very important. It is one of those positions that I think is kind of a natural leadership position. You see how everybody has set himself around you. You are the first one to break the huddle. When you walk to the line, everybody else walks to the line. If you are running to the line, they are running to the line. It is a natural leadership position. Now, at different times, we have a lot of responsibility. We have blocking assignments to make. We need to be sure that we can protect the quarterback or if there is a run play, to make sure that the run play is successful. I enjoyed it. Of all the positions on the football field, that is the position that I wanted to play.

I would have played anywhere, but that position was something I always gravitated toward. When I was coming up there, was a Center with the Minnesota Vikings, Mick Tingelhoff. I never got a chance to meet him, but he was a guy whom I kind of watched. I watched all the great Centers of course ... Mike Webster, Jim Langer, and Jim Ringo. I always gravitated toward the Center position.

Bear Bryant

Coach Bryant was probably the right guy for me at that time in my life. I went to the University of Alabama not expecting a whole lot, wondering if I could even play there, and if I even deserved to be there. Coach Bryant got us in training camp and that is where he pretty much broke us all down. He let us know that it was great we were good in high school and it is great to feel good about ourselves, but we were all starting there on an even level. It depended on how hard you worked, what you did, and the decisions that you made as to how good a football player you'd become at the University of Alabama, and what you'd do for the rest of your life. He was the right guy to come into my life at that time. I enjoyed him.

Don Shula's Coaching Style Compared to Bear Bryant

They were very similar and also very organized. There was no lollygagging at their practices. Both practices were very, very organized. They would go over game type of situations. They did not leave much to chance. They controlled where we stayed, and everything. Those guys were involved in the details. They knew what was going on.

It was a great experience playing at the University of Alabama, seeing how Coach Bryant was dealing with boys. I mean, pretty much, we were older boys who were trying to be men. He kind of handled us that way, knowing that we need to be molded in the decisions we were going to make, like quitting or those types of things. You can't quit. If you quit once, it is easy to do it the next time. Those were the kind of things we learned at the University of Alabama.

When I went to the Dolphins, Coach Shula was molding men. Some of us had families. We had a lot more responsibility. He treated us that way, but he didn't leave much to chance either. When it came to the football games, he would go over situations. We would overlearn situations. One of his phrases was, "You overlearn it." Both coaches were highly organized, very competitive people, who taught us things we could use for the rest of our lives.

Don Shula Changing His Offensive Philosophy Thru The Years
He recognized the rule changes. You can't keep on doing the same things as, say, 30 years ago. The rules change, and I think Coach Shula changed with the rules. The passing game became more of an opportunity. Then you had Air Marino. No question. It was kind of like a match was made there. We were a good football team and Dan Marino was what we needed. We needed a guy like that. The guy was an awesome leader and competitor. He is just a guy who is tough. A really tough guy, physically as well as mentally. I mean, a very, very tough guy. I enjoyed Dan.

Dan Marino
When we saw Dan, we just saw something different about him. We thought, "This guy can throw the football." Then you watched him in games, and he wasn't afraid. I heard other people say that he wasn't afraid of making a mistake. He would go out there and try something.

If it didn't work he wouldn't necessarily say that he would never do that again. He looked at it like, "I only did this," or "I only did that," and the next time he would go out there and make the correction. He was a guy who was going for it. He wasn't interested in, I feel, almost getting there. He wanted to go for it and that was a great attitude to have.

At times you did want him to do his own thing. Coach Shula would be more open to hearing some of his wide receivers ideas, and let them try things. Dan would call his own plays at times, and stuff like that. Some times in the situation, especially in two-minute drills, you just have to go out there and make adjustments on the field. Dan was the right guy.

Importance Of Offensive Line

Any successful team realizes that the offensive line as a whole, not the individual, is very, very important. That offensive or defensive line decides who wins the game, for the most part. Coach Shula realized they were important, and the offensive line had a real great coach in Monte Clark.

In 1972, the Dolphins undefeated season, they put the emphasis on the offensive line. The offensive line did not necessarily have all #1 draft choices on it either. The guys really put it on the line every time they played. That is what you need to do as an offensive lineman. You have to have a guy who is not necessarily the most talented guy, but the guy who will literally put it all on the line every play and give you all he's got. That is very, very important. The offensive linemen are very important to the success of a football team. They are literally a must on the field, not just because I was a part of it, but they are usually the hardest working group on the field. If they are not on the field, they are in the weight room, studying plays, and trying to coordinate and make sure that they work well together as a unit.

Toughest Defensive Lineman

Joe Klecko is one of the strongest guys I ever played against, and one of the nicest guys. He is not in the Pro Football Hall of Fame, but he should be. He was an athlete who could play the run. He was a smart guy, and just one heck of a football player. He could pretty much do it all.

He could play the run as well as pass. When that defensive line had it going, they were the New York Sack Exchange; they were something. He was a special football player and a great, great guy.

Dan Marino And Isotoner Gloves

Dan Marino actually gave us Isotoner gloves. I think he might have given them to more than just the offensive linemen. He brought some into the locker room and made sure we got some. Dan was always taking care of the guys, like when we would go to dinner and that kind of stuff. He did those things for the team. He was a great guy. He wasn't standoffish. He would hang out with the offensive linemen.

Photograph copyright Associated Press

Chapter 25

Rickey Jackson

> College:
> Pittsburgh
>
> Career History:
> New Orleans Saints (1981–1993)
> San Francisco 49ers (1994–1995)
>
> 2010 Inductee Pro Football Hall Of Fame

College
Pittsburgh was on TV all the time, so that was great for me. Dan Marino got recruited my junior year. He lived with me. We had a lot of great times. He used to come down to Florida and visit with me all the time.

Russ Grimm
Russ Grimm could have played any position, but he settled for playing on the offensive line and he was a load. Opponents could not mess with him. I think he was the best lineman I have ever seen, you know as far as being around or being with.

Hugh Green
Hugh Green was one of the best college players that ever played. For him to come in second for the Heisman Trophy as a defensive player, that was pretty strong.

Jackie Sherrill
Coach Jackie Sherrill was a great guy. Everybody liked him. I cared for him a lot. He was a coach who was for the players. He always tried to keep a good team and keep a lot of good guys together. Nick Saban is just like Jackie. Nick keeps a lot of good guys around him.

Not Winning National Championship At Pittsburgh

It was really hard because two years in a row, we went 11-1. It was something that one game a year got us. We stayed around the top five in the rankings every year. It wasn't bad. You hate to lose and we struggled with losing. Our thing was that at Pitt, we weren't supposed to lose. Every year for two years, that one game did us in. It knocked us out of being where we wanted to be.

North Carolina beat us my junior year, and Florida State my senior year. We should have easily beaten those teams. But, we didn't play that well. We had a lot of turnovers.

Best Game In College

My best game in college was in the Gator Bowl. I had a lot of good games, but in the Gator Bowl, scouts were looking at Hugh Green and George Rogers. I had a chance to show my skills and my power. I felt that was the game where people noticed me. For the world to get a chance to see me, that was my marquee game.

Being Named MVP Of East/West Shrine Game

I took off from there. Everybody knew then how good I was. Lawrence Taylor always knew that I was real good. We were good friends and stuff, but a lot of people were just waiting to see what would happen when I turned pro. A lot of times when you're in college, you really don't know how a guy's going to turn out. Just like all these guys you see now, you think some of them are going to be superstars, but they end up not panning out in the pros. It's a whole different ballgame when you get to the NFL.

NFL Draft

We had about 13-14 guys get drafted off the 1980 Pittsburgh team when we came out of college that year. A lot of them made the NFL that year. Russ Grimm, my teammate at Pittsburgh, and I went into the Pro Football Hall of Fame together. You don't see stuff like that too often.

A lot of people said I was going to get drafted in the first round or early second round. I was playing basketball when I got drafted. I didn't even know I was drafted. I thought, when they take me, they take me, but I wasn't going to stay home waiting to see where I went.

New Orleans drafted me along with George Rogers, Frank Warren, Jim Wilks, Hoby Brenner, and Hokie Gajon. Johnny Poe also that made the team, and Russ Gary was drafted in second round. We had a lot of good players that were drafted.

Bum Phillips

Bum Phillips was a great guy. You could tell he was a players' coach. He brought Leon Gray, Ken Stabler, and Earl Campbell, all of whom had been with him in Houston with the Oilers. Those were guys with experience. Bum felt like he could use them for a year or two and win with them, so he brought them over.

Rookie Year With New Orleans Saints

We came out ready to play in the NFL after playing at Pittsburgh. You went up against some of the best guys in the country when you were at Pitt. Our running back, Randy McMillan, was a first round pick. He was the twelfth pick in the draft by Baltimore that year. We had a lot of great running backs we went against in practice.

You were going against Russ Grimm, Mark May, and Jimbo Covert. We had a lot of good players to go up against. Those guys were big football players, so if you could beat them, you were going to do well in the pros.

New Orleans Saints Linebackers Best In NFL History

I agree we were the best. The only thing we didn't get to do was win a championship. Everything else we had. We had all the accolades. All four of us went to the Pro Bowl. That will never happen again. Everybody thinks that you aren't great unless you win the Super Bowl. When teams came down to the Superdome to play us, the four of us were somehow going to get you. You were going to get your bell rung. So I think we had the best group of guys that you could put together. It was Pat Swilling, Sam Mills, Vaughan Johnson, and me.

The Giants linebackers played a different system than us. They played a system where there were four guys up front to do the most damage. We had three guys up front so our linebacker had to fill in and do a lot of stuff. Plus, Bill Parcells had a great coaching staff. They did well there. They won the Super Bowl a couple of times.

They had Carl Banks, Lawrence Taylor, and Harry Carson. They got two of them into the Hall of Fame, Lawrence Taylor and Harry Carson, so they had great linebackers too.

The Bears had some pretty good linebackers in Otis Wilson, Wilber Marshall, and Mike Singletary. I think overall we were more physical, faster, and made more plays.

One thing about us, we were cover guys too. We weren't one dimensional, and that was great. I think I was a better player against the run than most guys. We were great pass cover guys too.

136 Career Sacks As A Linebacker

You have to look at the tackles that I had. I had over 1,100 tackles. I look at that more than anything, and playing in over 200 games. I look at that more than the sacks and stuff. People talk about the sacks, but look how many games I played … that meant more to me. Having over 1,100 tackles over a career … you aren't going to find that too often. That's the kind of stuff that counts the most to me.

Best Game In NFL

The best game was probably a game against the Atlanta Falcons. Atlanta was trying to beat us and I had about four sacks that day. The last drive Atlanta was coming down the field, I jumped across and tackled the quarterback. We ended up winning the game. I was always trying to get the Falcons, 49ers, and Rams, in our division games.

Reason Joined San Francisco 49ers

The chance to win a Super Bowl and Eddie DeBartolo was a great owner. He let me know exactly what I could expect. He had always helped older players at the end of their careers and gave them a couple more years. You didn't have to practice a whole lot or do a whole lot. You got the chance to get prepared for the game.

It was just my time was up with New Orleans. They didn't want me anymore. Coach Mora got rid of me along with Vaughan, Sam, and Pat. He wanted to go with younger guys. He didn't want us anymore. We had to go somewhere else, so everybody left.

A lot of older guys went there for the chance to win a Super Bowl. Look at the team we had. Our team that won the Super Bowl should have won it two years in a row. I was playing with Ken Norton, Gary Plummer, Tim McDonald, Eric Davis, Bryant Young, and Dana Stubblefield. We had so many great guys on that team. That was an all-star team. Richard Dent got hurt that year, tearing his knee up.

On offensive, we had Ricky Watters, Jerry Rice, Steve Young, and William Floyd. We had an all-star team. We didn't have to practice against our offense too much. We didn't have to do a whole lot against each other out there as far as beating each other up.

Best Player In NFL History
I would definitely say Jerry Rice is in the top three. I really liked Earl Campbell too. I think Earl Campbell was a load. For the years that he played, I think he earned the ball. There are so many great ones. It's hard to say, but a couple of guys who were really great at their positions were Jerry Rice, Earl, and Walter Peyton. They had some great guys. Then Emmitt Smith came along. All of them are great guys.

Jim Brown, Joe Montana, and Dan Marino were great too. Every time I look at Mean Joe Greene, he looks like he still can play today. There are a whole lot of great guys. I also got the chance to watch Jack Ham, so I've seen a whole lot of great guys. It is hard to say who was the greatest. All of them were great.

Player Modeled Himself After
I saw Jack Ham more than anybody. I studied Jack Ham more. Jack Ham was just that guy. The only difference between Jack Ham and me was I was a pass rusher with everything else.

Pro Football Hall Of Fame Induction
It was late. I should have been picked a lot earlier. When you look at my stats and some of the guys who were in there before me, I know that I should have been in there a long time ago. I was thinking this morning, other people have your fate in their hands and you don't really know how it's going to come out so you just have to thank God for just getting in. Even though I know I deserved to get in and should have been in a long time ago, that's something I didn't have

any say in. You don't have a say in that, so you have to go in whenever they let you in.

Toughest Offensive Lineman
The toughest guy I went up against was probably Jackie Slater. He played for 20 something years. He gave me a battle. I knew that if I beat him, I was doing well. I always worked to get ready to try to beat him because I knew he was going to come with a good fight. Willie Roaf was tough too. I'd just go against him in practice. Those were the best two, Jackie Slater and Willie Roaf.

San Francisco 49ers linebacker Rickey Jackson rushes Philadelphia Eagles quarterback Randall Cunningham. Photograph copyright Associated Press

Chapter 26

Anthony Munoz

> College:
> Southern California
>
> Career History:
> Cincinnati Bengals (1980–1992)
>
> 1998 Inductee Pro Football Hall Of Fame

College Choice
USC was always the school I wanted to go to. When I first fell in love with USC, I didn't know if it was because of the football tradition or it was Traveler, the big white horse that runs circles around the field every time they score. I was aware of the great offensive linemen that played there, but it was more the tradition and the program.

Growing up 40 miles down the street, I watched USC football every Saturday afternoon. I also remember seeing them in the Rose Bowl all the time, and I wanted to be a part of that. It was about getting the opportunity to go to school and play football because financially, I don't think we would have been able to swing it.

Baseball was my first love growing up as a kid. I always wanted to be a major league baseball player, but I started to get recruited for football. Of course, the selling pitch of most of the schools I talked to was that I could play baseball there. USC had a track record of letting guys do that. I wanted to go there, and the fact that they were going to let me play baseball and football, made it extra special and extra attractive. I was going to play a sport that I loved as a kid in college. Those were the primary reasons that I was excited about going to USC.

Winning A Baseball Championship As USC

I was a member of the team that enabled Rod Dedeaux to win his last College World Series. I was able to make the trip to Omaha and win a national championship in baseball.

I hit pretty well in high school. Then in college, I became a relief pitcher. I was also playing first base and DH a little bit. I was still able to hit some. I'll never forget my first game as a JV player. We were playing Cal Poly Pomona. My first at bat, the pitcher hung me a curve ball and I hit a home run, which was pretty exciting. I hit a couple others in college. I wasn't a great hitter, but I could hit the ball pretty well.

Coach Dedeaux was unbelievable. He had so much baseball knowledge. I'd be on the bench charting pitches during the game or just sitting there watching, and he was constantly up and down the bench asking questions about situations. Even if you were a player on the bench, he made you really stay in tune with the game. And, personality-wise, the guy was just the greatest. He was unbelievable. I was very fortunate to play for Rod Dedeaux and John Robinson while at USC. I'm thankful.

Transition From College To NFL

Technically, I was well prepared coming out of USC. Experience-wise, was different. When you play one game your senior year, then all of a sudden you're at an NFL camp, you're wondering, "Okay, how's this going to go?" I was very fortunate when I got to Cincinnati. I had a good offensive line coach who started to teach me. I knew it wouldn't be easy.

One of the great things about going to USC, I learned work ethic from the coaches. We had John Robinson, Hudson Houck, and all the guys at USC. That's what it was all about: working hard, and trying to be the best. I knew if I came in with that work ethic and really turned it up a few notches, something good might happen. I didn't think it was going to be easy.

Working Out Against Forrest Gregg Prior To Draft

Having gone through three knee operations in four years at USC, Cincinnati was the only team that sent somebody out to scout me.

Cincinnati Head Coach Forrest Gregg, came out and put me through a pretty rigorous two-hour workout. Forrest was still in pretty good shape, a young coach, with a southern drawl and an intimidating look. He was about 6'5", and 260 lbs. He said, "Just relax. I'm going to make some pass rush moves. Just react." My reaction as an offensive lineman, when he faked me out and came in, was to try to get his chest. I hit Forrest right in the chest. He went down, and hit the back of his head. I was like, "Oh my goodness." I extended my hand and apologized. He just looked up at me, smiled and said, "That's all right, Anthony." All I could say was, "Oh." I went from being totally frightened to thinking that maybe it was good that happened. Hopefully that helped out. And it appeared that it did.

After Playing In The Super Bowl

After playing in the Super Bowl, I thought maybe we were going to have a run. I was used to playing in Rose Bowls at USC. I figured, I played in my first Super Bowl during my second year in the NFL and we might put a few together. You quickly become aware of how difficult it is to get to consecutive Super Bowls.

Even though Buffalo didn't win one, it's impressive the Bills got to four straight Super Bowls. It's so hard getting back the following year, after you've been to one.

Sam Wyche

Sam Wyche was unbelievable. I still believe he was one of the greatest offensive minds around. What we did offensively was amazing. He brought in the no huddle offense. He put together a great offensive staff with Bruce Coslet, Jim McNally, and Jim Anderson. It was just amazing.

I enjoyed both Forrest Gregg and Sam Wyche. They had totally different styles of coaching. Forrest Gregg was more the CEO, managing both sides of the football. He had his coordinators on both sides. They ran the show offensively and defensively. He had his plan for the team.

Sam Wyche was more the head coach, offensive minded, and involved with the offensive. Sam was an amazing coach. I still have a great relationship with Sam. He comes to my foundation event every summer. He made football for an offensive player very fun. For an offensive linemen like me to be able to catch some touchdowns, he made it extremely enjoyable.

It was his idea that I thought he was a little crazy at the time having an offensive linemen catch a football. After that first catch, it was like, "This is pretty nice." His rookie year, he started bringing in two extra offensive linemen in to tackle. Then he moved another linemen and me out to the tight end. He just started designing plays. They worked, so we weren't going to argue. The impressive thing was the yards per catch. I think I averaged a little over a yard per catch, which is very impressive.

Blocking For Ken Anderson & Boomer Esiason
Both were extremely smart. People look at the differences between having right-handed or left-handed quarterbacks. Things really don't change as far as formations. Most teams are predominately right-handed; meaning formations are usually strong right side. That didn't change a whole lot. The difference was the whole personality.

Boomer was a lot more outgoing, a lot more verbal. Kenny was more of the silent assassin. The guy was one of the most accurate quarterbacks. He didn't say a whole lot, but when he said something, it was pretty profound. Since I was the left tackle, we rarely had a tight end over on my side with either guy playing quarterback, even though one was right handed and one was left handed. So the adjustment wasn't that different.

Punting
Pat McInally was an excellent punter for us for years. Friday practice was always a light work out, so Pat and I would have punting contests. I got word from up top that they didn't want me punting in those. Paul Brown ended our punting contests pretty quickly. Anytime Paul said something you just ... did it. I enjoyed punting. I actually punted and kicked in high school and enjoyed it.

Playing Against San Francisco 49ers
I kept thinking why do we have to play them in the Super Bowl and regular season. I think I went hitless. I think I was 0 for 5 against them in the two Super Bowls and regular season. When I have

nightmares it usually includes Joe Montana, number 16, wearing that 49ers uniform.

Paul Brown

Paul was regimented. It was the same schedule all the time. He was very involved in what was going on. He was around and very connected with the team and the staff. He was very engaging with the players. One thing we could always count on is he would come into the locker room and just kind of interact with us. The thing I loved about it was that the questions led to stories, and we heard a lot of stories.

There was a perception that he was a tightfisted patriarch by one of the radio shows in Cincinnati. He was very innovative in what he brought to the NFL, and that was the impressive. During the ten or eleven years of my career that I was around him, he brought so much to the game, and added so much to it. It was just great being around the guy.

Toughest Defensive Lineman

I never really feared anybody or went into a game saying, "I don't want to play against this guy." One guy who probably wasn't the fastest, Mike Bell from Kansas City, was a guy I could never figure out. He wasn't the quickest, the fastest, the biggest, or the strongest. He just had a way about doing his job.

Durability

I had four years of high school where I played three sports, football, basketball, and baseball. During those four years, I never missed a game.

In college it was just one of those things, where I was at the wrong place at the wrong time. All three injuries in college were kind of these freak accidents.

Of course, my injury history was a concern of many people in the NFL. When you go through injuries like that you want to make sure that you're physically fit, and I took that very seriously. I was a workout fanatic with weight training and conditioning. I really didn't think about the injuries, but I knew that it was part of the game. I can't really say that my durability in the NFL surprised me because of my track record in high school. I was just in the wrong place at the wrong time in college when I got injured.

Acting
You're out there in that crazy place close to Hollywood. USC is known for their TV Department. You've got the George Lucas School of Theater on campus. You get some opportunities. Young guys who don't know a whole lot say, "Oh, let's check that out. It might be fun." You do it, and you think, "Wow, sitting around all day waiting for your scene … it's not for me." It's fun while you're doing it. I got to meet people like Charles Bronson, Ed Harris, Scott Paulin, and Scott Glenn. It's pretty cool being able to meet individuals like that.

Pro Football Hall Of Fame Induction
It's unbelievable. It's very humbling, thrilling, and exciting. It's one of those things where you think, "Bart Starr, Deacon Jones, Gale Sayers, Merlin Olsen, ... Anthony Munoz? Oh, man. This is pretty exciting." The fun thing for me was, I grew up in Southern California, played at USC, played my entire NFL career in Cincinnati, and then I actually got the word that I was going into the Hall of Fame in San Diego. It was kind of like it went full circle, when I got the actual announcement back in California.

Even now it's still kind of crazy thinking that I'm in the Hall of Fame. I walk around the place, and think, "My goodness, this is crazy." It's still hard for me to believe at times.

Most people don't forget where they come from, including me. I haven't forgotten where I came from. For my acceptance speech, it was easy for me to do a time line of 'thank yous' to the people who made it happen for me. I chuckle even today when I hear about self-made men. This guy is self-made. I haven't met anybody who is self-made. Everybody that is successful has a supporting cast starting from the time they're young. The easy and fun thing for me was selecting those who helped me along my journey. It was fun for me. The tough thing was making sure I didn't forget anybody along the way. That's the one tough thing I was concerned about, because there were so many people in my life that helped me. I had support from family members, coaches, teachers, and friends. Hopefully I didn't leave anybody out. That was the only tough thing about writing the speech.

Halftime Ceremony During Final Game

The one thing that made the halftime experience so great was that just about the entire stadium was filled with Bengals fans, guys and gals that had watched most of my games over my career. While the Hall of Fame experience is the pinnacle of a professional football career, you know that the audience is not all Bengals fan. The fact that I had that experience at the home stadium where I played all 13 years was really extra special. It was in front of my hometown. The Hall of Fame, of course, is very, very special, but it's a different setting. The only difference is that you're in front of fans of all football teams.

Photograph copyright Associated Press

Chapter 27

Mike Singletary

> College:
> Baylor
>
> Career History:
> As Player:
> Chicago Bears (1981–1992)
>
> As Coach:
> Baltimore Ravens (2003–2004)
> Linebackers coach
> San Francisco 49ers (2005–2008)
> Assistant head coach / linebackers coach
> San Francisco 49ers (2008)
> Interim head coach
> San Francisco 49ers (2009–2010)
> Head coach
> Minnesota Vikings (2011–2013)
> Special assistant to head coach / linebackers coach
>
> 1998 Inductee Pro Football Hall Of Fame

College Choice
Texas asked me to play running back. They wanted me to be a blocking fullback for Earl Campbell. I said, "Can I at least have an opportunity to compete to play middle linebacker?" I was told, "No. We're looking at you as a blocking fullback." I said, "No, thank you." That was it.

A couple of things caused me to chose Baylor. Number one was the coach. When I met Grant Teaff, I was sold. He was a wonderful man who had the ability to make you feel like he really cared about you and that he had your best interests at heart. I really felt good about that and he sold my mom. I was going there anyway, but the other thing is Baylor was the only other school outside of Texas that would let me play linebacker.

Adjustment From High School Football To College Football

In high school you think you're working. You have practice, but at the next level in college, it's like a job. You're going to school and you have your studies and then after that, you've got to get ready to go out and compete every day. If you're not competing at a very high level you're not going to play. Then you're not going to enjoy the game. For me it was just the intensity about practice. In high school, you go out and do what you have to do and you don't know what you don't know, but at the collegiate level it's a whole another ball game.

Starting As A Freshman At Baylor

When I left the poor neighborhood that I lived in with all of the broken dreams and everything else that I saw to attend Baylor, I made a commitment. I was going to number one, honor God and honor my family with every decision that I made, and just go full speed with everything I did.

I think that went a long way in really helping me to become a starter. In everything I did, I kept asking the coaches what do I need to be able to do in order to start? At first it was, "We don't really have freshmen come in and start on our team." I said, "Well I'm asking you what do I need to do in order to start?" Once they answered that question, I just went to work on what they told me.

After a while it just became a reality because I wasn't backing down. For me there was no other way. I was going to do what they said I needed to do and then it was up to them to keep their word. That's how it worked.

Process Of Becoming A College All-American

At Baylor I talked to my defense coordinator and I asked him, "What do I need to do in order to be an All-American. What do I need to do to be the best?" He said, "Mike, you know we're at Baylor, we're not at Oklahoma, Alabama, Ohio State, or any of those schools. In order for you to do that you're going to have to go outside of the realm, you're going to have to shatter everything that has ever been done, to even be mentioned in the category of All-American. You have to make every tackle with every opportunity you have."

That's what I did. I tried to make every tackle I possibly could. That really became my standard. Every time the ball was snapped, I wanted to be where the ball was and be responsible for bringing the guy down. That was kind of how that happened.

Breaking Helmets At Baylor
I was beginning to think man, am I just getting a bad deal on these helmets? I was the only one cracking them, so something was up. Once again it was going full speed, giving my full attention and everything in me into every hit. Whether it was in practice, games, or whatever it was, I always putting 100% into it.

Players Modeled Himself After
There were three players that I basically modeled myself after. When I watched the Cowboys the guy that I looked at was Roger Staubach. The thing about Roger Staubach that stuck out to me was he always seemed to find a way to win. He had the will to win. That's what I loved about the Cowboys, and particularly that's what I loved about Roger Staubach. As far as linebackers are concerned, there was Willie Lanier who was with the Chiefs, and Lee Roy Jordan. Those are the three guys that I looked at.

Willie Lanier First African American Starting Middle Linebacker
I studied Willie Lanier's history and how that whole thing came to be. I met him several times and talked with him. I really apprenticed what he stood for and what he brought to the game as a linebacker. He is a very sharp guy.

Winning Two Davey O'Brien Awards In College
I didn't even know what the Davey O'Brien Award was. It is given to the best player in the Southwest. It is a very special honor, so to win it twice was really cool. I am very thankful I was able to do that.

Realization Could Play In NFL
I thought I could play in the NFL when I was in high school and college. The same way I asked my defense coordinator in college what I needed to do in order to be the best, that's what I asked my high school coaches. The thought never crossed my mind that I couldn't do it as long as I was willing to work. A lot of times people

say things, but they're not willing to do the work. Well, I was willing to do the work.

NFL Draft
I knew that there was a possibility the Chicago Bears would draft me. There were several teams that talked about drafting me. I think San Diego was one that talked about the possibility of drafting me. So I thought, shoot I'm going to be gone in the first round. I didn't really think about it too much. When the Bears drafted me, that's what I hoped for. I just thought it was going to be in the first round.

Chicago Bears Hiring Mike Ditka As Head Coach
It was a big change, but it was a great change. When I first heard Mike Ditka was hired I knew that he was exactly what we needed. He was a visionary. He was very strong willed and he was very demanding. We needed that. The Bears, at that time, were a team that really did not expect a whole lot, we didn't get a whole lot, and we didn't give a whole lot either. He was a great addition.

Buddy Ryan
There were some special guys that we had on defense. Anybody that was smart and was a good football player, Buddy loved them and respected them. We had Alan Page, someone Buddy had in Minnesota with the Vikings. He loved Alan Page, Dan Hampton, and Gary Fencik. Those guys were our leaders during my rookie year. They thought, hey we need to keep Buddy. Of course, part of me said I don't know about that and the other part of me knew what they were saying was exactly right. I felt the same way. Buddy is just that way. He's the kind of guy that grows on you and if he likes you, you know it, if he doesn't you know it. That's just who he is.

1984 Raiders vs. Bears Game
The Raiders were a physical team and they were coming to our house. We were striving to be a physical team. We wanted to be the team that was the most physical in the league and we wanted everybody to know it. We didn't want to do it in a dirty way. We didn't want to really make a name for ourselves that way. We just wanted to go out, dominate, and be respected that way. I think it worked that way for us. It just worked out.

Origin Of "Samurai" Nickname

I just made a lot of different noises. I was always moving, always making noises and the guys just thought it was funny. Man, we need to name this guy "Samurai" or something like that because he makes so many noises. A very interesting name, but it stuck.

Sustaining Only Loss During 1985 Season To Miami Dolphins

I would never go back and say, man we should have won that game. As a matter of fact, I think the fact that we lost that game gave us a chance to win the Super Bowl because it brought us more into focus. I think it was more of a blessing then it was a curse. I'd think wow, I hate that we lost a game, but when I really think about it we were the youngest team to ever win the Super Bowl up until that time. The fact that we lost to Miami really woke us up and made us realize hey, it doesn't matter how many games we win. If we really want to make something special happen we have to win the big game. That means we have to get better every week and stop drinking the Kool-Aid. Let's go out there and get better each week so we can be ready for the Super Bowl. At the end of the day, that's really what it's about.

46 Defense

The 46 Defense comes down to the personnel. If the personnel are driven, you've got the right personnel to play it. If you don't have the right personnel, you can't play it. It's just as simple as that.

Personnel are the key. We just happened to have the right personnel. We had linebackers who could cover and we had a defensive line that could get off the ball and get to the quarterback. That's the combination you need to have a successful 46 defense.

Vince Tobin Taking Over As Defensive Coordinator When Buddy Ryan Left

We loved Buddy. He was a guy whom we believed in and he believed in us. I think that's a heck of a combination to have. We lost that, so it was an adjustment. It took time to adjust to just playing a regular defense instead of playing a defense that's exhilarating, exciting, ever changing, and always adjusting. It made a difference.

Reason Why Bears Only Won One Super Bowl

The biggest reason we didn't win another Super Bowl is just immaturity. We just took it for granted that we were going to win another Super Bowl because we were the Bears, not realizing that we had to work just as hard.

We were in a city that was so hungry for a Super Bowl. After winning the Super Bowl, it was just one of those things where everybody took advantage of every opportunity that came instead of saying we'll get more opportunities. Someone needed to have the wisdom to say we'll get more opportunities, let's just make sure that we get ourselves ready to repeat and do all the things necessary. All of us needed to be on the same page. We didn't have the foresight to do that.

Best Player Faced

I have to do it in categories. The best offensive linemen I ever played against would be between Dwight Stephenson and John Hannah. Running back would be between Earl Campbell and Eric Dickerson. Receiver is Jerry Rice. Quarterback, I'd have to say Joe Montana.

San Francisco 49ers

The 49ers ran a very, very efficient, disciplined offense. They were better on defense then most people gave them credit for. I really appreciated the execution they had in terms of really understanding the offense and knowing the strengths and weaknesses of the offense. They were able to put the ball into the hands of the playmakers. That's what that offense did.

Pro Football Hall Of Fame Induction

It was great. It was a very special day and a very special honor. Everything about that day was special. My family was there and all of the people that had given so much to me, allowing me to play the game at that level. It was just a really, really wonderful day. It was one of the best days of my life.

Photograph copyright Associated Press

Chapter 28

Ronnie Lott

> College:
> Southern California
>
> Career History:
> San Francisco 49ers (1981–1990)
> Los Angeles Raiders (1991–1992)
> New York Jets (1993–1994)
> Kansas City Chiefs (1995)
> San Francisco 49ers (1995)
>
> 2000 Inductee Pro Football Hall Of Fame

Career History
I was looking at a lot of schools. I was looking at schools all over California and I was looking at schools throughout the Midwest. John Robinson decided to recruit me, and I thought it would be a great place for me to go. So, I chose to move in the direction of a lot of great Southern California players, and decided to go to USC.

It wasn't a tough sell. The reason it wasn't a tough sell was even though I wanted to go to UCLA, my high school coach said, "Look. If you really want to play football, and it is definitely really what you want to do in your life, you should go to USC. You're going to get a great education and you won't only be a Trojan for four years, you'll be part of the Trojan family for life." I realized right after my coach said that, it was the right thing for me to do.

Possible Position Change At USC
I started off as a defensive back, but when they lost Charlie White, they were looking for a tailback. At the time they had Marcus Allen, Dennis Smith, me, along with a host of other defensive players. They

thought, "You know what? We should try one of these guys and see if they can play."

I think they chose the right guy. Marcus Allen was pretty good. Marcus was great on defense. That was the problem, though. He was great at whatever he did.

USC Talent
We had a lot of talent on that team. We had an offensive line that was arguably better than a lot of pro lines. We had phenomenal athletes and guys who loved the game, loved playing it, and worked very hard at it.

Biggest Rival Of USC
Notre Dame was and will always be, for a lot of reasons. Both teams have great athletes. They had a group of guys over the years that I learned to love and hate competing against. When you are competing against the likes of Joe Montana and others, it makes your life really very difficult.

John Robinson
John Robinson was a great coach, and arguably the best coach I ever played for. Bill Walsh was an exceptional coach. I really enjoyed what I learned from Coach Robinson and all the things that he brought in terms of his enthusiasm and his passion for wanting to win.

Difference Between John Robinson & Bill Walsh
The difference was you had one guy who talked about competing, and you had another guy who talked about execution. I think Bill focused more on execution and the way the game was played. John just said, "Look. You've got to out-compete the guys. You've got to find ways to impose your will." I think that attribute was something that resonated with me. I think that was one of the differences that allowed me to be a great football player.

Transition From High School To College
It was very difficult, because there are things that you had to learn that you didn't learn in high school. And, you have to get ready for the size and the speed of college players.

Big Games Played In College
A lot of games were big games. Obviously, playing against Notre Dame was great. Playing against teams like Stanford and Bill Walsh, UCLA, Alabama and Bear Bryant, were just as exciting.

There were a lot of great games that we played at USC and a lot of great teams that we played against. I would say that going on the road and winning on the road were some of the best parts about playing sports.

Charles White
Going up against Charles White in practice was very tough. Charlie was one of the great competitors, one of the most dominating backs in college football.

Jerry Attaway USC Conditioning Coach Convincing Bill Walsh To Draft You
I'll be the first one to tell you, it happens when you have somebody who trained you, worked with you, and helped you. Jerry Attaway was essential to helping me develop as a football player at USC as well as helping me develop as an athlete with the San Francisco 49ers.

NFL Draft
I wasn't confident. I did not know the 49ers were going to draft me. I think they chose three defensive backs in the first three rounds at that time, because they felt like they needed to find ways to shore up their secondary and shore up their defense. I know that the year before, they'd had a lot of challenges with the secondary. They had a lot of injuries. I think they wanted to go young. Thank God they went young. We were all excited to play together and come together. It turned out that playing with those guys was the best part of my life, because all of them were great guys.

George Seifert
George Seifert, our assistant coach, made sure that we were humbled and we stayed on task every day. I think that the focus was for us to continue to do the things that we were capable of doing. George was the taskmaster and made sure that all we did was focus on the game of football.

I think what happens is you find yourself realizing every day how you've got to get bigger, faster, and stronger. Every day you had a lot to work on.

Playing In Four Super Bowls
Obviously, I think of all the Super Bowls, and about all the things that went on. I think about the one in 1989, when we came back and beat Denver and how that went. The Super Bowl playing Cincinnati was a very close game.

In 1984, we played against Dan Marino. That was a phenomenal, phenomenal game for us, playing in front of a home crowd and playing in front of our fans. That was a lot of fun. You had a chance to stay with your family and friends. You didn't have to go to a hotel that week. There were a lot of things that made that week very, very special. At the same time, it was also one of those weeks where you were nervous, because nobody had ever played in his hometown before. We were able to go out and win convincingly.

The thing that people forget is that team was very, very special, because it didn't lose a lot of games. We found ourselves with a lot of great football players. Some of the football players on that team were some of the best at their positions. What I loved is that we didn't have Jerry Rice on that team. We had "Big Hands" Johnson. We had Louie Kelcher. Those were the best at their position at one time or another.

We had guys who really supplemented, helped, and complemented our team. When we got down to the end, it was really our defense alone in that game that put on a show and allowed us to win. It was just wonderful execution by guys playing great football.

When I think about the first Super Bowl I played in and how it played out, it's unbelievable. The reason I think it was unbelievable is we had so many things that went well that day. It was a phenomenal day. I think the first one's always the best one, because there are so many things that you accomplish that day, and so many things that make you feel really good about it.

When you think about those moments and you think about all the things that you're trying to accomplish, the first one is the hardest one. The reason it's the hardest one ... nobody knows that you can get there. Clearly, we didn't know it. We didn't walk into the season that year saying, "Boy, we're going to the Super Bowl." We walked in that year saying, "Man let's just make sure we can play great football." We ended up playing a lot of great football that year, and it became a phenomenal year.

Having Finger Amputated During Game

In 1985, we played the Cowboys the last game of the season. During that game I may have smashed my finger. I ended up deciding that I was going to play the following game. The doctor said I shouldn't play. I said, "Look. I've got to play."

I ended up playing against the Giants in a playoff game. We ended up losing in New York. That was a tough loss. We went there and gave our best effort, but Joe Morris and the Giants prevailed that day. After that game, everybody was saying, "I can't believe you played in the game." I was, like, "Those are the things that we do in life." The doctor said to me after that game, "You have to amputate the finger." So I ended up amputating the finger during the offseason. I realized that I was going to have to continue my career playing with my finger cut off.

The story is a Paul Bunyan story. A lot of people have said a lot of different things about it, but it was not a part of the '84-'85 season.

Transition From Playing Cornerback To Safety

It wasn't a tough transition. I went to safety in 1985, around the fifth game of the season. The coach said, "Look Lott, we want you off the corner position. We want you out of there. We'd like for you to go back and play the safety position. We think that's better for you. We think that you'll have a better opportunity to have success there."

I went to safety and made the most of it that year. That was the one-year I didn't make the Pro Bowl. So that was a tough year for me, because I lost out. I had to regroup. I came back the following year, and ended up making the Pro Bowl. I had a phenomenal year and played really well.

The 1985 season was a very difficult for me, because there were a lot of things that didn't go well, like the transition of going to a new position.

Pro Football Hall Of Fame Induction

Anytime that you feel that you have a shot of making the Pro Football Hall Of Fame, that means that you've worked your tail off and you've given a lot to the game. So many things have to fall in place. The only thing you know is what you did. What you don't know is what other people are going to think about your body of work. You don't know how people will judge it.

Unfortunately for me, I had friends telling me that there was no way that you're going to make it your first year. There were some guys that said, "Hey, you might have a shot." I ended up getting lucky and going in the same year with Joe Montana. I think that the momentum of him and Dave Wilcox carried me in. That's what got me into the Hall of Fame.

Edward DeBartolo

He's one of the best, if not the best, owner ever. He set the tone for how ownership should be; how they should interact, help players, and find ways to enhance their lives. He did an incredible job; he still does. He still continues to help people and finds ways to enhance their lives. He's just a very phenomenal leader and a phenomenal person. I'm forever indebted to him because of all the things that he was able to accomplish.

Favorite Moment Of Career

The favorite moment for me was in 1981. That was the defining moment to me. We learned a lot about what we could do and how we could get better. I think we applied that each and every year. I think that everybody who was associated with that year realized that there was so much more that we could do.

Looking at that year, at the guys, and what we were able to accomplish, I realized that, man, we set a new tone for the game of football. We were guys who constantly believed that we could always be better and we could always accomplish a lot for the game of football, and more importantly, for the San Francisco 49ers.

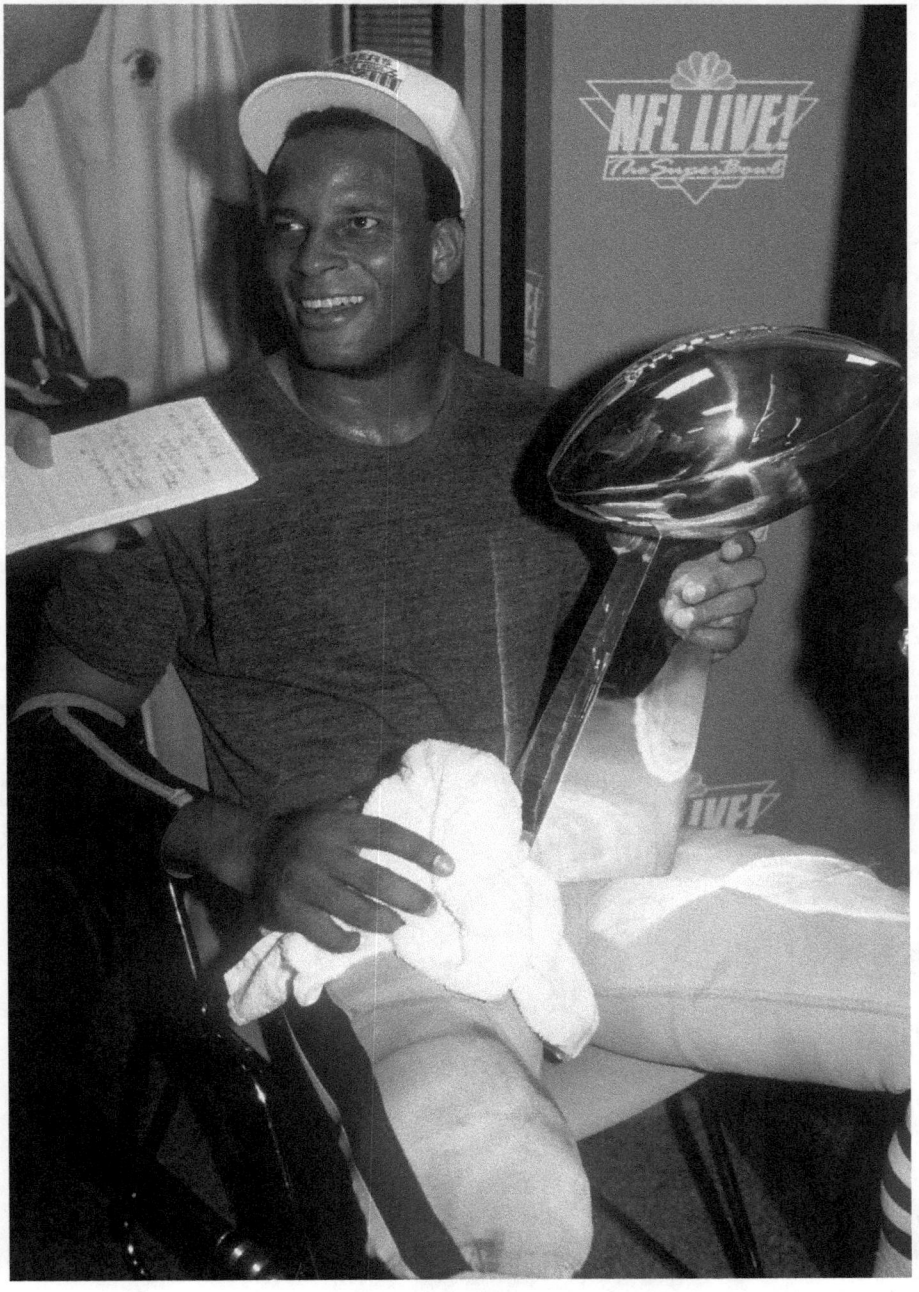

San Francisco 49ers safety Ronnie Lott smiles while holding the Vince Lombardi Trophy during a postgame press conference after winning the Super Bowl XXIII against the Cincinnati Bengals on January 22, 1989 in Miami, Florida. Photograph copyright Associated Press

Chapter 29

Howie Long

> College:
> Villanova
>
> Career History:
> Oakland/Los Angeles Raiders (1981–1993)
>
> 2000 Inductee Pro Football Hall Of Fame

<u>College Choice</u>
I was living with my grandmother in Charlestown, Massachusetts. The desegregation busing rides started my freshman year of high school. I missed the majority of my freshman year because of that. At that point, I grew up right under the 'L' tracks in the city and played in the street every day. I played basketball, baseball, and mostly street hockey. I wanted to be Bobby Orr, but I had never played organized sports of any kind.

My Uncle Billy, had grown up in Charlestown and worked for the Boston Housing Authority, the projects in the city, his entire professional career. He had lived a kind of "American dream." He was the first person in the family to graduate from high school. He had moved to Milford, Massachusetts. I went to Milford to live with him at my grandmother's request. He had two kids of his own and two adopted kids and took me in at 13 years old.

The high school football coach saw me walking down the hallway and asked who I was and if I was interested in coming out for the football team. Once I figured out how to put the equipment on, it kind of grew from there. I was a raw, big kid.

By the time I got out of high school, I was 6'5", 225 and had scholarship offers from Boston College and Villanova. My grandmother made a very sage decision that was probably best for me, given the turbulent circumstances of the area that I grew up in, to head down to Pennsylvania to go to Villanova. They were both

Catholic schools, and she was very heavily Catholic, an Irish Catholic, from Boston.

Villanova

Villanova was great. It was the perfect place for me. I probably had the opportunity to go to some other schools that were probably smaller, but never really considered or thought about it.

I was 6'5", 225, when I went to summer school down there prior to my freshman year. I had a meal card and was working out for the first time. By the time I got to training camp, I was 6'5", 262, and went from probably playing outside linebacker to nose guard in a three-man front.

I started every game my freshman year and took every snap. It was just the right level for me. We never played on television. We bused to most of our games. We stayed three to a room on the road. They were the best of times.

I made a lot of great friends there. I met my wife, Diane, there. To this day, we have four or five really, really good, close friends and a number of friends that have been kind enough to support causes that are directly associated with the university. They're supporting an older coach who needed some help and the university program. It's been great.

Being Heavyweight Boxing Champion In College

The majority of the time, I would get there and whomever I was supposed to fight would kind of walk away. So, it really wasn't much of a title.

I enjoyed boxing. I boxed in high school. There were four or five of us in high school who would just box regularly in the basement of the high school. Still, through my NFL career, I always had a heavy bag and a speed bag somewhere on whatever property I lifted in.

The only thing that boxing really helped me with regarding football, was conditioning. If you think you're in shape and you think you understand what taking yourself to the limit is, get in a boxing ring and go three minutes.

I was holding out from the Raiders in 1983, and I trained with a trainer by the name of Richie Giachetti. Richie worked with Larry Holmes. As part of a contract ploy, I was kind of dancing with the idea of turning pro as an alternative to laboring for what I considered to be less than consistent wages for services rendered as a football player, but it didn't work out real well.

NFL Draft
If you're at a big school like Oklahoma or Texas, they schedule a Pro Day and every NFL team sends a representative there. Players do their drills, whether it's the 40-yard dash, vertical jump … all that stuff. They do it one time for the scouts. By the end of my senior season, I really wasn't on a lot of people's radar.

I played high school football with a kid by the name of Joe Restic Jr., who ironically went on to Notre Dame and ended up captaining the team at Notre Dame. His dad was a very famous Ivy League coach at Harvard, Joe Restic, Sr. Joe Restic Sr. was on the Blue-Gray All-Star Committee. I think a player got injured or pulled out or something, and they needed someone to step in for that player. Joe Restic Sr., I think, was responsible for getting me selected to the Blue-Gray All-Star game. Ironically the coach of that game was Jimmy Johnson, who was the head coach at Oklahoma State. That was in December of 1980, in Alabama.

I ended up winning the MVP of the Blue-Gray game and then suddenly I was on everyone's radar. Since small schools don't have a Pro Day, I probably ran the Pro Day drills 25 to 30 separate times for different scouts.

A scout knocked on my St. Mary's dorm room door on a Sunday. St. Mary's was the name of the dorm that I lived in. He wanted me to run on the front lawn of my dorm with sneakers on. I ran for everyone. I ran in the rain and in the snow.

Before Villanova changed their facility, if it was snowing or raining, I had to run inside the old Jake Nevin Field House, which was not a big place. If you ran a 40-yard dash, you had to start in the hallway of the facility with the double doors open and run kitty-corner across the gym into the other hallway at the other corner.

I ran at least two or three times on really rainy days for scouts or coaches. Obviously all those scouts or coaches put me through a battery of tests. A Raiders' coach came by, eyed me up, talked to me for a couple minutes, and wasn't particularly friendly. There were a couple of other scouts waiting. He had me get in a stance, take two steps, come off the ball, take two steps, plant, and come inside. Then he left, and I wrote them off. As it turned out, that was the team that ended up drafting me.

Joining Raiders
It was incredible on a lot of levels. I went from Villanova to the Super Bowl Champion Oakland Raiders. It was a team that was larger than life. Walking into that locker room as a 21-year-old was pretty shocking. I went from Villanova where there was a priest on every floor, to the Oakland Raiders locker room, and it was amazing.

Art Shell, Gene Upshaw, Cliff Branch, Jim Plunkett, Ted Hendricks, Lyle Alzado, and Lester Hayes were there. The list goes on. Cedrick Hardman was my roommate my first year. He was Joe Greene's roommate in college at North Texas. He played on the defensive front with the San Francisco 49ers and was a great pass rusher. I think they called the San Francisco defensive line the Gold Rush with Tommy Hart and Cedrick.

I had no idea what greatness looked like before I walked into that locker room. The one thing about the Raiders is if you dare to envision yourself being great, you certainly knew what it looked like because it was all around you. Whether it was the owner, Jim Otto, Fred Biletnikoff, Art Shell, or Gene Upshaw, greatness was all around you. Those are the guys who brought me up.

Practicing Against Raiders Offensive Line
Early on, it was kind of like going to graduate school. Art Shell and Gene Upshaw were just so physically dominant. They took great pride

in, for lack of a better term, breaking a young guy in. Those lessons learned during my first year were really greatly appreciated. The further away I get from it, the greater the appreciation I have for having guys like that. I think it's something that's missing in many cases in today's game because of the salary cap. You can't have that 33, 34-year-old guy around to mentor the younger players telling them, "This is how you play. This is how you act. This is how you handle yourself. This is what it means to be great." I had that all around me, which I was fortunate to have.

Al Davis

The Raiders are one of the iconic franchises in NFL history. Al had an impact on the game over many decades, whether it's the AFL or coaching the Raiders in the early part of his tenure there. He hired John Madden, a guy nobody else was considering. John ended up being one of the most iconic presences in the history of football, both as a coach and as a broadcaster. I would like to say Al was the conscience of the NFL, making sure that the game was treated, played, and thought of the right way.

He got so many great players from small schools, like Art Shell from University of Maryland Eastern Shore. The Raiders were kind of the Ellis Island of the NFL. The writing on the Statue of Liberty states, "Bring me your tired ..." I'm not sure of the exact quote, but that might as well have been on the front door of the building.

Whether it's Jim Plunkett, Lyle Alzado, or Cedrick Hardman, the list goes on and on of players that he brought in. These were guys who were great contributors and yearning to be great, not just individually, but collectively. And, they wanted to win championships. Championships end up defining your career as a player. I think relationships are built when you win. Those were all great players who performed well. The Raiders have always had a great connection with those players.

Super Bowl XVIII Win Against Redskins

Michael Strahan and I have had this conversation. Michael went to a Super Bowl early on in his career and lost badly. He was fortunate enough to win a Super Bowl in his final season. I won early and thought to myself, "I've got Marcus Allen, Jim Plunkett, Cliff

Branch, Ted Hendricks, Rod Martin, Lester Hayes, Mike Haynes, and the list goes on and on and on. Boy, this Super Bowl thing is easy. We'll do this every year."

We had lost to Washington, interestingly enough, earlier that year, and it was kind of a shootout. We had a number of players who were out, including Marcus Allen, Cliff Branch, who pulled a hamstring early in the game, and Vann McElroy who missed the game. It was a really hot day up in Washington, and they ended up beating us. I believe it was a long screen pass to Joe Washington. Joe was just an amazing talent.

Ironically enough, fast forward to the Super Bowl, we had them on the ropes early. Joe Washington came into the game with Washington backed up on second and long. What ended up happening is we substituted Jack Squirek for Matt Millen. His job was to spy Joe Washington. Jack read the play perfectly, intercepted the ball, scored a touchdown, and the game was over. So it was a contrast from the earlier game, particularly defensively. We were dominant.

I have a great deal of respect for that Redskins team, and particularly their offense, because they were very physical, with two and three tight ends. They pounded you with a lot of counters. They were a team that ended up winning three Super Bowls with three different quarterbacks, and could have won more. The Redskin team that we beat that year had set a scoring record that stood from 1983, until that Randy Moss-Chris Carter team in Washington broke it. Can you believe that?

You could still be very physical within five yards of the line of scrimmage, and our corners were. You can look back at that game as a how-to play corner. Mike Haynes was so good, he was boring. When they talk about the great cover corners of all times, you rarely hear Mike Haynes' name, but people inside of football know who Mike Haynes was. Lester was the consummate riverboat gambler. A lot of bump and run; he really rolled the dice a lot, and more often than not came up a winner. That performance those two cornerbacks had in the Super Bowl was amazing, really amazing.

1984 Raiders vs. Bears Game

I think that that Bears defense was, if not the best, one of the best of all time. It was the perfect marriage between talent and scheme. No one knew how to block the 46 defense. Then you couple that with the group they had on defense talent-wise, and it was a prescription for disaster, particularly when you're playing on the road.

During the game we lost two quarterbacks, and the emergency quarterback was either going to be Marcus Allen or Ray Guy. Ray Guy would occasionally quarterback the scout team for us. Ray was a great athlete and could throw the hell out of a ball. Guys were breaking scot-free. David Humm blew his ACL; guys were just beat up.

That was a very physical game. For our offense it was as physical a game as they had ever played, because the Bears brought so much pressure. If you left five in, they brought six or seven. If you left six in, they brought seven or eight. If you left seven in, they brought eight. They always brought more than you had, and you were guaranteed at the very least, a one-on-one matchup if not breaking scot-free, and more often than not, somebody got turned totally free.

Then people figured out the 46 defense. Like the spread read option, where teams really struggled with it for a couple years and it was going to be the new wave in the NFL. Then people figured it out and it went away. It was the same with the 46 defense. Nobody runs that anymore. Really you can't.

Raiders Deserving To Be Enshrined In The Pro Football Hall Of Fame

Jim Plunkett won two Super Bowls. Jim's a great story. When you're the number one pick in the draft, you go to the worst team in football. Jim nearly got killed up in New England, ended up signing on with San Francisco, and got beat up there. Al Davis took a chance on him, and it ended up resulting in two Super Bowls.

Lester Hayes is another guy that should be up for consideration. There are a lot of really good players from those teams. Cliff Branch threw the fear of God in every defense, and look at Cliff Branch's numbers in playoff games and Super Bowls.

I would compare Cliff to Bobby Hayes. Cliff had better hands. Just look at the numbers and compare the two careers. Cliff won three Super Bowls.

Here's the irony of it. Tom Flores won two Super Bowls with a pretty drastic change in personnel across the board. That team that won in 1983 was completely different than the team that won in 1980, for the most part, particularly on defense. Marcus Allen was on the 1983 team. It was just a different group of players.

Pro Football Hall Of Fame Induction

It's kind of a surreal feeling. It's … I don't want to say a confirmation of your career. I mean, I don't know if you necessarily need that. I think when you've given everything you had to the game and your career, you went till you couldn't go anymore, and you rode off into the sunset, I think you're at peace with that.

The process is a very tough process, particularly for guys that have to wait five, 10, 15, sometimes 20 years to get in. Look at the top 10 finalists from last year. Each and every one of them, you could make a case, is definitively a Hall of Famer. It's just a question of when.

At some positions it's more difficult than others. The wide receiver seems to be a position where there's a real conundrum in terms of today's numbers versus the numbers from years ago. When you're playing for the Steelers - Lynn Swann and Jon Stallworth - and they're throwing the ball 22 times a game, you're not going to put up the kind of numbers that teams are putting up now, but they were big time players in big time games.

It's a tough job the voters have. When you get the call that you've been chosen, it's really special.

Toughest Offensive Lineman

Not as much an offensive line as much as maybe a system. With San Francisco, everything was angle blocking, odd blocks, and trap blocks. The passing game was three steps up, five step drop, ball's out, get the ball to the receiver on a slant or quick out, and let the receiver run for yards after the catch. So you play in a game, they put 30 points up.

It's a totally different feeling when you're playing the Redskins. It's the "Hogs". It's two, three tight ends, John Riggins. You know you've been in a football game.

San Francisco was just more surgical. The tackle influences blocks outside, the fullback comes from the inside. Or the tackle influence blocks inside and the fullback comes from the outside and takes your legs out. A lot of high low blocks and things like that. San Francisco was probably the biggest challenge looking back on it, but it was more schematic than it was personnel.

People have to realize that when you're playing against John Elway, you can't go inside on the tackle. Let's say you're rushing the quarterback. You have to stay outside or just bull rush. So your numbers aren't going to be great, and the way you rush the quarterback is not going to be great because you have to account for John. The Broncos with John Elway and his ability to run and extend plays, and help his offensive line out was very difficult.

Talk about an era of great quarterbacks. Jim Kelly, Dan Marino, Warren Moon, John Elway, Joe Montana, and Steve Young … the list goes on and on.

John Elway was as difficult as anyone to deal with. Joe Montana was surgical. It was death by a thousand cuts. With John, when his pocket broke down. John would spin out to his left, reset his feet, and throw the ball 70 yards across the field for a touchdown. That's John.

Whereas Joe would take a three steps drop or five steps drop, and hit whomever in stride, whether it was Jerry Rice or one of their other great receivers, for a touchdown.

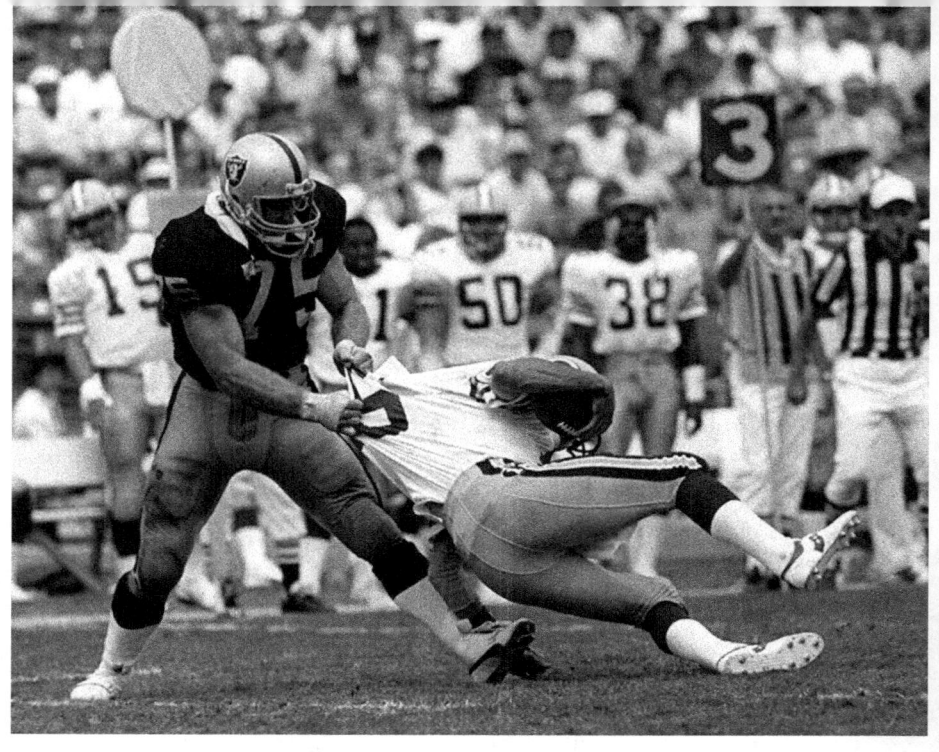

Los Angeles Raiders' Howie Long takes down Green Bay Packers Randy Wright. Photograph copyright Associated Press

Chapter 30

Jim Kelly

> College:
> Miami
>
> Career History:
> Houston Gamblers (1984–1985)
> Buffalo Bills (1986–1996)
>
> 2002 inductee Pro Football Hall Of Fame

College Choice
Lou Saban was the Miami head football coach back then. I was told they were going to run a pro-style offense and I thought that was what was going to happen.

I wanted to go to Penn State, but at the last minute Joe Paterno told me they wanted me as a linebacker. I was like you've got to be kidding me. I said, "No, thank you." Miami seemed to me to be the best fit. Unfortunately, Lou Saban was there for only one year.

I shouldn't say unfortunately, because what happened was Howard Schnellenberger came on as head coach the following year, and brought in Earl Morrall as the quarterback coach. Earl was a former quarterback with the Dolphins and the Colts. It was a blessing for me that happened. That's when I really got the opportunity to show that I could play quarterback.

I wasn't mad that Joe Paterno wanted me to play linebacker. To be honest with you, I liked playing linebacker because I was able to dish out the hits. I grew up in a family of six boys. We had to fight every day of our lives not only for food, but in anything we did. We used to drive my mother crazy. I'll put it this way, my high school football coach moved me from linebacker to free safety my senior year, because I wanted to make every tackle. I wanted to make sure that whomever I hit remembered what number and what person hit them at the end of the game.

You earn respect that way. I've never been a dirty player. Don't be dumb, don't be dirty, but you want to make sure that when you walk off that football field that those guys know who they played against. My father taught that to me early in life. Play to your ability every play. One of the things he always told me, which is now probably an old cliché, "Every time you walk out this front door son, remember you represent the Kelly name." My five brothers and I always took that to heart and we tried not to tarnish the Kelly name.

I went to football camp my junior and senior year. I thought I showed Joe Paterno enough of me playing quarterback. Anyway, it all worked out pretty good, so I have no complaints.

Howard Schnellenberger
One of the good things, from my point of view, was Howard Schnellenberger was like a drill sergeant. He was a noble guy. He demanded respect. He didn't even need to say it; you knew just by being around him what type of guy he was. He was no nonsense, but he knew how to talk to players. He knew how to get us motivated, especially me. Coming out of high school, some players need that. They need a little kick in the butt, and I'm sure I did at the time. He knew how to get the best out of players.

Of course the old cliché, again, is you're only as good the players around you or the coaching staff around you. Howard brought in a bunch of big guys, some big coaches, and he wound up winning a National Championship at Miami.

As you get older you start learning, you mature, you start thinking that maybe I don't know it all. It's a good time to start listening a little more. I'm sure that works with coaches too. I'm sure looking at some of the guys that have been behind Howard, that I'm sure they learned the same thing. For me, I've been very blessed. From high school to the NFL, I was blessed. I had great head coaches.

Miami Practices

Back in the late '70s and early '80s when you asked for a water break, they said, "What are you crazy. You get one water break. Be happy with it." Nowadays, you have to give kids water. Anytime they want it, you've got to give it to them. Back then we were taking salt pills because you'd sweat so much. In Miami we used to hide water bags underneath the yard markers just so that we could sneak some water.

My teammates would say, "Jim you need to put an ice bag on your shoulder." I'd get ice to put on my shoulder right after team drills, because I knew I wasn't going to practice anymore. Whether I wanted it or not, everybody wanted me to have an ice bag because they were able to bite the tip off of it and everybody was drinking the water out of the ice bag. By the time the practice was over, there wasn't much ice left.

Decision To Sign With Houston Gamblers Of USFL and Not Buffalo Bills Of NFL

The USFL said we need to get top quality players in here. They had already signed a couple Heisman Trophy winners. They said, "Tell me where you want to play; Chicago, Tampa Bay, Houston. Where do you want to play?" I took trips to those cities and I decided that Houston was the place for me with their domed stadium. There would be no wind or rain to deal with. It was exciting to maybe be able to start something that could last forever.

Unfortunately, the USFL only lasted three years. I can't really complain because that's pretty much where I probably learned the passing game. We threw the ball 35-45 times a game.

Mouse Davis

Number one, he's awesome, almost like a father figure. Number two, he definitely helped increase my quickness and worked on my footwork. The offense was more of me sprinting out and throwing on the run. I had to learn that from the beginning because I really wasn't that type of passer. It taught me how to read a defense. I learned a lot from Mouse, there's no doubt about it.

Joining Buffalo Bills
Back then I was just praying that it would work out, and that the owner, Ralph Wilson, would bring players in like he said he was going to. Boy did he ever. Andre Reed was already there. They brought in Thurman Thomas, Kent Hull, Will Wolford, Cornelius Bennett, and James Lofton ... I can go on and on naming all the great players. We wound up having a lot of Hall of Fame players. I'm not sure if there's any team that ever had as much fun as we did playing the game of football.

Marv Levy
Marv Levy was a blessing for me. He was the kind of coach that let his players be themselves, but we knew what our guidelines were. We knew the limitations. When we were on the football field during practice, we knew what we were doing. It wasn't like we had two-and-a-half or three-hour practices. We practiced for 100-145 minutes because we knew what we had to get accomplished. We knew that we wanted to be the best.

They were called quality practices not quantity, not having to do it over, and over, and over. We did it right to begin with. Marv allowed us to be ourselves. We knew our limitations. We knew that if we stepped out of line he'd be the first one to get in our face. He wasn't a big rah, rah type of guy. He always said the right things at the right time.

Origin Of Buffalo Bills No Huddle Offense
It was against the Cleveland Browns in a playoff game in 1989. We wound up running the no huddle offense pretty much 95% of the time the next season. That's why we went to four straight Super Bowls. Our offense was clicking. We tired defensive linemen out. We rarely substituted. We had an idea of what type of defense they were going to run.

When Coach Levy allowed me to call my own plays, I knew where to put Andre Reed. I knew where to line Thurman up, knowing he was great against linebackers one-on-one. Andre was a lot better receiver inside than he was outside. It's something I'm very passionate about. It took colleges and the NFL years to really understand that the no huddle will work and give some of these quarterbacks the freedom to go ahead and call the plays.

Playing Professional Football
I would never call it work. I just loved the game. I thank God that they paid players a lot of money when I played and that they still do, to play the game that they enjoy. If the salaries had been a lot less I would have still played. I would have played for whatever they were paying, because I just enjoyed it.

I grew up in a family of six boys. Whether there was snow on the ground or it was pouring down rain, we always had a football in our hands. That's what we did all day. We always wanted to play and we always dreamt about doing that.

For me it was always just a joy to get out there and have fun. At times I would lay out some licks. Unfortunately, well I should say fortunately, I wound up being a quarterback and it's gotten me to where I'm at today. I've been very blessed.

Running No Huddle Offense
Marv Levy knew that I was smart enough to handle the no huddle offense. He put his job security on the line. He knew that if I screwed it up it was his job too. He knew what style quarterback I was. He knew that I thrived on it and knew how to quick pace the offense. That's pretty much the type of person I am. My mother always used to tell me, "Son you need to slow down." I've never been that way. I've always been a guy that was full steam ahead. Let's do it, let's go. I'm not a very patient person. It worked out; I think it worked out pretty good for all of us. We've got a bunch of Hall of Famers in Canton, Ohio.

Playing In Four Consecutive Super Bowls & Not Winning One
I don't care what it is; it's never easy when you lose. The good thing is the resiliency we built up and how we went through it. It would be different if we went to one and then skipped two and then went to another one, skipped one, and played in four Super Bowls over a 10-12 year period. We played in the Super Bowl four years in a row.

The resiliency our team had, the mental toughness that we had to put what we had done in the past behind us and move forward. Even though we didn't win one, I'm so proud to say that I played for the Buffalo Bills.

The more people I talk to, whether it's a reporter or people that didn't pull for us, they look back and say, "Wow. I can't believe you guys were able to accomplish playing in the Super Bowl four years in a row, which will never be done again." When you lose, that lingers on for so long. With a good Head Coach in Marv Levy we were able to focus. The mental toughness and the mental preparation we had before every season and every game was unmatched. I'm just proud to say that I played in that era.

We would have liked to win one or two, but it didn't happen. If you look at my career, Bruce Smith's, Thurman Thomas', or Andre Reed's careers, we all know we were very successful whether we won one or not. Trust me, a lot of guys out there would have loved to be in one Super Bowl let alone going to four. I'm still very proud of our accomplishments. I would never sit there and cry over it. I'll put it that way.

We all knew we wanted to be best. We all wanted to do well. We enjoyed winning even though the last game of the season was a loss as far as when it came to Super Bowls. But the thing is, we were professionals. We knew how we had to get prepared for the following year and try to do it again. I even remember our motto one year was, "Let's piss everybody off. Let's go back to the Super Bowl again."

I still thank God that for my teammates because I was surrounded with great players, but more than that players with great character.

Toughest Opponent
My brother Pat, when I was in Junior High. Pat was a good kid. I'm serious it was always my brothers. Everybody was tough. When you play professional football as long as I did you get to play with a bunch of great players like Joe Klecko, Howie Long, Andre Tippett, and Neil Smith and Derrick Thomas from the Chiefs. I don't want to start throwing out a bunch of names, but there were so many great players when I played.

I played college football with Fred Marion, whom a lot of people probably have not heard of. He intercepted more passes playing for the Patriots against me, than anyone did. It was always tough but I always enjoyed it. I always enjoyed the task ahead and being able to compete.

Pro Football Hall Of Fame Induction

It was something I had never dreamt about. I dreamt about playing in the NFL, but not the Pro Football Hall of Fame. I thought going into the Pro Football Hall of Fame was reserved for guys like Merlin Olsen, Deacon Jones, Joe Namath, Johnny Unitas, Bart Starr, Bob Griese, and Terry Bradshaw. Then all of a sudden, I'm right alongside them. It's pretty cool, plus my son was there. For me, that was a dream come true and a blessing that my son was able to be there the day I was inducted.

Buffalo Bills quarterback Jim Kelly and Miami Dolphins quarterback Dan Marino talk after play. Photograph copyright Associated Press

Chapter 31

Eric Dickerson

> College:
> SMU
>
> Career History:
> Los Angeles Rams (1983–1987)
> Indianapolis Colts (1987–1991)
> Los Angeles Raiders (1992)
> Atlanta Falcons (1993)
>
> 1999 Inductee Pro Football Hall Of Fame

College Choice
I think I was in the ninth grade and a guy said to me, "You're one of the best athletes we've ever seen in these parts in the last 25 years." I didn't get it. I'm like, "Really?" He said, "Yeah. You can really do things." I didn't know what he was talking about.

I started playing sports at an early age. I played football and ran track from seventh grade on. Ron Meyer recruited me. He came to my hometown of Sealy several times. He came to watch me play when I played in the State Championship game. Yeah, that's how I ended up going there because he recruited me so heavily.

College
We were not a passing football team. We were mostly a running football team. I think a lot of people looked at "The Pony Express", and thought that was the main part of our team. We had such great defenses. We really did. We had great guys on defense. I always say that our defense was so underrated and they were so good. I think just because of the notoriety that the "Pony Express" had back in those days people overlooked the defense.

Ron Meyer As SMU Head Coach

Ron Meyer was a very good coach. I think Ron was an even better recruiter than he was a coach. He knew how to get a talent. Ron pretty much could sell your mom, your grandmother, and the whole family on the school and you were going definitely. If you didn't think about SMU before he came to visit, it was at the top of the list for sure after he left the house.

"Pony Express" (Eric Dickerson & Craig James)

Craig James and I weren't in the backfield together that often. As a matter of fact, because SMU was in the offset on offense, we would alternate. My fullback was Charles Drayton and his was Mark Crites. Sometimes they would just switch the fullbacks out. Really, Craig and I alternated. He'd take a series and I'd take a series. You'd run your series and if your series scored a touchdown, you'd stay in that whole time. That's how we did it. It worked for us.

I think Russ Potts came up with the "Pony Express" name. He was the Athletic Director. When we got there it was "Mustang Mania". Then all of a sudden, they switched it up and started calling it the "Pony Express".

NFL Draft

I knew the Rams were trying to get me and they made a trade. I think the trade took place with Houston and Seattle. The Rams called me the night before and told me that I had a ticket at the airport for me to take a flight out to LA. They were going to draft me the next morning. I actually heard that I got drafted when I was in the car on my way to the airport.

When I got drafted I asked my mother and my grandmother, "Which one do you think I should go to, the Los Angeles Express of the USFL or the Rams in the NFL?" I won't forget my mother's reply. She said, "Which one has been around longer?" I said, "The NFL." She said, "That's where you should go."

John Robinson

I liked John Robinson. John was a coach who knew how to run the football. He was a player's coach, and knew how to talk to the players. He was just a really good coach.

John recruited me to Southern Cal, where he was the coach, while I was in high school. When the Rams drafted me he walked up to me and said, "I finally got you."

There was a little bit of a temptation to go to Southern Cal, but Southern Cal is so far from Texas. I was born and raised in Texas. I am a Texas boy from a small town, and Southern California is a long ways away. I took my first official visit to USC, but I didn't end up going there.

Los Angeles Rams Offensive Line
It was never all you as a running back. You got to have the help up front. We had a great offensive line; Jackie Slater, Kent Hill, Doug Smith, Dennis Harrah, David Hill, and Bill Bain. We had a lot of great guys on that line. We had an outstanding offensive line.

The running back has to have help. We had a coach who knew how to run the football. His scheme was to put the other guys and me, in good situations.

When I was younger, I always felt like anytime I got my hands on the ball, that I had a chance to take it all the way. That's what I was. I was a long run hitter, like a home run hitter in baseball. Football is different. I always went for the long run. I didn't look for five or six yards because I had the speed to outrun most guys.

Joining Los Angeles Rams
When I first got to the Rams, we had a two back set. We played the Redskins in the preseason. I'll never forget, they beat us to death in the second pre-season game. We came back the next day and John Robinson said, "Forget everything you learned. We're going to go to the one back set like the Redskins. Eric is my running back." That's when I got a chance to start.

Reason Wore Goggles
I am blind. I can't see. I have to wear glasses. That's where the goggles came from. I still wear glasses to this day. Without the goggles I couldn't have done anything.

A running back goes by feel a lot of times. Stuff happens in a flash, real fast out there. Everything is not done just by vision.

Field Preference
I didn't really care, grass or turf, it didn't make a difference to me. I could run on either one. At that time, the turf fields were not great. They make you feel faster. It was good to have a mix. I think if I had my preference to play on one for a full season, I'd take grass like most players.

Some of the turf was like painted concrete. The field in New England at the time was a terrible field. The Astrodome had a bad field. A lot of fields were not really good fields.

Trade To Indianapolis Colts
It was business. I didn't really want to leave LA, but I had to leave for the money. I felt like the Rams underpaid me, for sure. I was only making about $250,000. A lot of guys were making triple my salary and they weren't even playing up to my level.

A lot of teams, not just the Rams, were big on messing up the players by underpaying them. They thought it was a game, but it wasn't a game to us. That's what they did to you. There was no free agency. You couldn't go anywhere. You were just stuck and you could take it or leave it. That was their motto.

I know there were a couple of teams that wanted me. One was the Redskins. I really wanted to go there because my cousin played for the Redskins. He was the one who called me and told me that the Redskins were after me, but I knew the Rams weren't going to let that happen. They were not going to trade me to a NFC team at that time.

Ron Meyer As Indianapolis Colts Head Coach
Ron Meyer was the Colt's coach. Ron's a good friend of mine. He took care of me in college. He is just a good man. I can say I really love Ron. When he recruited me coming out of high school, he told my mother, "I'll treat him like he's my own son." He kept his word.

Favorite Moment Playing In The NFL

I had so many. One of my favorite moments was when I got drafted. The year that I rushed for over 2,000 yards was another favorite moment. When I made my first Pro Bowl, I was really excited about that. I had so many moments. I can't say one particular moment was my favorite. I never got a chance to play in the Super Bowl, but I have so many great memories and moments in the league.

Playing On Monday Night Football

Playing on Monday night was special for every guy at that time. Every player would look forward to playing on Monday night. When the schedule came out you wanted to see how many Monday night games you had. There weren't all these other stations like ESPN, ESPN1, ESPN2, NBC, ABC, or CBS televising games on days other than Sunday. Monday night was it. All your peers got a chance to watch you play. The whole world got a chance to watch you play that one game. I think playing on Monday night was a very special night for all players back in those days. Now, I think players take it for granted.

Opportunity To Break Walter Payton's Record For Most Career Rushing Yards

If I would have stayed with the Rams my entire career I think I would have broken it. It just didn't work out like that. Walter Payton, Lawrence Taylor, and I were doing an episode of "Coach" and Walter said to me, "I want to thank you for something." I said, "What?" "I want to thank you for getting traded. You would have broken all the records." We laughed about it.

I thought I had a chance at the record, but honestly when I played, I didn't think about that kind of stuff. I just liked playing football and that was it. I enjoyed the sport and I played it. There comes a point where you figure out the business and the ugly side of it, but it is what it is.

Top Running Backs Of All Time

Most definitely I have got to put O.J. Simpson and Jim Brown in there for sure. Barry Sanders has got to be in there. Walter Payton has to be in there. It just depends on which player you like; that's what it comes down to.

Eric Dickerson NFL Single Season Rushing Record

Someone might break it one day. I hope it lasts for another 25-30 years. Maybe I'll be dead and gone by then. I have a little son who is one-and-a-half. Maybe he'll come along and play football and break my record. You want your records to last as long as they can. There's nothing selfish about that. I'm honest about it. If a guy gets close, that's great, but honestly no guy wants his records broken. I don't care if you have a jump rope record in high school, you don't want your record broken.

Pro Football Hall Of Fame Induction

I didn't know I was going to be elected to the Hall Of Fame my first year of eligibility. I had the numbers. For me, that is what it should be about, the numbers.

I didn't even know what the Hall of Fame was my first two years. After my second year in the league, after I ran over 2,000 yards, I was at the Pro Bowl. Rickey Jackson said to me, "You're going to go into the Hall of Fame if you keep playing like you're playing." I was waiting for him to elaborate what the Hall of Fame was because I didn't know what it was. Finally, he stopped talking and I said, "Listen, I got a question to ask you. What's the Hall of Fame?" He said, "Eric, you don't know what the Hall of Fame is?" I said, "I have no idea." He explained it to me and I said, "Oh. Okay."

I didn't know I was going in. When the moment came and I was chosen to go in, it was a proud moment for me. It kind of solidifies your career as a player saying that you were one of the greatest that ever played that position. I always wanted to be a great player no matter what I did, whether it was running track, playing football, or playing baseball. I wanted to be great at it. I didn't just want to be good; I wanted to be great. I thank God for my talent because that's where it came from, God. I just dealt with the talent he gave me. I worked with it.

Keys To Success For A Running Back

To play running back you can't just be fast. You've got to know your position and work with what you have. You have to know how to slow it down, speed it up, and hit it when the time is right.

The greatest thing for a back is when you get an open field. I didn't look over my shoulder. I didn't look back. If you caught me, you caught me, but I didn't believe in looking back.

When I was in high school a coach told me, "Hey, don't look back. The goal line is that way." I never looked back again after that.

Toughest Defense
The toughest defense, for me was the New England Patriots. They always gave me fits. People would think it was the Chicago Bears. Year in and year out, I don't care if it was with the Rams or Colts, the New England Patriots always seemed to give me fits. When we played in the NFC Championship Game against the Bears they were a tough defense that day. On average, I always played well against the Bears. We didn't fear them and we played well against them. As far as for my career, the team that gave me the blues would have to be the New England Patriots.

Uniform Numbers
I wore number 19 in college. The Rams had numbers 32, 34, 29, 45, and 25 available. I couldn't choose number 19 since running backs weren't allowed numbers in the teens. So I took number 25. When I got drafted I was holding number 25. When I got back to Dallas that night my best friend said, "So, what number did you choose?" I said, "I chose 25." He said, "Why did you take 25? That's a slow number."

I told him the numbers again, he said, "Why didn't you take 29? I'm like, "Okay." I called back the next day and talked to Todd Hewitt, the equipment guy, and I said, "Mr. Hewitt I want to switch my number." He said we already got you in the paper as 25, I don't think we can change that number." I said, "Well, if you all don't change it I'm not coming." He said, "Well, I think we can change that number." That's how I became 29.

Photograph copyright Associated Press

Chapter 32

Richard Dent

> College:
> Tennessee State
>
> Career History:
> Chicago Bears (1983–1993)
> San Francisco 49ers (1994)
> Chicago Bears (1995)
> Indianapolis Colts (1996)
> Philadelphia Eagles (1997)
>
> 2011 Inductee Pro Football Hall Of Fame

College Choice
I didn't get recruited much in football. I found out later that I had an opportunity to play basketball at Alcorn State, but my high school coach, William Lester, never told me about it. I probably would have played basketball there. I have to be happy with the road that William Lester put me on.

I really didn't start to play football until I got in the 11th or 12th grade. One of my buddies lived a couple doors away from me; he knew I loved the game and he sacrificed himself to play the game to get me out there. I was working and taking care of my own business. My buddy told me, "You know Richard, you can work the rest of your life. Why don't you try your dream one time?" That statement put me where I am today.

Tennessee State
What happened was I noticed that I probably wouldn't be playing any time soon as an offensive lineman at Tennessee State. I did a head count of the number of offensive linemen and doing the math, I figured it would probably be my senior year before I played.

I looked at the defense and saw Joe Gilliam coaching over there. If a guy was performing, Joe was going to play you regardless if you were a rookie, a senior, or whatever. I came there to play ball. I didn't go there to sit around and watch.

I decided to make the transition to defense. During that time when I was practicing on the offense side, I took that time to start preparing myself to be a defensive ball player. I started screwing up offensive plays and making the offense run them over and eventually, I guess, the offensive coaches got tired of me and told me to go over to defense. After spending a full season and spring practice on offense that summer, I was told, "Okay, you're going to defense." Maybe they thought I was going to go away after the season.

I really wanted to play tight end but they wouldn't go for that. I went another route and eventually got pushed over to the defensive side of the football.

<u>1983 Chicago Bears Draft (Jimbo Covert, Willie Gault, Mike Richardson, Dave Dueron, Tom Thayer, Mark Bortz)</u>
That was an amazing draft. Dennis McKinnon was a free agent signee that year. It was one of the top draft years for a team of all time.

When I came to the Chicago Bears, I wasn't used to losing. At Tennessee State I lost five games in five years. With the Bears from 1984-1988 we only lost ten games. We only won one Super Bowl. I was disappointed with that, but outside of that we had a great run.

I had a great time and played with a lot of great guys. Initially my teammates didn't know much about me and I didn't know much about them. You have to show people what you're about and either they'll catch on or you'll catch on to them or whatever. The main goal is all about going out winning, competing and being the best that you can be.

Going into the draft a lot of people were saying I was small. I just wanted to get an opportunity to play in the NFL. Kids today bitch and whine about how they lost money when they don't get drafted as high as they think they should have. It's not about where you should get drafted, it's what you accomplish after you get drafted.

1984 Los Angeles Raiders vs. Chicago Bears Game
I can remember the 49ers, Cowboys, and Raiders players were all calling me saying we're going to get you. That Raiders game was a coming out game. The Raiders had just won a Super Bowl. That day I saw Al Davis walking on the field. I said, "Al, you know you're getting an ass whooped today." He looked at me real crazy. He got whupped. Whupped to gum. That was a 4½ sack day for me. I should have had five, six, or seven on that particular day.

First Training Camp With Bears
Everybody has butterflies. You go through things and you have to build up to that moment. I can remember looking at Keith Van Horne who is about 6'7", and I'm like, "Oh God. Maybe I'm in the wrong league." As soon as I put my hand down to play, your memory comes back that you can play. It's not about the size or anything. You put your hand down and you forget about everything. It's getting to the target; what I'm trying to hit, what I'm trying to protect and play. You have those thoughts while you're standing there. The next thing you know, you get the equipment on and you get out there. You forget about those things. It was probably in the spring or summer we did some stuff, but there wasn't any contact. I was getting off the ball so fast the guys could hardly even touch me. I was running by them.

Some of the older guys were teaching me. They said, "You've got to use your hands." I'm like, "Dude nobody can put their hands on me." Eventually they caught up to me.

Then we got into training camp and I was going up against Jimbo Covert. I got about two or three sacks on him. He was the starter. He joined the Bears just like me in 1983. I knew I was beating him.

I got hurt after the first preseason game in practice. I tore my hamstring and rolled up on my ankle really bad. It was really rough for about a week and a half. Week to week just taking baby steps, it was tough. The last game of the preseason I started to strap it up. I wasn't ready to go; I wasn't 100% as far as running and doing some of the stuff I was expected to do on the special teams.

By the end of the season, my legs came back. The next year the Bears finally started me about game six. That's when things took off.

Competing Against Al Harris For Starting Position

It was Al Harris and I going at it for the starting position. You ask for opportunities for success. You see the team had an investment in Al Harris. It's evident to the team and me that the team's got money in this guy. They want to see this guy come about. I can understand it. He was a first round pick, a couple years before me. Here I am, a guy the Bears paid hardly anything for. I was performing way better than him.

As a businessman, I understood the Bears had money in this guy and wanted to see this guy come around. So they gave him a lot of chances.

It's not a player's fault, but sometimes players don't understand those situations. You have to understand all of what's around you, who's going to support you, what you are supporting so you can understand this is a business. A sports industry is a 600 billion dollar industry. You only make 30% of the 600 billion. That's a lot of jobs in sports.

I basically asked for an opportunity and eventually got the opportunity. My first year I was basically just playing pass rushing downs. I probably wasn't ready at that time. The next year I was pretty much ready. I could have stayed on Buddy Ryan's sideline. After game six I played the last ten games. I didn't have one sack after 6 games, but I end up leading the league with seventeen and a half sacks. In ten games I came up with 17½ sacks. We went to the NFC Championship.

The next year I did the same thing again. I had 17 sacks. We won the Super Bowl. After that they didn't renew Al's contract. They offered him more money but I guess it wasn't what he wanted. That's up to the player. Management and coaching staff eventually made a decision, and decided to go with me. It took them a minute. I can understand that but sometimes athletes don't know what they're really getting into.

Winning Super Bowl MVP

It was a great feeling but it also was a lonely feeling too, in a way, if you can believe that. I don't know how they went about choosing the

Super Bowl MVP. I thought it was over all the playoff games. When I thought about that and I sold myself on that conclusion, I said, "Well hell, I've had two hell of a games." First game I had about three sacks, the next game I had a two. I had four forced fumbles and eight or nine sacks in three playoff games.

My Super Bowl performance, I thought, was my worst performance compared to the first two playoff games. I look back and see that my forced fumble there turned the tide. The Patriots had gone up three points on us. I forced the Patriots to fumble and we got the ball. The offense went 13 yards and scored.

I had that thought the night before. I told my roommate Tyrone Keys, that I was going to be on ESPN. I started to say, "I see myself winning the Super Bowl MVP." I thought, I won't be that cocky. I've never been that type of guy. I'm cocky about what I do and how I do it but I don't have to talk about it; actions show it.

Super Bowl Shuffle
Doing something different was cool. We did the Super Bowl Shuffle right after our first loss so it was probably a good time. We were licking our wounds. Before the taping of the video, I was like, "Why am I here? I thought you are doing this for the charities, raising money, and those things." That made the situation a little bit more fun. We got back in town at 3:00 a.m. after losing to Miami. At 2:00 p.m. the next day, I was at the studio filming the Super Bowl Shuffle video. The lyrics were all ready. It was fun.

I've got two grown girls and they crack up about it now. It's funny to them. No one ever did something like that, and I think that's the special thing there.

To put something like that out three or four months before the Super Bowl, was pretty cocky. We talked about doing the video and were able to do it. We committed ourselves to it. We lost a major game the day before the video shoot. In the video, we said we were going to come back and win everything hands down. We said we were going to come back and kick everybody's tail and bring home the Super Bowl.

1985 Chicago Bears vs. Miami Dolphins Game (Bears Only Loss Of Season)

Mike Ditka wanted to throw the ball to win the game. Miami was 27th in stopping the rush. Obviously, you run the ball since Miami was near last in stopping the run. We had Walter Payton, who had seven consecutive 100-yard rushing games in a row, entering that game. Walter finally got 100 by the end of the game. I think Mike got tied up trying to be like Don Shula. He wanted to do as good as or better than Shula, who liked to throw the ball everywhere at that time.

Buddy Ryan was telling Ditka to run the ball, and Ditka was telling Buddy to stop blitzing. They were going back and forth like that. What do you do as a player? Sometimes we had to take over the game ourselves because the sideline was out of whack. When you're out of whack you say, "We'll talk to them on Monday. Right now, let's go out here and win this game."

They had every ghost on the sideline out there, I was tripping over stuff that wasn't even there. It was one of those games. We realized that there was an opportunity for us to possibly go undefeated. At that point, it looked like they were the last team that we would be playing that could maybe stop us.

We wanted to go to Miami earlier in the week and practice, and get ready for the game. Some of the guys asked Buddy to ask Mike if we could go to Miami earlier. If Buddy came up with a idea and Mike didn't, Mike wasn't going to do it. So we didn't go. There was a lot of bitching here and there, it was crazy.

Miami was the first team to spread us out. Dan Marino would do a half roll from me. He would make a little roll away from the side I was on, and get rid of the ball. The idea there was, let's match up. They made Gary Fencik come up from his usual position, and the matchup was a go to Nat Moore. Then Nat Moore was going against Wilber Marshall or Gary Fencik in the slot. Dan hit Nat in the slot quick, and made us tackle Nat. That's what you can do against the 46 Defense.

When you're losing or the game is not in your hands, the opposing team has more of a repertoire to reach out to see what they might want to do with you.

Favorite Coach

I enjoyed John Merritt and I enjoyed my high school coach. I appreciated what Joe Gilliam, Sr. did, which was prepare me not for just the game, but for life in general. To me it's not about the university where I send my kids to school. If he's going to school, he's going to school. It's the teachers and the university itself. When they're going to play sports, those coaches become the second fathers, you would hope. Kids need to be pushed to a limit that they don't know they have.

Once you've been pushed to that limit, your mind opens up and you appreciate what you have been pushed to, and what you accomplished at that moment. Now your vision comes in play. Now you start to visualize all you can do. You just took a big leap and put yourself in a spot that you thought you never could get to. You get there, and now your vision comes in place even stronger to see whatever else you might want to do, and how you want to do what you're doing. How much farther can I take this? What level can I take this to?

When you know what's about to happen, you can be moving at 60 to 70% and look like you're running at 120%. You can do this because you know what's going on and you know what's about to take place.

Not Winning More Than One Super Bowl

That's the killer. That's why I think that our so-called leaders, the head coach, management, or general manager; they all played a part in us not winning more than one Super Bowl. You should know what makes people go, what makes them tick. Mike Ditka tried a different way to try to make me tick. He didn't need to work on me to make me tick.

I met a man that taught me about life through football, and that was Joe Gilliam. He was the best ever. I never slept in his meetings. His vocabulary, his education, was so strong. He is a person who will always be a memory in my mind along with all that he had given me to accomplish.

The Bears did not have a quarterback for the length of time we needed. Jim McMahon was a great quarterback. He was injury prone, but he had something great between his ears. He could make it happen. When McMahon went down, that's when the team tried to get another All-American white kid in Doug Flutie. Mike Ditka was thinking that he could win with a quarterback he just put on the team, with about five weeks left in season, and go to the playoffs. Ditka was saying the defense could do anything.

The defense knew that we couldn't give up more than 10 to 13 points. That was our model. Our kicker could kick the field goals, but we knew it was going to be hard for the offense to get into the end zone. The defense knew that we could get turnovers, which would lead to field goals. We knew Kevin Butler was good for three or four field goals. Thirteen was a tough number. We couldn't score more than 13 points.

The point was we had two guys. Why didn't Ditka just give Mike Tomczak a chance to start instead of Flutie? The same thing with Steve Fuller; give him a chance. They didn't want to make someone big and have to deal with that situation. It's a brewing storm. You don't want to be in it.

Favorite Moment In NFL
My mother couldn't get to the Super Bowl. She met me at the Pro Bowl after the Super Bowl. That was a great moment. We played the Jets on my 25th birthday. That was pretty cool.

In 1984, right after I visited my mother for her birthday, we played the Redskins. That was a good old fashioned, hard-hitting game. There was something about that stadium and playing in Washington that was always great.

Joining San Francisco 49ers
I went to the 49ers to win and pick up some Super Bowls. I thought that we missed out on some opportunities with the Chicago Bears. The 49ers organization was different from the Bears. They took that extra step.

With the 49ers, you would check into a hotel and there was a fruit basket and Gatorade there. They would pay for all the meals. If we were flying over two or three hours for a game, the team would leave the night before to get ready for the jet lag. The 49ers were more sophisticated.

When I went to the 49ers, I thought that I probably could play there at least three years, maybe four. It was possible I could have played until about 2000. That was very possible with how the 49ers went about things. It wouldn't have been that brutal on me. I could have started there for two or three more years, and then went to a third down role.

Pro Football Hall Of Fame Induction

It was a great feeling. I was happy that I could thank some people who were a part of and helped my journey. My high school coach was an important part of my career. I went into the Georgia Hall of Fame with him, and I was able to say thanks to him before he passed away.

Coach Gilliam treated everybody the same. He had a love for human beings and was able to help one to overcome. Here's a guy who sent over 140 guys to the pros, including Claude Humphrey, Ed "Too Tall" Jones, Cleveland Elam and his own son, Joe Gilliam, Jr. Here's a guy that in 1948, was a quarterback at the University of Indiana and part of the first black backfield. You just don't run across that kind of guy very often. To have him on stage with me for my Hall of Fame induction … I appreciated that more than the induction.

People had been giving me love and appreciation for what I had done. It's nice to see that award take place because it was the first award for my career. We won the Super Bowl and I got the MVP of the game. That's a onetime event; that's not your career. That's not your season. To get the first award for your career or anything related to your career and it's the Hall of Fame, was pretty cool. I guess it's best to say, if you stay on track you're going to be all right. I've always said, "Stars always shine. It may be cloudy, but I'm always going to have some shine."

Chicago Bears' defensive end Richard Dent puts pressure on Miami Dolphin quarterback Dan Marino. Photograph copyright Associated Press

Chapter 33

Chris Doleman

> College:
> Pittsburgh
>
> Career History:
> Minnesota Vikings (1985–1993)
> Atlanta Falcons (1994–1995)
> San Francisco 49ers (1996–1998)
> Minnesota Vikings (1999)
>
> 2012 Inductee Pro Football Hall Of Fame

University Of Pittsburgh's Success
Pittsburgh was an independent. We played against some tough, tough teams. You've got to be on your game every week. It seemed like somewhere along the road there would be a bump and we just couldn't recover.

I have fond memories of playing football at Pittsburgh. My first three years in school, the team was 33 and 3, which is pretty impressive.

I know one loss was to Penn State. In 1981, we played Georgia and beat them. If they had won, they would have won the national championship. I think we lost to Florida State one year.
When you're an independent, you're playing the best teams that are out there at the time. I look back on those years often. I made a lot of friends and memories. Those were just wonderful times.

College Choice
Penn State recruited me. I was just never a Penn State guy, even though I grew up in a Penn State environment. I looked at Penn State

almost like a cult. You just didn't have the freedom. Penn State is a great school, but I see their uniforms matching their personalities.

There was nothing that stood out. Everybody was programmed, they did what they were supposed to do, and had success. They didn't want to deviate from that plan.

I grew up probably 100 miles from Penn State. The coaches were never warm and fuzzy. I don't remember their coaches coming in and spending time with me. Everybody recruited me. I might have got a letter from Penn State but that was about it. I don't know if they expected kids to run to Penn State and ask, "Hey are you going to recruit me?" Sometimes if you live too close to a school, they know too much about you and they're just not turned on by you.

Teammates At Pittsburgh
When I got a chance to go to the University of Pittsburgh, I played with some great guys like Bill Maas, Tim Lewis, and Bill Fralic, who played in the National Football League. Pittsburgh just had that family fun environment that you think a college should have.
We had so many great players, it wasn't even funny. We had Dan Marino, Carlton Williamson, Lynn Thomas, Pappy Thomas, and Tim Lewis. The Pittsburgh class of 1980 had 12 or 13 guys drafted by the NFL. We were practicing against some of the best players in the country. We expected to win, give great performances, and all the stuff that our players tended to show once they got into the pros and really developed and refined their skill set.

Herschel Walker
We played against Herschel Walker and Georgia in the 1982 Sugar Bowl. We played those guys in New Orleans and we beat them. On our closing drive, Dan Marino threw a pass to James Brown. He caught it, scored, and the game was over.

NFL Draft
First of all, the pressure is on the team. It's not on the player because the team drafted the player, the player didn't draft the team. You have a situation where the team felt that you were good enough to play at the NFL level. I think as a player, you owe them the respect to do everything you can to meet their expectations. If you can't

meet their expectations, you just can't. You can't get water from a rock. If a guy can play, he can play; but if he can't, you can't hold that against him. He might have maxed out in college and he'll never become the guy you thought he should have been. That has happened.

The NFL spends millions and millions of dollars scouting guys. It's a situation where the teams might need to adjust because there may be too many opinions. They're missing on too many players right now.

I could have very easily been the second pick in the draft. Buffalo chose Bruce Smith with the first pick. Minnesota had the second pick, and Atlanta had the fourth pick. Atlanta and Minnesota traded picks. So Bill Fralic went to Atlanta with the second pick. Then, Ray Childress went to the Houston Oilers with the third pick. I went to Minnesota with the number four pick. There could have been Hall of Famers drafted with the first and second picks.

Position Change From Linebacker To Defensive End
Basically my first two years in the NFL, I played linebacker. We were making a run for the playoffs late in my second season. We had two or three games left to play in the regular season and our defensive line was pretty beat up. The coach said, "Hey if you could step up there and rush the passer on fourth down, it will help us out a great deal." I said, "Thank God." It got me back to doing what I did in college. It was somewhat difficult. In 13 years, I amassed 150 and a half sacks, I was on a roll. I wonder what would have happened if I'd been playing for the 49ers my entire career, or if I'd been a defensive end from the time I came into the league.

Minnesota Vikings Defensive Line
Man we were a talented group. We were a talented group in the sense that we were so good, John Randle couldn't even get on the field. He was playing behind Keith Millard. When you look at that and realize how great the players and the coaches we had were, we knew we had something special. That has been the backbone of Minnesota for a long time. Everybody's team is built differently. Some teams feature a strong quarterback, some do a great job with

the running back, and then there are teams that do a great job with defensive line. Minnesota's definitely one of those teams.

Carrying A Briefcase Into The Locker Room
I felt that they were paying players like executives so players had to act and conduct themselves like executives. Even though I had my hands in the dirt and it was blue-collar work, I always had a thing, I wanted to look good, feel good, and play good. I always respected that. That was how I approached my craft. That was probably what motivated me to carry a briefcase. I grew out of the gym bag stage. I was no larger carrying my wrinkled notes in a gym bag. I was beyond the gym bag stage and needed to act like that. I wore pants now.

Best Coach
I would probably say Bud Grant because Bud didn't talk a lot, but I remember every conversation I had with him. I remember there was a guy on our team who was getting a lot of penalties on the kickoff and special teams. He told this guy, "You're going to play yourself off this team." That stuck with me. He didn't tolerate a lot of nonsense. It was about business. It was about being a professional.

Toughest Offensive Lineman
That would be Gary Zimmerman. We played together for seven years and we played against each other for about three. That was tough.

He knew how to do everything. Gary was a great. He is a Hall of Famer and was a great player. When I was inducted into the Hall of Fame, I credited him for me being in the Hall of Fame just as he credited me when he went in the Hall. This was the right side of the line on defense and the left side of the line on offense. On offense, the tackle was Gary Zimmerman and the guard was Randall McDaniel. On the defensive side of the ball on the right side were Keith Millard, John Randle, and I. Out of the guys I named, four of us are in the Hall of Fame.

If Keith would have been able to play longer, there's no question in my mind that he would have been a Hall of Famer.

Minnesota Vikings Trade For Herschel Walker
The Vikings gave up way too many good players when they traded for Herschel Walker. No player is worth 11 guys.

I had known Herschel since college and there was no way in the world that Herschel could meet all their expectations. He would have had to score three touchdowns in every game. There was just no way that he could be as good as they thought he could be. I don't think it would have even mattered if it were a quarterback. I don't think they could have survived that scrutiny.

Only Missing Two Games During A 15-Year Career

I only missed two games during my 15-year career through, the grace of God. God blessed me with a strong body to go out and play week in and week out. If it were a cold or the flu, you better keep guys away from me because I would get sick in a heartbeat. But physically breaking down, breaking bones, tearing ligaments, tendons, and all that other stuff, wasn't an issue. I could catch a cold in a heartbeat, though.

Pro Football Hall Of Fame Induction

When I found out I was selected for the Pro Football Hall of Fame I thought, "Is this real?" Was my body of work that good that they would consider me one of the best that ever played the game? Was I really good enough for this award? Do I really deserve this award? It's very humbling. It's hard to believe that your bust is going to be in Canton forever, and it's hard to believe that you are part of a very small group of guys who have made the game great.

Having my son as my presenter at the Hall was amazing. I played while he was growing up. He didn't see my whole career but he got a chance to see just how good I was; how much of a professional I was. He was just totally blown away by it because to him, I'm just dad. Now, I'm part of NFL history and it's a little more than just dad, but he still treats me like just dad. There are no perks out of the deal.

I've made not only my parents and my family proud, but I made the Minnesota Vikings, the University of Pittsburgh, and the people that followed me and supported me along the way proud. I'm happy and appreciative of that.

Minnesota Vikings Hall of Fame defensive end Chris Doleman pressures Chicago Bears quarterback Jim McMahon. Photograph copyright Associated Press

Chapter 34

Gary Zimmerman

> College:
> Oregon
>
> Career History:
> Los Angeles Express (1984–1985)
> Minnesota Vikings (1986–1992)
> Denver Broncos (1993–1997)
>
> 2008 Inductee Pro Football Hall Of Fame

College Choice
In high school, I played both ways. Back in those days you always did that. I was recruited by almost everybody in the Pac-10 except USC at that time, and they wanted me to play offensive line, but I wanted to play middle linebacker. I was also recruited by Harvard, Utah State, and Hawaii. I picked Oregon because I thought I was going to play middle linebacker. But, looking back at it, I guess they did me a favor.

When I got there my uniform number was 75. I said, "That's kind of a funny number for a middle linebacker." After the first practice they said, "Well, we're going to move you over to the offensive line." I made lemonade out of lemons there. A lot of kids would have quit, but I stuck it out and worked my way through it. It was actually a benefit for me in that I had to fight through adversity. As it turned out, I met my wife at Oregon.

College
Oregon was rough. It's not like Oregon nowadays. They were just building a program back then. Things were different. It was right after the Vietnam War. We were told not to wear our athletic stuff

around campus because people were mad we went to school for free. It was a totally different era. The athletic department couldn't give you anything. They'd pick up our old shoes and throw them in the dumpster. They couldn't give them to us. We got nothing, as far as handouts, like they do today. It was a good experience because I was really focused on football and school, because there wasn't anything else to do there. There were no cell phones or computers around then. So you went to school, you worked, and you worked out. That was basically all you did back then.

Biggest College Rivalry

I'd have to say it was Oregon State. The Civil War is kind of a big thing in Oregon, but every game was a big game to us cause we were underdogs every game. Oregon State was kind of our bowl game, cause we'd been on probation. So it was always the Civil War, the pride of Oregon. The big rivalry back then was with Oregon State.

Draft

I was over in Hawaii for the Hula Bowl, and my dad called me. The Los Angeles Express wanted me to stop by on the way back to Oregon, because I flew back thru Los Angeles. I stopped by, and they kind of threw me out of the office. I thought it was over then, but they ended up drafting me. I knew they wanted to draft me, but I thought I made them mad when I was there that they wouldn't. It didn't work out that way.

Los Angeles Express

I think the idea was for the USFL to try to build a league to compete with the NFL. So, they were trying to snag all the big names. That was their plan.

The USFL was probably the most important period of my career because coming out of college; I was a center and guard. During the first game, Mark Adickes, the left tackle, blew out his knee. That's when I became a left tackle. I spent two years learning how to play left tackle in the USFL. I think those were the two most important years of my career learning how to play the left tackle position.

With the L.A. Express, the first year we went pretty hard in practice. The difference between the USFL and NFL was there were some players in USFL that wouldn't have made it in the NFL. You had lesser quality players, and you didn't have the high quality players at every position. So, I would say that was a little easier. But, the first year was tough back then. They had 8mm tape, and they'd film the practice session. You had to wait for the tape to get developed.

The second year, the team had some money issues. The team ran out of money, so they had no film. We'd come in and practice, then be done and out of there by noon. The first year was just like the NFL, but the quality of the players was not quite the level of an NFL team.

The Express owner had financial issues and the L.A. Express went broke. They told us, "This is our last game Sunday. We ran out of money." After the game, we took our belongings home. Then they called everyone up on Wednesday and said, "Hey, we found some more money." The rest of the league kind of floated us. The league hated us because they were paying our salaries too. I guess they needed us because we were in the L.A. market. A lot of the players went and cashed their checks quickly. I got my money up front so I didn't have that issue. I didn't have to worry about that.

Steve Young and all the older guys kind of knew that the odds of something going bad were pretty high. I think some of the guys who could demand that kind of contract, got it. But if you were a guy just looking for work, you couldn't get that kind of deal.

Sid Gillman

Sid Gillman was the greatest. My flight was late my first day with the Express. When I arrived, the team was in a meeting. The room was dark and Sid was running tape. I heard him say, "Who's that number 63 or something?" Someone in the room said, "Rogers" or whatever his name was. Sid said, "Good job. Rogers." Then a couple of plays later he said, "Who's that number 72?" Somebody said, "Alex" or whatever. Sid said, "I want you out of here tomorrow. You're horrible." It was an eye-opener seeing him cut someone right in front of everybody, right there in the meeting. So that was kind of awesome. That kind of got my head in the right place.

Another story about Sid that sticks with me is in the USFL, there were always guys wanting to tryout. Someone was coming in for a tryout. Sid was going to time him in the 40-yard dash. The kid started running, and about 20 yards into the 40, Sid just walked off the field and said, "Hell with him."

Those are the things that stuck with me. Sid was kind of a no-nonsense guy. If he liked you and you worked hard, you got along good. If you didn't work hard and didn't do your job, you were gone. That was the kind of mentality back then, and it stuck with me for my whole career.

John Hadl was the head coach, so we had quite a tandem. My line coach was Sam Gruneisen, who played with the Chargers for 10 or 15 years. Jeff Hart was playing on the offensive line. He had played in the NFL. So we had a lot of NFL guys there. We had a lot of NFL experience there.

I was making the transition from center to tackle, so I really wasn't examining the offense that much. But just learning the tackle position and having Steve Young sure helped out. The first two years I had a left-handed quarterback in Steve Young, so he didn't have to rely on my blindside so much. It was a great time in my career. Those two years were some of the most fun and some of the craziest I've ever had.

Joining The Minnesota Vikings
It was different. I was nervous. The first day I walked into the facility, I was walking down the hall with all of my stuff and Jerry Burns came down the hall. I went up to Jerry Burns and he said, "What's your name?" I told him and he said, "Awe hell, you're too little to play in this league." I was 284 pounds.

The Vikings' practice was harder than the game. It was brutal. It took a lot of years off my career because we pretty much hit everyday. Going against Chris Doleman and John Randle everyday was tough in Minnesota.

Difference Between Minnesota Vikings & Denver Broncos
Position by position the Vikings were probably the best team I ever played on. One year we had 22 guys go to the Pro Bowl. I mean it was ridiculous. We could never win the big game because we were so worn

out by the end of the season. Back then we really didn't have a game plan. We just had a playbook and they ran it.

When I went to Denver, they game planned everything. The Vikings put the whole playbook out there and called the plays that we ran. The games weren't really game planned. The Vikings' defense was number one in the league for a bunch of years. Our offensive line was also well thought of. The offensive line was Randall McDaniel, Kirt Lowdermilk, Todd Kalis, Tim Irwin, and me. We had one of the better lines back then. We were ... maybe a quarterback away from winning the whole thing.

Toughest Defensive Lineman
Derrick Thomas was hard because he was so quick off the ball. Richard Dent was tough. Bruce Smith was a handful. I always said the toughest guy is the guy you play every Sunday, because there are no slouches in the NFL. Every week you're playing against the best guy. I thought they were all great, and that's the way I approached it. I approached it as it's going to be an uphill fight for me just to hold my own. That's the way I approached it.

If you get where you're behind, you have to go to a passing situation. That's a bitch. If you can run the ball, you can play your game. So it's just kind of situational. You don't want to get in certain situations with certain guys. They were all great. Every guy in the NFL is a great guy. And there's not much difference between a great guy and a good guy. Everybody is pretty talented, but there are a few guys that just stand out. Thomas was so quick off the ball. When you couldn't hear, if you were half a second late, it was over. I played with a lot of great players over the years. For me it's hard to pick one guy, because they all gave me trouble.

I've always said that Chris Doleman put me in the Hall of Fame. Going against him everyday ... neither one of us liked to lose, so I'd come up with something to beat him and he'd counter that and come up with something to beat me. We went back and forth. I think it just made us both evolve. We got better and better, because we were constantly trying to outdo each other.

Trash Talking

Back then, there were a few guys like Tim Harris and John Randle who trash talked. Those are the only guys that I can really think of who did it. I think it was different back then. You had mutual respect and you didn't really do that kind of stuff. I don't know, I guess the times have changed and the mentality has changed. I don't think it was really that common when I played.

Jerry Burns

Jerry Burns was different. I don't think he knew anybody's name on the team. All the linemen were "Big Boy". He would say, "Run that play where you run behind Big Boy. Run that play where you throw the ball to A.C." He was an old-school coach. He hammered the hell out of us all week. A lot of the time we were in the playoffs, but we never went very far. I think we were just worn-out from beating the hell out of each other for 20 weeks or whatever it was. We had tough training camps. He just wore us out. That's my take on Jerry.

Dennis Green

Dennis Green and I didn't get along, because I could tell right away that he was phony. He could talk a good game, but he couldn't coach a good game. He could rile you up with good talk, but when you look at his staff and some of the stuff that happened there with the Vikings ... I only played for him for one year. One of the reasons that I ended up out of there was because we didn't get along.

Joining Denver Broncos

I was retired for six months; so going to the Broncos gave me a new life. It's like a dog that goes to the dog pound, and then someone adopts you. After that you have total loyalty to them. That's the way I feel. When I went to the Broncos, it was the first time I had ever met a team owner. I was with the Vikings for seven years, and I was never in the same room with the team owner. Pat Bowlen, the Broncos owner, would be down in the locker room everyday, coming out to practice everyday, and he'd talk to you. From the top-down, Mr. Bowlen just ran one hell of a program. It was unbelievable. I wish I played my whole career there.

Smaller Offensive Linemen
Back in the day, when I first got into the NFL the linemen weren't that big. It was Dallas that started the "slobblocker", where you get the guy who's just so big that nobody could get around him. At Minnesota, we were kind of a technique team. We worked on technique everyday and prided ourselves on having good technique. Dallas brought in huge guys who didn't have that good of a technique, but they had the size. So, we prided ourselves on being technicians.

After I went to Denver and Alex Gibbs got there, it was like heaven. He was a technician type guy too. He believed in mobile guys, and I just fell into what he wanted. If he wanted a big guy, I wasn't the guy. It just happened to work out. That was his philosophy—having athletic mobile guys.

Wade Phillips
I thought Wade Phillips was a great coach. I think his downfall was that he was too nice. I think what happened was people took advantage of him too much. I think people could get away with things you couldn't get away with, with other coaches. I loved playing for Wade. I think his mentality of being so nice kind of bit him in the butt. He treated us as men. He always said, "I want to treat you guys as men." Of course there's some guys that will always push the limit, and that's what happened. Players realized that they wouldn't get in too much trouble with Wade. I think that kind of got him. I loved playing for him, because he was a great coach. There were guys in the NFL just to get a paycheck. Then there are guys there who want to win. It depends on what kind of guy you are, whether you liked him or not. Some people took advantage of him.

Super Bowl Denver vs. Packers
Nobody gave us a chance. Green Bay had these great big guys who people thought we wouldn't be able to handle. The Green Bay players were going to eat our lunch. It kind of stuck in our gut, all of the offensive line. I wish we were allowed to bet on games back then, because I knew a week out that we were going to win that game. Our team was an older team, and everyone understood how hard it was to get to the Super Bowl. I had played 12 years and had never been to one. There were a lot of guys on the Broncos that were

older and had never been to one. We realized this could be our only shot at it. I think we just took it a little more seriously than Green Bay. Green Bay thought they were coming in to pick up the trophy, I guess.

It was both exciting and frustrating, because everything was so different. It was like when you get into a routine where you do everything at a certain time. Then the day of the Super Bowl, we couldn't go to the stadium early because we had to have a police escort over there. They wouldn't allow us in if we had come earlier, by cab. Our timetables were changed up. After all the hoopla the week before, I didn't like that. My whole football career I had never won a championship, and there it was. It was my one shot at it. I was in the playoffs so many times, that people don't realize how hard it is just to get to the Super Bowl, let alone win it.

I just think we were focused for the Packers. Nobody gave us a chance. All the things were in our favor, yet nobody gave us a chance. So, we were kind of proving to the world that we could do it. It was a great game to end your career on.

Mike Shanahan
I always say that's when I learned how to win. In the past, we'd have our meetings and the coach would always say, "Our goal is to win the conference and the division, then work our way to the Super Bowl." When Mike Shanahan came in he said, "Our goal is to win the Super Bowl. Anything less is a failure." Right there, he set the tone. To me, that makes a huge difference in what they expect. Mike carried a book, and in that book you could see every hour where we were going to be the whole season. It was unbelievable. He had every practice with laid out times. Every meeting time was laid out.

I'm a structure guy, so it really fit me well in that he was so structured. I heard other guys didn't like it because it was too structured. I think it was good, because we had meetings at 10 o'clock at night at training camp. All the guys hemmed and hawed, because they couldn't go out drinking. He kept a tight reign on the team and I liked it. Our goal was to win the Super Bowl and I think that permeated and everybody knew what the goal was.

Decision To Retire After Super Bowl Win Versus Packers
I wanted to come back so bad. I told Mr. Bowlen, "If I came back I'd just be taking your money." My shoulders were so shot, I was getting injections before every game. My wife was mad I was doing that. My body just couldn't take it. Then I thought what if I lose a shoulder and I can't play with my kids the rest of my life? I've got one ring. What good are two rings going to do? They'll just both be in the safe deposit together.

Honestly I wanted to come back, but I knew better than to do that. I knew something could have happened. So I wanted to come back, but I didn't.

Pro Football Hall Of Fame Induction
It was a shock, because so many times I was a finalist and it didn't happen. It's the greatest single individual honor I've received. Never in my whole life have I ever dreamed of being in the Pro Football Hall of Fame. It just never entered my mind that I would enter the hall. To get in there and meet the guys I watched growing up was just unbelievable. I go back every year now. To see those guys is like a renewal every time I go back. I get to talk to those guys; it's amazing how many thoughts everybody has. People tell stories and I can say, "Hey, I feel the same exact way." It's kind of weird. Everybody has a common thought process.

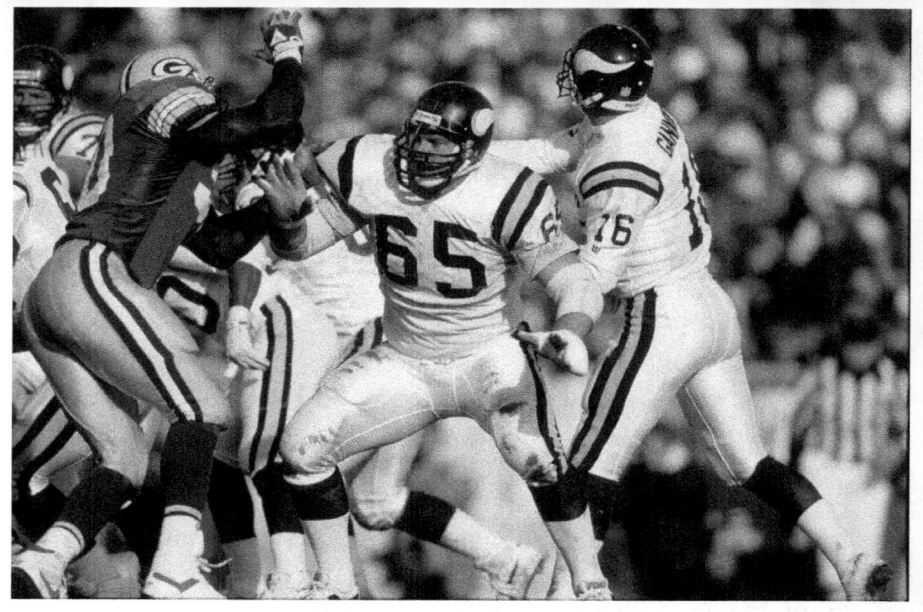

Photograph copyright Associated Press

Chapter 35

Kevin Greene

> College:
> Auburn
>
> Career History:
> As Player:
> Los Angeles Rams (1985–1992)
> Pittsburgh Steelers (1993–1995)
> Carolina Panthers (1996)
> San Francisco 49ers (1997)
> Carolina Panthers (1998–1999)
>
> As Coach:
> Green Bay Packers (2009–2013) (OLB)
>
> 2016 Inductee Pro Football Hall Of Fame

College Choice
My mom and dad were from Choccolocco, Alabama, and they grew up Auburn fans. When you're born in Alabama, you're born either into an Auburn household or University of Alabama household. My mom and dad were in the military. Because of that, my older brother Keith and I were born on the road. Since we were born into an Auburn household when it came time for college, there was no question where we were going. We were going to Auburn.

I went to high school in Granite City, Illinois, which is considerably north of Auburn, and Auburn didn't really recruit in that area. Plus, that high school was really known for its soccer team. We were soccer state champions four years in a row. Anyway, the football team wasn't really well known. We were average, but competitive. I sent my films down to Auburn, and they replied with a letter. They said, "We've filled the spots for linebackers. We'd like you to come down and walk on." Essentially, that's what I did.

Auburn Running Backs
We had great running backs during my years at Auburn. We had Bo Jackson, Lionel James, Brent Fullwood, Tommie Agee, and Tim Jessie. It was like Running Back University. It was hard, and I learned a lot.

Bo Jackson got me a number of times. But, I wasn't the only one he was running over, so I felt good about that. I was trying to lay leather on Bo. He was a special cat. I knew that practicing against him at Auburn was going to make me better. I just knew he was special. You could see it from the way he moved and how fast and how hard he hit you. It made you a better player.

That's the way you've got to look at it. You're going to improve as long as you go against people that are better than you. You won't get better if you go against people that you can beat up on all the time, if you think about it. It was really cool playing against Bo and Lionel James, another fine back that played multiple years in the NFL, in practice. It was great.

Auburn's Biggest Rival
There'll never be a bigger opponent than Alabama. Auburn-Alabama is such a huge rivalry that it dates back freaking centuries. I'm sure it goes back to the caveman days. So of course, it's Alabama.

Charles Barkley
I remember Charles Barkley being such a good dude. Charles didn't really know me from Adam, since I was a walk-on at Auburn. I wasn't really known. I was not a scholarship guy. Charles was just as kind and nice to me as if I was a big time famous college player like he was. Charles had such a great heart. He was just a fine person.

Bo was as good as Charles was. He didn't have an ego and he didn't have an attitude. They were just great, classy individuals. They were just both great, special young men.

Auburn
I never earned a scholarship. I did not start until the starting outside linebacker went down. His name was Joe Robinson, and he was a fine player. He would go on to be a first round draft choice with the

Minnesota Vikings. He went down about three-quarters of the way through my senior year. Then Coach Pat Dye put me in as a starter. I started making things happen and I ended up leading the SEC in sacks my senior year, 1984, and was Defensive Player of the Year. That's when I really started to step up my play at Auburn. So it was just a blessing. You don't want to wish injuries on anybody, but in that case, it really opened the door for me at that time.

Why would Pat Dye spend a scholarship on a walk-on who was basically just playing for two years? It just didn't make sense, and I understood that. That didn't take anything away from my experience playing for Auburn. I totally understood. My mom and dad could afford to put me in Auburn and keep me in Auburn, so that wasn't a deal breaker by any means. I mean, good God, I had a chance to play for Auburn. It was a phenomenal opportunity. I'm just blessed that Coach Pat Dye recognized something in me, got me in the mix, and got me on the field. I did some good things for them. So that's the way I look at it.

Draft
I was just hoping to get drafted. I really didn't know if I would. I was already a second lieutenant in the Army Reserves, so I was tracking a military career as my folks did. I remember during the season ending interview Coach Dye had with the seniors in 1984, I asked Coach Dye point blank, "Coach, do you think that I can play at the next level?" He told me, "Yes, Kevin. Absolutely. I think there's a place for you somewhere in the NFL."

That's really all I needed. Now I started thinking, I'm going to start running more and training harder. I am going to be ready to potentially walk on somewhere if I get a chance as a free agent in the NFL. I'm going to give it my best shot. We've only got one life to live, and I said, "I'm going to give it my best shot."

I was the first player picked in the fifth round by the Rams. I thought, "Oh my gosh. I've actually got my foot in the door." It was just unbelievable for me as a former walk-on to get drafted. Un freaking real. It was crazy.

The Birmingham Stallions had drafted me in their territorial draft. It was a backup game plan for me. When Coach Dye told me, "Yes, absolutely, I think there's a place for you somewhere in the NFL," that's really what my focus started to hone in on. Being drafted by the Birmingham Stallions was a blessing, too. I had a chance with them, but Coach Dye told me I really had a chance to run on the same field with the big boys; the big guys. So that was really where my focus was.

Earning Playing Time With Rams

Coach John Robinson had me at linebacker with the Rams. I was an outside linebacker at Auburn. We ran a three-four defense at Auburn and we ran a three-four with the Rams. So I just slid into the three-four outside backer position. Coach Robinson had me running down on kickoff team cracking noggins, the kickoff return team, punt team, and punt return team. I paid my dues my first three years playing on all the special teams. Then during my fourth year, I got my first start. I responded with 16½ sacks that season.

With the Rams, we had the same defensive coordinator. His name was Fritz Shurmur, and he was just a fine individual. I really loved Fritz. I think Fritz and John Robinson said, "We've got to find a way to get Kevin Greene on the field 'cuz he's running down on the kickoff team and he's crushing people." The first three years they started getting me in on third down and long to rush the passer. They wanted to see if I had any pass rush skills and stuff like that and I responded.

My second year in the league I had seven sacks as a part-time, third down pass rusher. I was a special teams guy primarily. My third year, I had 6½ sacks in a strike-shortened season. I think we only played nine or ten games that year. So they came up with an idea to get me on the field, and that idea was what they called the Eagle Defense. That put me in a position to rush the passer. They figured out a way to get me on the field.

1986 Los Angeles Rams vs. Chicago Bears NFC Championship Game

The Chicago Bears were tough, no doubt. It was a chilly game, but I felt pretty good. Our quarterback was Dieter Brock. He had played in the Canadian Football League, and he played really well for us that year.

We had Eric Dickerson at running back. I knew Eric Dickerson was special. I figured we had a chance to go into Soldier Field and win.

Chicago was rolling with their 46 defense. The Bears got ahead and then the crowd got into it. The wind started whipping off the water, it started snowing, and it was just brutal. It was a tail thumping. It is what it is. It was really cool to go to the championship game my rookie year.

Los Angeles Rams Change In Defensive Coordinators

Coach Robinson brought in a new defensive staff. Fritz Shurmur was let go, and they brought in Jeff Fisher to coordinate the defense. Jeff really didn't know how to play me. He played me for six games at right defensive end, four games at left defensive end, and six games at outside linebacker. My previous years, in '88, '89 and '90, I had 46 sacks. I was killing people. We didn't have a good year team-wise in 1990, and I think that prompted Coach Robinson to let Fritz and the staff go. Individually, I had a good, productive year in 1990, with 13 sacks. So I struggled and was I only able to get three sacks in 1991.

In 1992, the entire staff was let go. So the Rams brought in Chuck Knox as head coach and George Dyer as defensive coordinator. George put me as an outside linebacker in a four-three defense. I had more coverage responsibilities and less pass rush opportunities. I led the team in tackles and sacks as a part-time pass rusher on third down. He let me rush the passer. I knew I really couldn't have an impact in games as a four-three outside linebacker. I really needed to be attacking to have a direct impact in a game.

Signing With Pittsburg Steelers

Then in 1993, the first year of free agency, I signed with the Pittsburgh Steelers. They put me back as a three-four outside backer. So I was just really blessed. The Lord works in mysterious ways and he orchestrated my steps. I flew into Pittsburgh. Their starting left outside linebacker, Gerald Williams, wanted out of Pittsburgh. Gerald went and signed a free agent contract with the San Diego Chargers. Steelers Head Coach Bill Cowher, really needed a left outside linebacker in Defensive Coordinator Dom Capers' three-four pressure blitz-on package. It was just a perfect fit for me. It was what

I basically played those three years that I was highly productive with the Rams from 1988-1990.

Bill Cowher said, "Hey. We're going to put you back at your old position and let you do what you do." I said, "Cool. I'm all about it." I just loved playing for the Steeler Nation. With Greg Lloyd on the other side of me, he was slobbering as much as I was slobbering. He's freaking out as much as I'm going gonzo. We hunted together extremely well. The Steelers had a fine defense and fine offense. Those three years at Pittsburgh really defined my career.

Signing With Carolina Panthers
It was tough to leave Pittsburgh. I wasn't ready to ride the pine after the 1995 season. We lost the Super Bowl against Dallas. I was going into my 12th year, and Coach Cowher clearly wanted to play a young fellow named Jason Gildon. Coach Cowher wanted me to take Jason under my wing and teach him tricks of the trade and show him how to watch film. I just wasn't ready to be a backup to anybody.

So, I left and I signed with Carolina in 1996, which was my 12th year in the league. It just so happened Dom Capers' was the head coach. He said, "Hey, Kevin. I'm going to put you back where you belong, at outside linebacker. Just do what you do, and help teach the three-four pressure to the rest of the brothers on defense." I said, "Okay. Let's do it." I led the league in sacks again. I was a First Team All Pro and Linebacker of the Year again. I really wanted to stay a Steeler, but I wasn't ready to really ride the pine at that point in my career. I knew I had some more football left in me, some high level stuff left in me. So I had to leave.

Edward DeBartolo
Eddie was great. Eddie was wonderful. That was probably my 13th year in the league when I was a 49er. He was a great owner and it was a great organization. I really enjoyed my time during that one year in San Francisco. I think Eddie did a good job of bringing together a lot of talent to make a run at the Super Bowl. We just fell a little bit short. We actually played the championship game there in 1997, against the Green Bay Packers. Favre beat us, and I think they went on to lose the Super Bowl. We had Steve Young, Jerry Rice, Chris Doleman, and Rod Woodson there. We had Hall of Famers on that team. Brett Favre

was in the peak of his career and they came into Candlestick and beat us.

I had just a wonderful time in San Francisco. It was essentially a blip on the radar as far as my career was concerned, just one year, then I was back in Carolina. It was great playing for Mr. DeBartolo and that organization for a year.

Favorite Game
It was just a blessing. Good Lord, one weekend I was looking into the eyes of Joe Montana, the next weekend Dan Marino, the next weekend John Elway, Troy Aikman, Brett Favre, and then Steve Young. The list of great quarterbacks just went on and on and on. I knew they were Hall of Famers. I knew they were special when I was lining up on the other side of the ball from them, looking at them. I knew. My job, of course, was to hunt their tail. They didn't even have to pay me to do it. I just knew I was living a dream. I was totally in touch with reality at that time, and I knew that they were special, special cats. My job was to hunt them down and crush them and I did. It was just an unbelievable dream come true.

Sacking Joe Montana 4 ½ Times In A Game
I sacked him 5½ times in the last game of 1988. One of my fellow defenders, I'm not going to mention his name, got called for holding on one play and one of my sacks was nullified. So I ended up with 4½ sacks on Joe Montana in the last game of 1988, to help get the L.A. Rams into the playoffs. That was a surreal game. Obviously that was a big game for me.

I had a lot of big games. I was just blessed to play with a lot of great players that helped me along the way; great coaches and great players. I mentioned, some of those great players that helped me along the way.

Referees
I always thought that I would have more sacks if the referees would make more holding calls. Very few offensive tackles blocked me within the rules and regulations of the game. I've got this saying. It's what I taught my kids in Green Bay as a coach there for five years. "If they can't hold you, they can't block you." So I always thought

I'd have had more sacks if the refs would have specifically looked at me and whoever was in front of me, trying to block me each and every play. They couldn't do that. Plus, they want to let the big boys' play. They want to let them play and they know the fans at home don't want to see a lot of holding calls, yada, yada, yada. So that's the way football goes.

Waiting To Get Inducted Into The Pro Football Hall Of Fame
It was confusing more than anything. I just didn't understand the criteria for induction in the Hall of Fame, that's the bottom line. I just didn't understand what qualifies a man to be inducted. They were clearly putting in people that did not play as long as I did, and essentially we played the same position. They didn't have anywhere near the same production, statistical numbers, and impact I had on four different teams. So I was just scratching my noggin. More than anything, I was confused about the process. I wasn't going to get stressed about it. I was patient about it.

I just kept praying about it and trusting in the Lord that my time would come in God's time. Not when I want it, but it's going to happen in His time. It happened in His time and it was the right time in my family. It was definitely the right time in my life for it to transpire. It really doesn't matter now. I'm in and I'm part of an elite fraternity. So it doesn't matter. It doesn't faze me now.

Winning A Super Bowl As A Coach With Green Bay Packers
It was extremely fulfilling. I always wanted a Super Bowl ring. It's something that I fought tooth and nail for during my 15 years as a player and I came up short for 15 years. I went to six championship games as a player and lost five of them. The one championship game we won, we lost the Super Bowl. It's just so hard to go to the Super Bowl, much less win the thing. So as a coach my second year up in Green Bay, to win a Super Bowl was just unbelievable, but bittersweet because we beat the Pittsburgh Steelers. So it was bittersweet to beat the old team that I owe so much to in the big show.

I am grateful to Coach Mike McCarthy for giving me an opportunity up in Green Bay to coach for him and his staff and get a Super Bowl ring. I'm just really grateful to Coach McCarthy and that entire organization.

Favorite Coach

I have been blessed to be surrounded by a lot of good coaches. It started at Auburn. I had a great coach in Coach Pat Dye. What a fine coach he was; a hard, physical coach. I just loved playing for him. My position coach there was Joe Whitt, another good coach.

Then I went into the NFL with the Rams, and John Robinson was the head coach. Fritz Shurmur was a great defensive coordinator who actually created a defense to get me on the field. My position coach there, Fred Whittingham, played in the NFL for a number of years at linebacker. He was just a great position coach. Then I go to Pittsburgh with Coach Bill Cowher. Of course, we all know about him. Dom Capers was there as the defensive coordinator, and my position coach at Pittsburgh was Marvin Lewis. I mean, good Lord. Dick LeBeau was on that staff. Then I go to Carolina and Coach Dom Capers is the head coach there. Billy Davis was my position coach there. Billy Davis has been a long-time defensive coordinator in the NFL.

It just went on and on and on. Wonderful coaches and great players surrounded me. I was just blessed all along the way. I truly was.

NFL Team Most Identify With

There's a part of me that bleeds a lot of different colors. During my eight years with the Rams I was a good player, a Pro Bowl player. Part of me bleeds blue and gold. It surely does. When I went to Pittsburgh, they really put me on the stage and my career really took off there opposite of Greg Lloyd. I was working with Rod Woodson. So, I bleed black and gold. Then I went to Carolina, and was with Lamar Lathon, Sam Mills, and all those guys. I bleed a little bit of that teal blue and black. So I bleed a lot of different colors.

If you look back at my career, there's no question I stepped up on stage there in Pittsburgh. It was a whole other level that we played at as a defense, and what we were able to do as a defensive unit. So I bleed a lot of colors, but it was great to be a part of the Steeler Nation.

Photograph copyright Associated Press

Chapter 36

Bruce Smith

> College:
> Virginia Tech
>
> Career History:
> Buffalo Bills (1985–1999)
> Washington Redskins (2000–2003)
>
> 2009 Inductee Pro Football Hall Of Fame

College Choice
There were a number of different factors that convinced me to attend Virginia Tech. Mainly, I wanted to stay in the state of Virginia, I wanted to be a part of something special, and I wanted to be close to my father who was ill at the time. Those were important factors for me. I wanted to be able to get home at a relatively quick pace if something happened to my father.

Ohio State, Michigan, you name the school, they were recruiting me. I had never been a great distance away from the state of Virginia and the city of Norfolk before, and I was really gun-shy about leaving the area.

Virginia Tech
As a kid growing up in Norfolk, Virginia I had never been on a plane before. Because I lived in a small town, I didn't know the world was so vast and worthy of being explored. So my first of many experiences was going to Virginia Tech. The first time riding on a plane, I was scared to death. Just the whole college experience was amazing—getting an education, being a student athlete and playing football at a level that I had never experienced before, and just making a lot of my dreams come true.

Virginia Tech was remarkable. Once again, I was part of something special. At that point, we were in an independent league and didn't get a great deal of respect, but it was big time college football; the atmosphere, the environment, the surroundings, the excitement of football, and some of the best athletes in the country. To be a kid who grew up and played sports in Norfolk, Virginia at Booker T. Washington High School, to be able to attend a major university, and become the number one pick in the 1985 draft after leading the nation in sacks two years in a row in 1983 and 1984, that speaks volumes. I accomplished this via goals that I set out to accomplish. I wanted to be a part of something special.

Winning Outland Trophy

Winning the Outland Trophy was certainly the icing on the cake after being a consensus All-American, on every All-American team that existed. It was certainly special winning the Outland Trophy.

When I went out to [I believe it was] Seattle and received the Outland Trophy, they had lost it. They could not find the Outland Trophy and years later, they had to make a replica and get it to me. It was the darndest thing I had ever heard of in my life. I was at the award ceremony and prior to that they had told me that they didn't have the actual trophy. Being a 20-year-old kid, I didn't understand how in the hell could you lose the Outland Trophy. Now that some years have passed Virginia Tech has a replica of the Outland Trophy sitting in their trophy room.

Draft

The Buffalo Bills were deciding between Ray Childress, who eventually went to the Houston Oilers, and me as the first pick in the draft. I think about two months prior to the draft they sat me down with my agent and said they were going to make me the number one pick in the NFL draft in 1985. It was a foregone conclusion on draft day. My walking out on stage and being announced as the first player picked, was just a formality. It was certainly something that was worked out well ahead of time, although the contract wasn't worked out.

The USFL's Philadelphia Stars tried to get me to come out of college after my junior year. They had my rights but it just wasn't enticing to me. I wanted to stay in school, continue my education, and finish out my senior year, which ended up being very enjoyable. It was just an exceptional time for me with my teammates, assistant coaches, and coach Bill Dooley.

Things were happening so quickly. I didn't understand the process of being drafted and all the expectations and the pressure that's placed on someone in that position. I was just happy to have the opportunity to do something I loved to do. I didn't realize the work ethic and the commitment it would take until my first year playing in the National Football League, My first year I had Kay Stephenson as head coach. We had six weeks of training camp. I never worked that hard and that long before in a training camp period.

Later that season, Hank Bullough came in and took over for Kay Stephenson. It was just an eye-opening experience for me. It helped to build my character and make me the person that I am today. I appreciate that opportunity, the hard work, and the lessons that were learned. I truly believe it's helped to put me in the position that I'm in today.

Marv Levy
When Marv Levy arrived it was like a breathe of fresh air. He wanted us to act like men and he treated us like men. He was very soft spoken and very rarely raised his voice. I probably can count on one hand the number of times he used a few choice words to get his point across. He was a constant professional, the perfect gentleman. I always tell people, Marv taught us how to be successful on the football field, but more importantly, he taught us how to be successful in the game of life. Those are the things that stick with you throughout your life. Your career in football is relatively short, but life itself and paying attention to details and the values is not. He taught us to not be late for meetings, to put in an honest day's work, to make sure we are prepared for any challenge or task, whether it is on Sunday or going to work on a day-to-day basis. It was just an incredible experience and learning lesson that I was taught by Marv Levy, and quite frankly, the whole coaching staff. I learned a great deal from Marv Levy.

Mentors With Bills
There were a number of guys. One gentleman who stands out is Ben Williams. He was very encouraging; he took me under his wing. One

of the first things that I remember he told me was about the offensive lineman. He said, "If he can't grab you, he can't hold you." I took that, literally, to heart and I started working on things. I started to emulate the way he used his hands to keep an offensive lineman from holding him. I think that was one of the things that made me successful.

There was also Lucius Sanford, Darryl Talley, and a host of older guys taking the younger guys they saw had great potential, under their wings. It was a process for me, and I had to be committed. I had to work diligently and extremely hard. There was a nucleus of guys, coaches, teammates, and Rusty Jones, who handled the nutritional and conditioning aspects. When you put all those pieces together, in addition to my desire to be the best, that's when you create something special.

Playing In A 3-4 Defense
There was a constant double and an occasional triple team on pretty much every play. Teams can scheme against a 3-4 dominant defensive lineman a lot easier than they can in a 4-3 defensive system.

In a 3-4 defensive system, defensive front guys aren't known for getting a lot of sacks. They're known for getting a lot of tackles. It's rare a defensive end is able to get a lot of sacks and a lot of tackles for a long time in their career playing in a 3-4 defensive system. You just get beat up because there are double teams coming from all different angles and it just creates a lot of wear and tear.

First Mini-Camp In Buffalo
It was an eye-opening experience for me. It was roughly May 15, and I was walking out to the first mini-camp practice. The stadium is in the middle of the Snowbelt, right off of Lake Erie. I noticed the clouds in the distance and within 15 minutes it started raining, then it started hailing, then it snowed, and then the sun came out about 20 minutes later. I thought to myself, "What in the hell have I gotten myself into?" That was the lake effect snow in that particular region, and to be quite honest, I became quite fond of it after a short period of time because I enjoyed playing in the cold weather. I enjoyed playing in the elements. We used it to our advantage and it became a state of mind over matter. When we used to get teams from down South or out West that came to play against the Buffalo Bills, we knew we had that advantage.

Favorite Game

I think there are a number of games that actually stand out, but probably my favorite game was against the Houston Oilers. It's a great experience to watch that game to this very day and see the resilience, the overcoming of obstacles, and a group of guys who just would not quit. We were losing 28-3 at halftime. When we went into the locker-room, I remember Darryl Talley stood up and said to the guys, "Yeah, they think they're hot shit right now, but we've got them right where we want them." After halftime was over, we went back out and I believe the Houston Oilers only scored one touchdown and one field goal. We scored the remainder of the points. We ended up winning that game 41-38.

Buffalo Bills Transformation To Super Bowl Contender

The first sign of that was in 1986, when we were able to acquire Jim Kelly. The ownership and the front office made a committed effort to make a run. In 1985, they drafted Andre Reed and me. They already had Darryl Talley so we had a few bright stars. We needed to get a few more, and management was committed to doing that. In 1986, they went and got Jim Kelly. In 1987, they traded for Cornelius Bennett, and in 1988, they got Thurman Thomas. That was pretty much the nucleus of the team they would build around and we were off to the races. I think we all thrived and wanted to be a part of something special. We wanted to make the Bills something to cheer about and be proud about. Our mindset was to make this an enjoyable experience for western New Yorkers.

First Super Bowl

It was an incredible experience. The country was at the height of the Gulf War and there was a heavy military presence at the game. Whitney Houston sung the National Anthem. It was just an incredible atmosphere, one in which we thoroughly enjoyed. I wish we had come out on top. I wish we could have made the field goal, but it was still an incredible experience

That game could have gone either way. The first one is always the sweetest, so to speak. We had the ball in our court, but just missed the field goal. We win as a team and we lose as a team.

Comparison With Reggie White

My body of work speaks for itself; what I meant to the team, the contributions that I made, being the all-time sack leader against the odds of the double and occasional triple teams. I guarantee you that no one on that defensive line was double-teamed more than I was under that system. You can go to the 4-3 system or whatever type of system it is. I've even had conversations with Reggie White when he was alive and he said, "Bruce, if you ever played in a 4-3 system you would have never gotten touched," because he thought that highly of my athletic ability and the way that I was able to run.

We were two totally different players. Reggie was just a man-child. He was a powerful giant that had brute force. I was more on the athletic side. I could run, I used finesse, I had some power, but not as much as Reggie. Reggie was 295-300 pounds. I was more of a player that used my quickness, my speed, and my agility. We were two totally different players, but I have a great deal of respect for Reggie.

Deacon Jones Honoring Me

Deacon Jones had an event out in California to recognize me as being the All-Time NFL sack leader. Deacon and I were very good friends. I called him one time when I was in a slump. I hadn't had a sack in about five or six games. When I talked to him, he gave me advice and encouragement. I was honored to be among the greats in Bills history

I had a great relationship with Deacon. Certainly he didn't have to concede. I respected Deacon both on and off the field. He did acknowledge that I was the all-time sack leader.

Pro Football Hall Of Fame Induction

I was on cloud nine knowing that it wasn't necessarily just about me, it was about all the other people who played with me and took part in my reaching the pinnacle in my career. It was about my mother, father, sister, brother, my high school football and basketball coaches, Cal Davidson and Zeke Avery, and all of the other individuals who saw more in me than I saw in myself. They encouraged me, guided me, and taught me. It was just an incredible experience and opportunity for me to say, "Thanks to those individuals who believed in me and kept giving me the opportunities to succeed, and to Virginia Tech and

Booker T. Washington High School." It was an opportunity to pay homage to them for what they did for me.

Bills Wall Of Fame Induction
That was exceptional as well, to be among the greats in Bills history. On the wall is Thurman Thomas, Ralph Wilson, Marv Levy, Jim Kelly, Bill Polian, Andre Reed … the list just goes on. I'm just happy to have my name etched in stone in Ralph Wilson Stadium.

Photograph copyright Associated Press

Chapter 37

Charles Haley

> College:
> James Madison
>
> Career History:
> San Francisco 49ers (1986–1991) Dallas Cowboys (1992–1996) San Francisco 49ers (1998–1999)

<u>College Choice</u>
Initially my options were Liberty or James Madison. After the East-West All Star Game that I played in, other colleges wanted me. A big school middle linebacker was on the All Star team. I was also a middle linebacker, so I had to go play at my second position, which was tight end. I lit the other team up in the All Star Game, so schools were looking at me to play offense after that game. I wasn't gong to do that because I didn't like getting hit.

I'm one of those guys who didn't like being exposed on the field where I was going to get rocked. I took some big hits during that game and held onto the ball. I was ecstatic about going to James Madison. I think for me, a small town guy, going to James Madison was the perfect fit.

<u>NFL Draft</u>
People told me the 49ers and the Giants came down and looked at me. One thing I had going for me, was my 40-yard dash time. I was 6'4½" and weighed 200 pounds at the time, so I guess they saw something more than I saw.

As the draft came on, people were saying I was going to be drafted in the second or third round. When those two rounds finished, my girlfriend and I biked down to the movie theater and watched a movie. Then my roommate came down and said, "You've been drafted by the 49ers." I had no idea who played on the 49ers. All I knew was that I had to travel across the country and that was kind of frightening for me.

Bill Walsh

Bill Walsh was amazing. I still remember him up on stage giving a boxing analogy, telling us they hit the champ a couple of times but in the end, the champ knocks them out. When we go play, the other team is going to make some plays just like boxing champs, but we will win in the end.

The other thing that he did was, bring in great people who were winners, like Olympic gold medalists, singers, etc. They would talk about their journey and how they became great. For me, that was better than having somebody stand there, talking about things he had never done. When those people get up there and talk to you, it inspires you to be great.

He also brought back former players who had won a Super Bowl. I never thought that you weren't supposed to win playing football, because the expectation was always to win.

George Seifert

George Seifert micromanaged, but I loved him for that because he made me study. The Monday after every game, we studied for two and a half hours. We would go over everybody's position and everybody's responsibility. After about the third game, I sat there and learned every defensive alignment, as well as everybody's position on the field. That gave me the opportunity to take chances. Plus it empowered me. The more you know how other people are going to play, the better you can play.

Training

Ronnie Lott was fiery and led by example. I've never met anybody like that, or that intense.

He took me under his belt and showed me the way. We did karate. He would show me how to do a lot of the drills and stuff. The best part about it was that I didn't train with the linebackers, I trained with the defensive backs. I trained with people who were faster than me and who had more of a skill set. My goal was not to get to that skill set, but to get as close to it as I could. Each time I did that it made me better.

I worked out with Roger Craig and Jerry Rice once. After about 30 minutes, I went home. They had flight jackets on, weights on, and they were just running. I was thinking, "Oh my God." I thought I could run, but nah, that wasn't for me. So I went back to doing the things that I could do to be great.

Nothing is easy. Every year I tore something or hurt myself. I never lifted weights. I don't know if that was the cause of it, but every year I played with pain. After a while, I could control the pain mentally. I didn't need pills or anything like that to control the pain. What I believe is, the more you can control your mind and control your breathing, the more you can be explosive and the longer you can stay on the field.

First Super Bowl
My first Super Bowl against Cincinnati was amazing. With about three minute left, we were losing, but we got the ball on the 8-yard line. The first play we got a holding call, so we were backed up farther. I was sitting over there thinking, "God, why did you bring me here to lose?"

I forgot that we had Jerry Rice, Roger Craig, Joe Montana, and Brent Jones. I was sitting there moping and ready to cry, and I heard the fans start cheering. I looked up and within about five or six plays, we were dancing and were the champions of the world. From that day on, I always believed in my teammates.

Joe Montana
Joe Montana was great. What made Joe great? Joe was not like any of the other quarterbacks who were stuck up, stuffy, and didn't want to talk to other players. Joe was an everyday guy. He played jokes on people did all kind of crazy things. He didn't make anybody feel

small. We were all on the same line. He would get in the huddle when we were losing and tell jokes. He would get everybody's mind off of losing, and then we would go and win. One time he threw the ball and somebody hit him hard. The only thing he asked was if the player caught the ball. I've seen quarterbacks just go off because they got hit. I loved him, man. He was the best quarterback I've ever played with.

Edward DeBartolo

Eddie DeBartolo treated us like family. He took us to Maui. He's done many great things for players when things get rough for them. He takes care of them. I don't think anybody can ever measure up to Eddie D. Jerry Jones comes close to Mr. D, but Mr. D is in a class all by himself because of the way he treated players. He took care of them. His word meant something. When he said yes, it meant yes. I respect a man who makes a decision and is willing to stand behind it. That's the kind of man he is.

Trade To Dallas Cowboys

I was dejected. At one point I wanted to leave the 49ers and then when it came time for me to go, I had buyer's remorse. I didn't know what to expect. The best thing ever happened was Jerry Jones picking me up from the airport. He told me the vision that he had for the team. He told me what his expectations of me were. I never had an owner do that before. I bought in right then and there. He did not make you feel like you were beneath him. He is a great man.

When I walked into the practice facility, I saw Troy Aikman and Coach Jimmy Johnson. Troy was out on the field throwing the football. I said, "Troy, you ain't no Joe Montana." He was throwing the ball in those little three-hole things, way out there. He stepped back and threw it in the hole the first time.

I said, "Man, lightening can strike once." He went back and threw it right down the middle into the hole again. I shut up after that. I've said things to guys just to get underneath their skin. Sometimes you needed extra motivation to go out and do your job. I tried to provide that for guys.

I went out and did my job. I didn't need to talk trash. I let other people do it because that's what helps motivate some people. Nothing that somebody says can motivate me because I believe in who I am. I motivate myself. Whatever goals anybody set for me, I reached even higher. I don't believe that anyone should set a goal for another person. We should always over achieve.

I had great coaches. I was the luckiest guy in the world to have Bill Walsh, George Seifert, Jimmy Johnson, and Barry Switzer. It doesn't get any better than that.

Jimmy Johnson
Jimmy Johnson was great for me. He kept his foot on the guys' necks. I think he should be in the Hall of Fame because he took the youngest team to the Super Bowl twice and won. He might have done it three or four times if he continued as coach, but it didn't happen like that. Jimmy's motto was, "Repetition is the mother of learning", and we did a lot of repetition. If things didn't go right, he started the whole practice over. He trained us to be disciplined.
The bottom line is, the great Jimmy Johnson went out and the great Barry Switzer came in. You can't slight Barry because he's not Jimmy. Barry inherited the talent that Jimmy had left, but you still have to know how to deal with players and to motivate them year, after year, after year. After you win two Super Bowls, most of the time, guys lose their focus or you lose most of your talent to free agency.

Super Bowl XXX
I came back two weeks after major back surgery and played in Super Bowl XXX. I told the defense I'd never forsake them and I had to be a man of my word. I couldn't just leave them out there. I had to be a part of it. When I look back, maybe that was a selfish thing to do; maybe I should have taken the game off. My career would have lasted longer. I'd rather do what I did and have my career shortened than to sit there and watch my teammates lose, or not be a part of the winning.

Decision To Retire
If I had known then what I know now, I would have never gone back to the 49ers and played that year. The repercussion of that was that I

had to get a back fusion. I had to get cages put in and that was probably the worst surgery I ever had. But, it was also the best surgery I ever had because I don't have the back pain any more. I'm happy the doctor performed it on me.

More Pressure Playing For Dallas Than San Francisco

The game is a game, is a game. Whether it's the Super Bowl, a playoff game, or the fourth game of the season, for me all of them are the same. It doesn't matter what team you play for, it's the standards that are set from the beginning. If high standards are set from the beginning, then they can't be lowered, they can only be raised higher.

Coaches dictate how players play. When you've got a fiery coach, you know you're going to have a team that is very determined. You have to look back at those things.

Bill Walsh was not a yeller. He didn't get on guys. He made guys become men by letting them make their own mistakes and their own choices. I don't like people telling me what to do, and he never did that. I would do dumb things to get in trouble and I would say, "Coach, why don't you just tell me what to do." He'd say, "You never ask."

I never thought about that. I never thought that all I had to do was ask somebody. I was always just doing it and taking control of my own destiny. I said, "Coach, that's all I've got to do?" And he said, "Yeah."

From that point on, I was not afraid to ask. I was never afraid to ask my D-line coach what I needed to do to be great. Most people are afraid to ask a coach what they need to do because they don't want to hear the answer.

Being In Cowboys Ring Of Honor

I never expected that. For me, I never expect anything and then the next thing I know I get it. Jerry said he couldn't spell Super Bowl without Charles Haley, so I guess he put his money where his mouth is when he put me in. Jerry is a man of his word. I don't know why he did it. It's like I tell people, I don't know why a lot of great people help me, but they do.

Not Wearing Super Bowl Rings

I'm not a flashy guy so I don't put my rings on. During my playing career, I never put them on because I always wanted to win another one. Now that my career is over, I want people to see me for who I am now, not just see me as a football player. I want them to meet the real Charles Haley. I want to be judged on what I'm doing now in my life and how I'm impacting the community, how I'm helping others. That for me, that's what it's all about.

Favorite Moment

Having my kids was my favorite moment. Just being there with them and taking them from California by myself, back home to Virginia. Just spending that time with them. That is the most important thing for me, family. It's always been family.

Toughest Offensive Lineman

Jackie Slater was the toughest offensive lineman I faced. I always did two things. I would always speed rush to get by guys, and would beat them on the inside. Then I would power rush in that combination.

One game during my rookie year I played against Jackie. I did a couple of speed rushes on him, and then I went to the power rush. When I power rushed Jackie, he hit me with his head and my head went backward. My knees hit the ground and I saw Jesus Christ in all three forms. I went to the sideline and sat down on the other side of the bench. I put my helmet where I couldn't find it. I did not want to go back out there. I was sitting down evaluating whether I should be in this game or not. That gave me a little time, five or six minutes, to get myself together. I went back on the field.

The thing I learned to do is use my speed. I just put my speed on Jackie because he couldn't handle that. I didn't try to muscle him anymore from that day on. I picked my poison. Guys that did the head butt stuff ... I didn't power rush those guys, I used quickness.

That time I got hit, I went on my knees to pray, "Good Lord, God help me." He said get off the field then, and I ran up off of it.

San Francisco 49er Charles Haley rushes Falcons quarterback Chris Miller. Photograph copyright Associated Press

Chapter 38

Andre Reed

> College:
> Kutztown University
>
> Career History:
> Buffalo Bills (1985–1999)
> Denver Broncos (2000)
> Washington Redskins (2000)
>
> 2014 Inductee Pro Football Hall Of Fame

College Choice

Coming out of high school I just thought I'd go to school locally. Kutztown University had a pretty good football program and was a good academic school. I was a homebody. I look back on it now, and it probably was the best thing for me. I could have gone to a bigger school and tried to walk on the football team, but you never know what could have happened.

Kutztown University is in eastern Pennsylvania. It's about an hour and a half to two hours outside of Philadelphia. It's a small Division 2 school. If you look at a lot of NFL rosters now, there's a lot of D2 kids on NFL rosters. Back in the day it wasn't like that, you just didn't see them on NFL rosters. Some former D2 players are NFL Pro Bowlers.

Draft

I was projected to be drafted between rounds 3-6. Back then there were twelve rounds in the draft instead of the seven that they have now.

On the first day of training camp, there were 125 guys on the practice field. I think now you can only have 90 players. So that's thirty-five more players that were on the field, which diminished players' chances of making the team. But, times change, things change, and that's how it was.

Position Change From High School Quarterback To College Wide Receiver

When I got to Kutztown they had a pretty good quarterback there that was an All-American. He was a senior and they had a guy behind him that was a junior. Coming in as a freshman who knew if I was going to get any playing time or not. I got some great advice from people at Kutztown. They saw me in high school and saw that I could handle the ball, and do all of that stuff. They wanted to know if I could catch the ball. I said, "Yeah, anything to help the team. If I can get on the field and play, I would love to contribute any way I can." The offensive coordinator at the time, asked me if I would make the switch to wide receiver and I said, "For sure." That obviously was the best switch I ever made.

Marv Levy

The Bills were in transition and they just had back-to-back 2-14 seasons. They hadn't been in the playoffs since the 1981 season, and there was a change being made. I think bringing Marv Levy in as head coach that fourth game of the year was the change that the team needed.

Marv was just a good guy. I think he was more than a coach, he was kind of like a father figure. He really had a great rapport with his players and that was the good thing about it.

Jim Kelly

Jim Kelly had a great career with Houston Gamblers. He was a very feisty guy. From day one, when he was in the huddle he demanded respect. You knew that he wanted to get stuff done. You look at some quarterbacks in their eyes, and it's like a deer in the headlights. Jim was a guy confident in his ability. You need that in a guy that's pulling the trigger. We believed in him. We had a bunch of good players around him in Thurman Thomas, Bruce Smith, and Darryl Talley. We just had a lot of good players at the right time.

No-Huddle Offense
The Bills coaches saw what Jim Kelly did in the USFL, how he threw for all those yards and had all those weapons. Ted Marchibroda was very instrumental in us starting to use the no-huddle offense.

One game we were losing and we just started saying, "Hurry up, hurry up." We ended up scoring a lot and almost won the game. We came back the next week and Ted was asked, "Why don't we do this all the time and put people on their heels all the time?" That's when all that started. We started running teams out of the stadium because they couldn't keep up with the pace.

Sometimes the defense hated the no-huddle. They said, "Man you guys are scoring too quick. We just rested for five minutes and we're back on the field." My response was, "Well, our job is to score, and your job is to stop them from scoring."

Success Running After The Catch
There are a bunch of keys why I was successful running after the catch. As a high school quarterback, we ran an option type of offense. I was able to handle the ball a lot and run with the ball. My college coaches saw that and when I went to college, they wanted to try and get the ball in my hands as quick as possible. That's when it all started. When I got to Buffalo, they gave me even more chances to do that.

I really worked on being strong, breaking tackles, and all that kind of stuff. It was really important to me the way I trained in the offseason to get ready for that. Our offense changed when Tim Marchibroda came. I had to be in the middle a lot and take a lot of hits. I had to be physically fit to do all that stuff. Again, I had some great teammates, great people behind me that made me better and vice-versa. What it comes down to is they gave me the opportunity to do everything. Again, just really taking pride in what I like to do and never being satisfied. That was a big key, definitely.

"The Comeback" (Houston Oilers vs. Buffalo Bills Playoff Game)
I think we had to get something going because we had a great crowd. Our 12th man was probably one of the best, if not the best, in the

game. We figured if we got a little bit going and the crowd got into it, we would start to make something happen. Plus, the Houston Oilers were making some mistakes. It's how you capitalize on the other person's mistake. We capitalized on every mistake the Oilers made and we turned it into points. The Oilers got a little complacent and that's what happens, you end up losing the game.

Toughest Cornerback
I can't say one guy or another, all of them were tough. You wouldn't be there playing that position if you weren't a pretty good player.

Playing Last Season For Redskins
I was with the Redskins for one year, the bulk of my career and accomplishments were in Buffalo. I always will be a Bill and remember that. I'm sure if you ask some of these other Hall of Famers, like Joe Montana who played the bulk of his career in San Francisco and he ended up in Kansas City. He's probably a 49er for life. I'm no different.

Not Winning A Super Bowl
Unfortunately we didn't win a Super Bowl. That's the way I look at it. That's what you play the game for, to get to the Super Bowl and win it. Some guys haven't even gotten to a Super Bowl, or to a playoff game, so that's really what your goal should be. When you step on that field in July, you want to be playing in that last game, at the Super Bowl.

I was blessed to be on that stage four years in a row, I don't think that is ever going to happen again. The outcome didn't turn out the way I wanted it to. If you look at those games, we have five Hall of Famers from those games. Obviously they think that the team was, not only individually what we did, but they think the team was very, very instrumental in changing the game at that time. We were pretty hard to contend with at the time. Opposing teams had to go through Buffalo most of the time during those years.

Pro Football Hall Of Fame Induction
The emotion was very, very ... it was a long wait, put it that way. I've told people, I'm very humbled by the accolade. I was only as good as

the people around me. I respected the process of the Hall of Fame and how they pick people. It's so hard to pick five guys out of, what do they start with, one hundred twenty-five guys? It's hard to pick five and say, "Okay, these five are better than those one hundred twenty." I think if you're nominated you're just as deserving as anybody else. I'm glad to be with my teammates and to be part of the greatest team ever assembled, and that's the Pro Football Hall of Fame. If you were to ask me in high school if I would be a Hall of Famer in the NFL, I would have probably laughed at you a few times.

This is what God made and God gave me the ability. I tried to work it and I think I worked it pretty good for him. Now it's time to be an Ambassador for the Hall of Fame, and be an Ambassador for kids and say, "Hey, you can do it. There's no limit to your ability. If you work hard, you can achieve the goals you want."

Reason Chose Marv Levy As His Presenter For Hall Of Fame Induction

Marvin Levy was my presenter. He's done a few. I thought about Bill Polian who is a great speaker and a heck of a GM. Jim Kelly was another possibility. It's not that Marv beat those two guys out. I think Marv is such an eloquent guy and really knows me as a player, what I'm made up of, and how I went about things. I'm honored to have him, not only as a former coach of mine, but he's a Hall of Famer too, so he knows what that's about.

Buffalo Bills wide receiver Andre Reed and teammate Keith McKeller celebrate Reed's third touchdown during the fourth quarter of "The Comeback" playoff game against the Houston Oilers. Photograph copyright Associated Press

Chapter 39

Randall McDaniel

> College:
> Arizona State
>
> Career History:
> Minnesota Vikings (1988–1999)
> Tampa Bay Buccaneers (2000–2001)
>
> 2009 Inductee Pro Football Hall Of Fame

College Choice
I was born and raised in Arizona. I always figured if I ever had the opportunity to go to college and play football at the school, it would be at Arizona State. They gave me that opportunity and I took it and ran with it.

There were other colleges more interested in me playing basketball than football, because I played both in high school. All I wanted to do was stay at home and go to Arizona State. So when Darryl Rogers gave me a call and said they were going to offer me a football scholarship, I immediately jumped on that.

Arizona State Tradition
There have been a lot of great players who came through ASU. It was nice to follow in that tradition and get an opportunity to play there and continue the tradition the Sun Devils have out there.

Position Change At Arizona State
When I went to college I was a tight end. I played my first year as a tight end. Then during my second year, I switched from tight end to guard and started from game six on. When the offensive line was struggling, they were holding tryouts for spots along the way. I just wanted the opportunity to play and show what I could do on the

field. I threw my hat into the ring and it worked out for me. I got in there, started playing, and I never looked back from that point on.

Changing positions wasn't that bad. The tight ends at ASU caught passes a lot, but they did a lot of run blocking also. My strength as a tight end at that time was run blocking. I thought I could block just about anyone they put in front of me. Then, I had an unfair advantage when I moved from tight end to guard because I was a lot quicker than all of the defensive linemen around. My speed helped out there too. I did power lifting along the way through high school and college. So I was just as strong as everybody else. I just wasn't as big as everybody else, but I could still get the job done.

Playing Basketball At Arizona State
I thought about playing basketball at ASU for a little bit, but when you've got Byron Scott out there on the team and some other guys, I figured football was going to be the better sport for me.

I knew all the guys who played on the ASU basketball team. I'd be out there playing pick up games before their practices and before our practices. I thought about doing both, but I figured I should concentrate on just football and get that done.

Transition To Minnesota Vikings
I had somewhat of an idea what it was going to be like to play in the NFL. ASU had guys who were drafted before me, like David Fulcher and some of the other guys that I played with. So I had an idea about it. I knew it wasn't going to be easy. I knew I had to work at it. I knew I had a lot of studying to do and had to learn to watch film. The transition went pretty smoothly.

I had a lot of great veterans on the offensive line when I came in. Kirk Lowdermilk, Gary Zimmerman, Tim Irwin, and all those guys who were the veterans back then, worked with me. They would tell me, "You're going to do it our way until you can do it better." They taught me a ton. I was very fortunate to join an established group. I just had to mesh with them, and I did.

Back then, first round picks didn't start a lot. You had to earn your way into the starting lineup. Even with all the expectations on you,

you still had to earn it. I remember sitting on the field one day and my coach was chewing me out. He offered me a bus ticket, a road map, and an apple. I thought I was gone.

You really knew when you got in there you were prepared. You knew what to expect. You knew the defenses. You knew what was going to happen if they shifted, before they shifted. So when I got that opportunity to step in the second game of that year, I never looked back. Once I got an opportunity to get in, I knew it was my job to lose and that's the way I played for all 14 years. It was my job to lose, so I went out and made sure I kept it.

Minnesota Vikings Defensive Line
We had some great defensive linemen; Keith Millard, John Randle, Henry Thomas, and Al Noga were there. I started with Doug Martin who was there toward the end of his career. Practice was like playing a game. So when you got to the game, it was like, I can take a breath now and have a little more fun.

Keith Millard and all those guys used to try to watch film of our practice so they could beat you in practice. In turn, we watched film on them and thought about what I needed to do to make sure Keith Millard, then later on John Randle, didn't have a good day in practice.

That was a nightmare. I actually told John after I retired that I hated practicing against him. I did whatever it took to make sure he couldn't get a rush or beat me in anything. If he were going to beat me, I would literally hold him and yank him down, and be like hey, you're never going to get there. It made the games so much easier. I give John and all those guys credit. They made practice fun. The work that I put into practice made the games a lot easier for me.

I think a lot of the guys used to wait to see John Randle and I go against each other at practice just to see what would take place. It got heated at times. At the end of each practice, we would both walk off the field and talk about it. We knew all we were going to do was make each other better, so we'd do it again tomorrow, and every day after. It just made both of us better.

There were times that there was no talking between us after plays. It was like okay, I got to get back at him for what he just did or he'll do the same thing. So it made for a rough day at practice sometimes, but when the games rolled around, whoever I was playing against, whoever he was playing against, we both kind of went okay, it's not against each other anymore so let's just take it out on somebody else.

John Randle's Trash Talking

I had an unfair advantage over him because I established myself early in practice against him during his rookie year. It was probably during one of those times when we got in a heated moment and I just made sure he knew I was in charge. I think that kind of stuck throughout our careers, but he never talked trash on me.

I know when I went to Tampa Bay for the last two years of my career, I thought he would talk trash, but he didn't do it. I tried to play head games with him telling him that I didn't have to hold back anymore. I said, "We're not teammates. I can finally just let it loose and finally go after you without holding back." He took it out on the other guard on the other side so it worked out.

Playing In 12 Straight Pro Bowls

I wasn't thinking about making the Pro Bowl when I made it after my second year in the league. All I was thinking about was the play at hand and doing well. When it happened, then it was okay, can I do it again? Can I put the work in to do it one more time? Each year it was always, can I get better to get back?

My wife said since I brought her to this arctic tundra Minnesota, I had to take her to some place warm every year in return. At the Pro Bowl she said, "You got to get me back to Hawaii." I could say I was playing for my wife, to make sure she got back to Hawaii every year.

I made a lot of friends along the way in Hawaii. I met a lot of people in Hawaii whom I still keep in contact with today. It was a good vacation. It was a good time to go see friends. It was always fun to play in the Pro Bowl.

Jerry Burns

Burnsy? I love him. He reminded me of Burgess Meredith. He was the Vikings head coach when I first met him. I learned a ton from him those first pro years. To this day, I owe Burnsy for taking a chance on [drafting] me. I was called the undersized lineman, and I was brought in when they didn't want to bring in a lineman. I owe Burnsy a lot for my career—giving me a start and an opportunity.

Dennis Green

Dennis Green was my head coach for eight years. The team did well. I finished my career in Tampa Bay with Coach Tony Dungy. I had a few different coaches along the way. You pick up what you can from each one and take it with you, and that's what I did.

John Michels

My first offensive line coach with the Vikings was John Michels. When I went into the Hall Of Fame, I'd made sure Johnny was there with me. I would say that he's the one who offered me the bus ticket, the roadmap, and the apple. I could've sworn I was going to be cut every day. Even when I started playing, I was still the person who took the brunt of the criticism in the meeting room because I was the young guy on the line. Johnny would go to battle for you, though. No one could talk about his offensive line. No one could yell at his offensive linemen, no one could get in his offensive line.

Basically, Johnny would just step up and do the job, but he made you learn. You had to know every defense against every situation and what the play could be. To this day, I still call him up and we talk. He actually chews me up for the first five or ten minutes of our conversation just to let me know he can still do it. He is amazing. Johnny, his wife Ann, and all his kids ... I still do stuff with his daughters who live here in Minnesota. John Michels is the coach that I owe a lot to.

Toughest Defensive Lineman

Besides my teammates, Jerome Brown was the toughest defensive lineman. He used to give me headaches. He is probably the one player I would watch even more film of than I normally would, just to make sure he wasn't going to have the upper hand on me. He was the first big guy inside, but he'd be considered small today. He was about 300 pounds, but he had size, speed, and quickness. He reminded me of John Randle, just a little bigger, and he used to give me headaches. I would never tell him that. After the game we'd talk and everything, but during the game it was all business.

Rich Gannon
Rich Gannon was a good player. He was a good student of the game too. He was that way when he was with the Vikings. He just didn't get the opportunity in Minnesota with everything going on.

When he went to the Raiders, he did what I knew he could do all along. He just got that opportunity and he ran with it. Gannon was fun. He ran when he was with us. He used to take off with the ball a little more. He was a student at the game, always studying, and always prepared. So it didn't shock me when he went to the Raiders and did what he did.

Prefer Run Blocking Or Pass Blocking
I preferred run blocking. I loved it when I could impose my will on the other guy. That's how you wear them down. You get to go out and pound defensive lineman for 70 or 80 plays a game. By the end of the of the game, if you were run blocking more than pass blocking, it took a lot out of the defensive linemen. You had to be able to pass block, but if I had my choice, I'd rather run block any day of the week.

I'll admit it now, I held on every play. If the defensive linemen were foolish enough to let me get my hands inside and put them where I needed to, I'd really put my hands in there.

It is easier to work with your hands a little more in run blocking because you've got more body, more surface. You try to get the defensive linemen to go where they don't want to go, but you can work the hands a lot more on the run blocking.

Favorite Running Back To Block For
I loved blocking for Robert Smith, Smitty. I don't know how fast that guy really was. It was like he was never going all out with the stride that he had. Robert was a great one to block for. I enjoyed it. I knew that if an offensive lineman opened a hole up, and in that brief

moment, if Robert got through it, no one was going to run him down. Robert was fun to watch for that.

I loved watching Terry Allen for his toughness. He'd bang it in there between the tackles and he tried to punish people. Between those two though, I'd go with Robert Smith.

Randy Moss
It didn't have to be an open field, Randy Moss just ran by everybody. I don't think anyone was quick enough to keep up with him. He came out in his rookie year in 1998, and introduced himself to the world. The guy was fun to watch. He had about 17 touchdowns as a rookie. He was just amazing.

I think that was the same year we set the scoring record. Moss changed the game. We had power receivers with speed. They could go deep. Moss was a game changer.

Pro Football Hall Of Fame Induction
I experienced a little bit of all the emotions: I was excited, humbled, and honored when I found out I was selected. It's something you don't plan for and never expect. You just go out and play and do what you do. I enjoyed my 14 years playing in the NFL, but to get that phone call on that day was something else. It still feels like it just happened yesterday.

Being in the Hall, I'm in a place where I don't think I belong. I can sit down and ask Tom Mack questions about what he did with Ram's back in the day. He can tell me all about Deacon Jones, if Deacon's not there to say it himself. I get to hear all the stories about Merlin Olsen. Then I can sit with Gale Sayers, Earl Campbell, and all those guys.

What a thrill it is just to be sitting in a room with all that history there and listening to their stories. It's been quite an honor. I still can't believe that I'm there, and I'm in there with them. You sit there with guys you played with and guys you sat and watched play with your dad beside you.

When I was inducted, my dad got to come to the Hall with my family. The most fun was when my dad was in the hotel with me, and all of the other Hall Of Fame players. My dad and I would meet every morning at six a.m. after I had my workout. I would ask him if he got the autographs that he was looking for. He would say, "Yes." I then asked, "Did you get them to sign twice?" He responded, "Yes. I got yours, too." My dad was collecting autographs for me too, and the guys did realize it. Some guys told me, "Your dad keeps asking us for two autographs." I responded, "Well, yeah, one's for me."

It was fun. It's fun to be around those guys. Any opportunity I have, whether it's a charity event or somewhere where there are more than five or ten Hall Of Famers, I just sit back and listen to them tell stories. It's fun to hear how they played and what they did. They're the ones who paved the way for all of us, and the young kids now playing. I owe them a ton for what they did and what they sacrificed to make the game what it is today.

Offensive Linemen Are The Smartest Players
Everybody says it's the quarterback who is the smartest player, but a lot of times the quarterback can't make his calls until the center and the line set the blocking. The quarterback can point everything out, but the linemen have to know just as much as the quarterback. We have to know who's blocking whom. We have to know where the help's coming from, where the help's not coming from. We have to see it before they see it. Then we have to do it all as one guy, five guys moving as one. It's fun seeing five guys who don't have to talk, working together. Sometimes you make your calls for the other guys so they know where they're supposed to go, but then nothing needs to be said from that point on. It's snapping the ball and everybody is working in unison. When you get a line that's been together, you can do that. It's just a fun thing to watch.

Decision To Retire (Next Season Tampa Bay Buccaneers Win Super Bowl)
I've always been one of those guys who once my decision is made, I don't look back. Playing in the NFL for fourteen years was good enough for me. I was ready to go. My body was ready to go. I told myself I was going to walk away while the game was still fun, while I

could still do the things that I loved to do, and that's what I did. I have no regrets.

I called Jeff Christy the night they won the Super Bowl and left him a message. I got a phone call the following day at three in the morning, with him screaming and yelling. He said, "I know I woke you up, but I just had to let you know, you should've been here." I said, "Jeff, I'm not supposed to be there. I'm where I'm supposed to be right now." I let him know I enjoyed what he did. I got to play with those guys for that long, so I had no regrets I walked away when I walked away.

When I retired, I told the team they should go ahead and win the Super Bowl. They had a good team coming back. Jon Gruden had come in as head coach and they were changing some things around. I told them they had a great opportunity, so they shouldn't waste it. They went on and did what they were supposed to do.

Favorite Player Growing Up
I'm going to get in trouble. When I was a tight end in high school and during my first year of college, I loved watching Kellen Winslow. Then, I got to meet him and do events with him. That was fun.

When I was in middle school, I did a book report on Gale Sayers. Now, I'm sitting at a table with him, poking Tom Mack, and telling him, "That's Gale Sayers sitting next to me!"

I have done some events with Earl Campbell. One time I was in Austin, Texas, expecting to take a cab to the next event. Here comes Earl with his brother-in-law. They picked me up themselves.

Bob Lilly, Mr. Cowboy, is one of my dad's favorites. I've gotten to do stuff with him and John Hannah, the guard of all guards. I really don't have one particular favorite. There are a lot of favorites, but if I had to pick one, I'm going to get me in trouble, I'll go with Earl Campbell. It's been fun just getting to know him and the things that he did, as well as the things he's doing now. It's just a thrill to be around him.

Starting 202 Consecutive Games

I thank the good Lord above for looking out for me. I was a kid who never missed a day of school, from kindergarten thru 12th grade. When my brother and I would go out and play games we could both run into a wall, but I was the one who would get up and laugh about it. The good Lord is looking after me. I have been fortunate and I worked hard. I loved working out, I loved being prepared, and I loved being ready. I still workout now. I'm just blessed. I have been fortunate to have the right opportunities and things with my wife. There were times I didn't think I was going to be able to play, but somehow someone was looking out for me and I was able to play.

Minnesota Viking guard Randall McDaniel blocks for running back Herschel Walker. Photograph copyright Associated Press

Chapter 40

Dermontti Dawson

> College:
> Kentucky
>
> Career History:
> Pittsburgh Steelers (1988–2000)
>
> 2012 Pro Football Hall Of Fame Induction

<u>Bryan Station High School Football</u>
I played football during my ninth grade year. I was on the team, but I didn't play in any games. I was basically a practice dummy. I really didn't care too much for football. Of course, after that I said, "No football for me."

Right before my senior year, Steve Parker was hired as the football coach at my high school, Bryan Station Senior High in Lexington, Kentucky. I was coming out of chemistry or biology, and he had mistaken me for an adult or one of the parents. He said, "Sir, can I help you?" I said, "I attend school here." He said, "Huh?" He put his hands on my shoulders and said, "Where have you been all my life? Son, you need to play football."

He was the one who convinced me to go out for football. Then he had two of my buddies who were on the track team with me, Marc Logan and Cornell Burbage, convince me to go out and try out for football. I did and the rest is history. Marc and Cornell played in the NFL as well.

We lost in the state playoffs against Christian County. They went on after they beat us, and won the state championship. We had a pretty good team. It's just we were outmanned against Christian County because they had so many players on that team. They had separate everything, separate special teams, separate defense, and separate offense. They were like a college team when they came to our school to play us in the playoffs. I couldn't believe it.

College Choice
Like a lot of us in high school, we have somebody that we are in love with—a girlfriend. I was a year ahead of my girlfriend in school. We wanted to be together. I said, "The only way it's going to work out is if we both go to Kentucky." So, that's how I ended up at Kentucky. We were married for 23½ years, and then got a divorce a few years ago.

Reason Named Dermontti
My dad's younger sister had naming rights of all the kids. She was the biggest influence on my mom. All my brothers have DD as initials. I'm the oldest, Dermontti Dawson, then Demarcus Dawson (four years younger), Deshawn Dawson (ten years younger and born on the same day as me), and then there's Deaaron Dawson (eleven years younger).

Kentucky
The football, track, and baseball teams all stayed in the same dorm. We stayed in the low-rise Kirwan Complex. We didn't have the walk-in lodge. That was for the basketball team. They had a pretty laid out little pad there on campus. We weren't privy to that.

I was redshirted as a freshman at Kentucky. The biggest difference that I saw between high school and college football was the physical part of it. I was about 250 pounds and the college guys were much larger, stronger, and faster than me. It was just a much faster and more physical game than what I was used to in high school, and the athletes were much better.

Replacing Mike Webster At Center
I was drafted as a guard and ended up starting in the fourth game of my rookie year beside Mike Webster. During the off-season after my rookie year, Coach Chuck Noll came up to me and said he wanted me to try me at center. He wanted Chuck Lanza, a third-round draft choice in 1988, and me to fight it out, to see who was going to take over Mike's position. We battled it out in mini-camp and training camp. At a certain point in training camp, I was named the starter.

I really didn't have time to think about the pressure in replacing Mike. I think the media made more fuss about it than I did. Mike was in his 15th year in the league, and was a legend in Pittsburgh. Of course, those are big shoes for anybody to fill.

I really didn't put any pressure on myself. I kept telling the media, "Just give me time to learn the position and go from there. Let me get settled in and just go from there." I did not put any pressure on myself because there was already enough pressure on me from everybody else. Why should I have put more pressure on myself? All I was going to do was learn the offense, learn the center position, and just go from there.

Playing Center For Different Quarterbacks

The voice inflection of all quarterbacks is different. It's just something that you get used to the more you work with the guy. Your hand position, the way they like the ball delivered to them, all of that stuff is a factor. Making the switch from one quarterback to another is a simple fix and not a hard transition. As long as the quarterback knows how you snap it, then you can accommodate him. It's not a big transition to a new quarterback.

Chuck Noll

I look up to Chuck Noll in awe because of who he was and what he accomplished as a coach. He was a very knowledgeable man about various subjects, and a great guy. He was one of those guys who had accomplished everything football-wise, in his life. I was just in awe and very, very proud that I had the chance to play under his coaching for four years.

Bill Cowher

The difference between Coach Cowher and Coach Noll was that Coach Noll had pretty much accomplished everything. Coach Noll was calm and relaxed. He would get upset every now and then, and let you know about his displeasure. Coach Cowher came in and he was much younger, not too much older than I was at the time. He still had that fire in his belly for the game. Not to say Coach Noll didn't have that fire, but it was a different kind of enthusiasm. Coach Cowher was right in the mix with all of the guys. He was running sprints right in the middle of a drill, yelling and screaming. He was just into it. He was a great coach to play for. I had the pleasure of playing nine years for Coach Cowher. All I can say is, it was a pleasurable nine years.

Uniform Number Not Reissued

The Steelers don't officially retire uniform numbers, but my number hasn't been reissued since I retired. It's a great honor for somebody not to have been assigned my number after I finished. That says a lot about the Steelers organization and how they embrace guys who have done well over their career. It's a big honor that nobody has been issued my number, but I wouldn't be mad if someone wore it.

To have your number not reissued to another player, is a sign of respect for the player who gave his all throughout his career. It's a big honor.

Favorite Moment In NFL

My favorite moment in the NFL was after we won that AFC Championship game against the Colts and we were going to play in Super Bowl XXX. It was always a dream of mine to play in the Super Bowl. Even though we lost the Super Bowl, we made it there. We didn't accomplish what we wanted, which was to win, but we made it there.

I thought that we would get back to the Super Bowl, but it was so hard. I don't care how well or how much success you have during a season, there is no guarantee that you're going to make it. There are so many different variables that play a role in making the playoffs or Super Bowl.

I was surprised we didn't play in another Super Bowl because we had a good run and played in AFC Championship Games. We lost two AFC Championship Games, then we finally won the one against the Colts. I thought we had a chance to make another run, unfortunately, it didn't happen.

Pro Football Hall Of Fame Induction

I found out I was selected for the Pro Football Hall Of Fame right before the selection show. The protocol was you needed to be by your phone right before the show came on. They would call you and let you know that you made it as an inductee.

I didn't find out until the selection show itself, after Jack Butler's name was announced. Stephen Perry, the President of the Pro Football

Hall of Fame was announcing the inductees and then he announced me. I was in pure shock. I just couldn't believe it and then my phone went haywire— phone calls, texts. I had a massive amount of calls and texts coming in.

Canton was special the year I was inducted. It was great to see all the Steelers fans out there. It was even more special for Pittsburgh, since there were four guys associated with Pittsburgh in one way or another who were inducted. That year, Curtis Martin, Chris Doleman, Jack Butler, and I were inducted. There was a ton of black and gold at that Hall of Fame induction.

Being enshrined is not something that you deserve. It's something that is rewarded to you based on your play, longevity, and consistency. It's an honor to be named and enshrined in the Pro Football Hall of Fame with some of the great players that I looked up to, and some of the guys that I respect to this day. It's just a great honor.

Technique Of Pulling From The Center Position
It really makes me feel old when guys say, "Our coach used to show us tapes of you playing to teach us how to pull from the center position." It's flattering that they use my tape as an example of what they want to accomplish on offense. It's a humbling experience and an honor as well.

Decision To Retire
It's always tough when you consider playing for another team. I think it's even tougher when it's not on your own accord. I had to retire due to an injury. Even after the Steelers cut me, I still had trainers who knew about my condition say, "We just want you to play on Sundays. We're not worried about you practicing in training camp." I said, "That's flattering, but I just don't think I can do it anymore."

At that time, I wasn't going to move my family. I didn't want to go thru all the pain and stuff that I'd suffered through with the hamstring tendon. To this day, my hamstrings still hurt and ache 24/7. I didn't want to have that be a burden on another team.

Photograph copyright Associated Press

Chapter 41

Thurman Thomas

> College:
> Oklahoma State
>
> Career History:
> Buffalo Bills (1988–1999)
> Miami Dolphins (2000)
>
> 2007 Inductee Pro Football Hall Of Fame

College Choice
Growing up in Texas, I wanted to go to the University of Texas. At the time, Fred Akers was the head coach. When I walked into his office and we started talking, his exact words were, "We're all set at the running back position. We'd love for you to play defensive back." I knew being 5'9½" there was no way that I was going to play defensive back. I left that meeting scratching my head because my idol, Earl Campbell, went to University of Texas and I followed them throughout my years in junior high and high school.

So, I went to Texas A&M next, where Jackie Sherrill was the head coach. I felt this has got to be the place in Texas for me. Jackie said the same thing, that he wanted me to play defensive back. So, I was thinking I have to go somewhere where they want me to play running back.

I got a call from Jimmy Johnson at Oklahoma State asking me to take a visit. I went there and Jimmy said to me, "I heard that Texas and Texas A&M want you to play defensive back. Well, I'll tell you what. If you come here you're going to be 6th in line for the running back position, and it's up to you to work your way up." I said

"Coach, you've got a deal. I'm coming to Oklahoma State." That's how it happened.

I'm just thankful that I was there a couple of years before Barry Sanders got there. He ended up winning the Heisman Trophy the year after I left. The two years I that I spent with Barry, I really didn't know that he was going to be that explosive. Once he broke through in college and went to the Detroit Lions, he just burst on the scene. He had an outstanding, fabulous career.

Pat Jones
Even though Jimmy Johnson recruited me, Pat Jones ended up being the head coach at Oklahoma State University when Jimmy went to the University of Miami. Pat was just a great guy. We used to run up the middle the entire time. I probably carried the ball about 35 times a game and 30 of the rushes would be right up the gut between the two guards.

He was just a tough individual. I think the first thing he said to us when he became head coach was, "We may not be the most talented football team in the NCAA, but we will be the most in shape guys in the NCAA." We knew at that point we were going to be running our tails off. He was a big proponent of being conditioned and being conditioned for the 4th quarter. He was just a great guy to be around.

Favorite Game In College
The 1987 Sun Bowl and the 1984 Gator Bowl, I would probably put 1 and 1A as my favorite college games. The 1987 season was the first 10 game season Oklahoma State ever had. We went down and beat South Carolina that year. We were nationally ranked and finished ranked 5th or 6th in the country that year. I was a freshman at the time.

When I was in the Sun Bowl back in my home state of Texas, I had a lot of family come down for that Bowl game. We went up against West Virginia. I think the Gator Bowl and the Sun Bowl were probably running neck and neck for my favorite games I ever played in an Oklahoma State uniform.

NFL Draft
I had no clue that the Buffalo Bills were going to draft me. I thought I might be drafted in the first round, but it didn't happen. The Buffalo Bills running backs coach Elijah Pitts, came to visit me at Oklahoma State, but so did a lot of running backs coaches from around the league. I actually thought I was going to be drafted by the Los Angeles Rams, Atlanta Falcons, or my hometown Houston Oilers. After I dropped down to the 2nd round, I got a call from the Buffalo Bills and they said, "If these next two teams don't pick you, we're going to pick you at number 40."

Being from the South, I had never been farther north than Oklahoma. I thought it would be pretty exciting going to New York. I'd be close to the Knicks and Yankees. I got to Buffalo and it was just a total culture shock. It is just so far away from New York City.

Weather In Buffalo
Sometimes during mini camp there was snowfall. It wasn't just flurries that would hit the ground and go away, they would stick. We had some mini camps where there was snow on the ground for a couple of days. It was kind of a culture shock for a lot of the young players.

Marv Levy
Marv Levy was awesome. He was just a genuine, great guy. He was a history major at Coe College. A lot of the stuff he said to us was regarding American History. He let his coaches, coach. Marv would come up to you after a game and tell you how great you did, or things that you needed to work on. More importantly, he was a guy who always asked how your family was doing. He was more concerned about how your family was, how you were doing, and how everything was going on and off the field. He was just an awesome coach and a guy who deserved to go into the Pro Football Hall of Fame.

Origin Of Buffalo Bills No-Huddle Offense
Jim Kelly and Ted Marchibroda, who was offensive coordinator at the time, said we work really well in the two-minute offense, why don't we try to do it for the entire game. Marv really didn't want it to do that, but we started running it, and were really effective at it.

Marv said, "Okay, if that's what you guys want to do, you go ahead and do it." Sometimes we would score within 30 seconds with one or two plays. Sometimes we would have drives of 10-12 plays, but we were still continuing to run the no-huddle.

There were some times where Bruce Smith and Darryl Talley said, "Hey man, can you give us a break? You are all scoring too fast." That was the pace we wanted. That was the pace that even the offensive linemen wanted. They liked the up-tempo offense, because they knew what they were doing, and the defense had to get set. The defense had to substitute and things like that. It was part of not just the two-minute drill, it was the entire offense.

Jim Kelly and Ted Marchibroda worked really well together. Even during the week, sometimes Jim would always call his plays. When we were out on the football field, it was all Jim. Ted had nothing to do with the plays that Jim called. Jim had a great feel for the game. If we were running the ball effectively, Jim was going to stick with the run. If we're passing the ball effectively, Jim was going to stick with the pass.

Jim had a great sense of what we needed to do at certain times. Our center, the late Kent Hull, was a big factor in it, too. Sometimes Jim would call a running play and it might be the wrong play to run. Kent would look back and say, "No, you can't run that. You've got to run something else." Jim would call all the plays 95% of the time. The only time Ted even got to call plays was when we were in a short yardage goal line situation.

<u>Houston Oilers vs. Buffalo Bills Playoff Game (The Comeback)</u>
Being down 35-3 to Houston at that point in time, you want to maybe score a couple of touchdowns, and make the game a little bit closer. Darryl Talley got as many guys as he possibly could on the sideline, and looked everybody in the eyes and said, "Now we got them right where we want them." Everybody was like, really? It's 35 to 3.

We started coming back, and all of a sudden the momentum shifted. The crowd really got into it. People who had left were trying to get back into the stadium. Once we got that momentum, man, it was something to be around. You could tell the Houston Oilers were kind of in shock by what was happening. I was just happy to be a part of it.

The one guy that I really felt bad for was Warren Moon. Warren had been a great friend of mine for the first couple years that I was in the league and living in Houston. We used to work out a lot together and I really felt bad for him.

They had an outstanding team. They had a lot of Pro Bowlers and a lot of guys who knew how to play the game. You could just see Warren's reaction after the game. It looked like a lot of the players really wanted to cry. They really wanted to know what happened, how did we not win this football game?

It was a great game for us, and a bad game for them. You feel bad for those guys. Even though we won the game, you feel bad for them for not putting us away. We were able to come back and win the football game.

Favorite Of Four Super Bowls
When you play in four Super Bowls and lose four, there really is no favorite. You only think about what you could have done differently to try to win one. That was the mindset of our whole football team. We talked about it after every Super Bowl. It's just not a good feeling to have when you lose the Super Bowl, or any game. You try to come back the following weekend to correct things. With the Super Bowl being the last game of the season, we knew that we had to wait a full off-season to come back and try to get back to the Super Bowl and win.

The good thing is that the players became closer friends. We really cared about each other and our families. Anytime you lose a big game like the Super Bowl, and lose four Super Bowls in a row, you're obviously going to be hurting not only for your teammates and your family, but you're also going to be hurting for the fans of Buffalo, too.

People Saying Thurman Thomas Should Have Been MVP Of Super Bowl & Not Otis Anderson

A lot of people have said that, but I don't think that would have been any consolation to how I feel about not winning the game. Sure, it might have been nice, but you still would have had that L next to your team name after the Super Bowl. If I had a fail and a loss with my team, even if I would have got the MVP, it still would not have been a very good feeling.

Pro Football Hall Of Fame Induction

Obviously it was great to be inducted into the Pro Football Hall of Fame, and be in there with some of your heroes that you watched over the years. I got to meet Joe Greene, another hero of mine growing up. I try to go back for the enshrinement every year. I got inducted in 2007, and I've only missed two years since then. One year I missed was because my daughter graduated from the University of Florida. It's exciting to go back and see the returning enshrines and the new inductees.

My favorite part is going to the Ray Nitschke Luncheon which is just for Hall of Famers—no outsiders, no reporters, nobody. A couple Hall of Famers get up and talk. Willie Lanier, the great linebacker from the Kansas City Chiefs, leads the luncheon. They do a great job of organizing everything. We sit in a room for about 2½ hours and just talk football, really welcome the guys who are going in that year. It's great to go back and see guys that you grew up idolizing and guys you grew up watching on TV.

Ralph Wilson

Ralph Wilson was great. He was an owner who loved football, knew football, and knew stats. He knew about the weather where we were playing and the history of other teams. He was just a great guy.

Throughout the '90s, he met us on the road for away games. He would come down from Detroit Thursday or Friday, and spend nights with the team at the hotel. He always congratulated whether we won or lost.

I remember after every Super Bowl he would come in the locker room and shake everybody's hand. I got to know Ralph really well. Ralph got to know some of the other players really well, too. They would say, "Mr. Wilson just came up to me and said hey, great game. We wouldn't have got here without you." He told that to almost every single player on the football squad. He wanted to make sure that every player knew that he was behind us. He was just a great owner to be around.

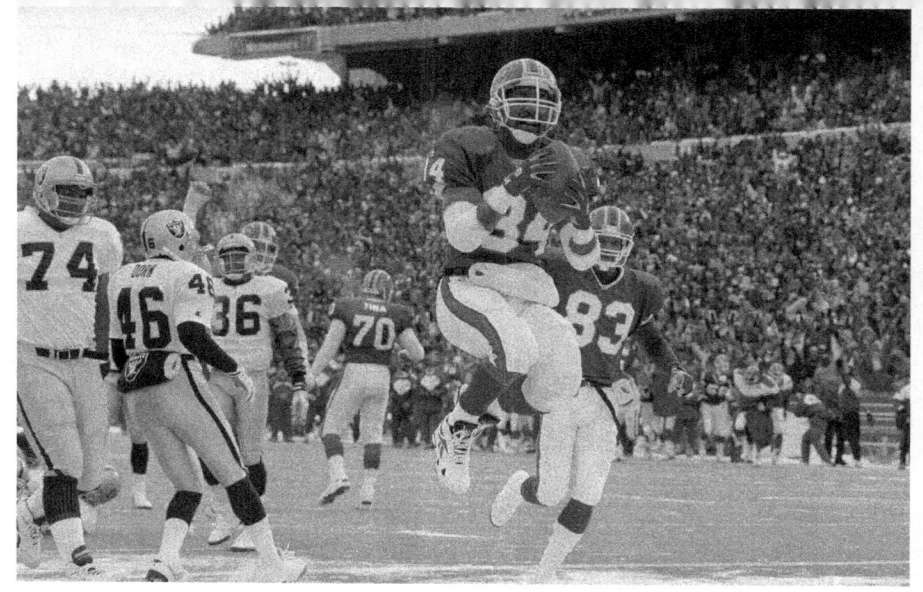

Photograph copyright Associated Press

Chapter 42

Tim Brown

> College:
> Notre Dame
>
> Career history
> Los Angeles / Oakland Raiders (1988–2003)
> Tampa Bay Buccaneers (2004)
>
> 2015 Inductee Pro Football Hall of Fame

College Choice
My parents and I were looking for a place where I would get a great education. The only school that came to the house talking about education, was Notre Dame. My parents were pretty impressed with their track record of graduating over ninety-eight percent of their athletes at the time. We didn't think I had a future in football so it was all about getting that education and coming back home and getting a good job.

SMU was attractive because I wanted to stay home and it's a great academic school. I knew if I went there, I would do well. With all the potential issues regarding SMU football that people were talking about then, my parents and I knew that it probably wasn't the best place for me to go. I graduated from high school when I was seventeen and I wanted to stay home. I wasn't ready to go fifteen hundred miles away to school. It came down to SMU and Notre Dame. With SMU and their potential problems, I really didn't have a choice but to go to Notre Dame.

First Two Years At Notre Dame
It was a pretty bad situation with the football team my first few years there. I told people I didn't go to Notre Dame for football. I went there for the academics. We had a tough two years. I think we went five and six both years. We just weren't a good football team. Unfortunately, they got rid of Coach Gerry Faust. He was one of the

greatest coaches I've been around as far as his ability to deal with players. On the field, it was just something totally different.

Lou Holtz
I knew right away that Lou Holtz knew exactly what he wanted to do and how he was going to get it done. The team felt as if we were a much more complete football team.

I think that his first year we went 6-5, but we really felt as if we had gone ten and one. We were really excited coming into my second year because we thought we had a chance. We were 8-1 until we met Penn State, and had a chance to go for the tie. We chose to go for the win and didn't get it. That knocked us out of the National Championship race.

Coach Holtz left it up to the captains and the seniors. It was our choice, whatever we wanted to do. If we wanted to go for the two points, we could. If we wanted to kick the extra point and tie the game, we could do that too. If we had tied, chances were we were going to be out of the National Championship race. Coach Holtz called the right play. Tony Rice just didn't pitch me the ball.

We were a great football team. Lou said when he first got there, that in three years he was going to win a National Championship, Sure enough, the next year after I was gone, they won it.

Touchdown Timmy
I believe it was the Notre Dame announcer who started calling me Touchdown Timmy. I think it was during a game when I scored that he said, "Touchdown Timmy". That was it; it stuck. It stuck with me throughout my NFL career too.

Winning Heisman Trophy
When I won the Heisman Trophy it was one of those moments that you really don't believe that it happened. I think by the time I got to the ceremony, I knew I had a good shot.

One of my teammates told me, "Well if somebody votes you third, then they shouldn't be voting anymore. You know everybody is going to vote you at least second. Don McPherson may win the East and

Gaston Green may win the West, but you're going to be second in all those regions. You're going to win this on second place votes alone."

That actually made a lot of sense to me but going into it, I still had no clue what was going to happen. It was an incredible moment, no doubt.

I don't know if playing at Notre Dame helped me win the Heisman or not. Jim Nantz asked me that question and I told him, "Look, I went to Notre Dame for one reason, and one reason alone—to get a great education. If it turns out that it helps me on the football field, then so be it."

I'm not apologetic for that. That certainly wasn't the reason I went there, but if it did help me with that, then God bless Notre Dame.

NFL Draft
I was hoping the Raiders would draft me. I was trying to get to them so I did everything I could to get to that pick. Once it got to the Raiders pick, I was hoping they would take me. They ended up taking me and it ended up being exactly what I wanted.

Early Seasons With Los Angeles Raiders
My rookie year I led the team in receptions because James Lofton and everybody else got hurt. I got hurt in my second year and missed fifteen games. I came back the next year and I was the third down guy and punt returner. I did that for two years and going into 1992, my fifth year, I was set to do the same thing. Then, Mervyn Fernandez got hurt the second or third game of the year. I ended up starting the rest of the year and the rest of my career.

Playing With Different Quarterbacks Throughout Time With Raiders
It was tough, but at the same time you knew that they had some ability. You just had to find out what that was and play to their strengths. That's what I was able to do.

Al Davis
Al Davis was great at times, and not so great at other times. I think that his overall legacy is going to be one of greatness and one of

excellence, because he won three Super Bowls and there are many Hall of Famers who played for him. You can't help but to be great, and he's in the Hall of Fame himself. So, from that standpoint it's a legacy of greatness and that's the way it should be.

Fred Biletnikoff & James Lofton
Fred Biletnikoff was my coach for fifteen years, so obviously I learned a lot from him. My rookie year, James Lofton stayed after practice with me and helped me get ready to play wide receiver.

Freddy and I spent many, many, many hours together in the classroom and on the field. Every once in a while, Freddy would drop nuggets of what he did when he played, or suggest to me what I should be thinking. He was very, very helpful.

Toughest Cornerback
Probably Dale Carter and James Hasty. Going against those guys twice a year was pretty tough. They were incredibly difficult guys to play against, but I managed to have some success against them. They sort of brought out the best in you.

Jerry Rice Signing With Raiders
I was really excited about Jerry Rice signing with the Raiders. I remember getting the call from Bruce Allen saying that they were going to do that. I said, "Do it yesterday and bring him in."

The next thing I knew, I saw Jerry Rice on CNN running routes with the Raiders. It was the right move. It was great for my career. I think we may have even have extended Jerry's career a couple years.

Playing In Super Bowl
It was great playing in the Super Bowl. It was year fifteen for me in the NFL when I got an opportunity to play for the World Championship. It was an amazing feeling.

We definitely had the better team that season, no doubt about it. We had the number one offense that year and our defense was ranked in the top ten. Everything that could go wrong just went wrong, and it ended up being what it was. It was still an incredible experience.

Defining Moment In Career
I don't know if there was a moment. I think for me, just being consistent for all those years was the thing that I may be known for rather than having one incredible, great year. I think I'm the only receiver in the history of the NFL that had ten years with seventy-five catches. I think that's good enough.

Waiting Six Years To Be Selected For Pro Football Hall Of Fame
The selection process is gut wrenching, and I wish there was a different way the Pro Football Hall of Fame could do it. I guess there isn't. If there were some kind of parameter list, I think it would make it a lot easier. Then guys would understand if you hit this number, it's going to take you two years. If you hit this number, it's going to take you five years. There needs to be something because this process is grueling, no doubt about it. I'm glad to see Charles Haley get in. I'm hoping that Kevin Greene (enshrined following year) gets in pretty soon. Kevin has been waiting nine or ten years. Haley waited eleven years. That's just way too long to be on the top fifteen list every year.

The wide receivers position is a tough position for the voters for some reason. I think it's only going to get tougher with all the guys becoming eligible. If they are having a problem deciding because of us playing in what they call the "Passer Era", I don't know how they're going to be able to navigate around these guys when they become eligible. We'll see what happens. It's just a tough deal. It took six years, but at least we got it done.

Photograph copyright Associated Press

Chapter 43

John Randle

> College:
> Texas A&I–Kingsville
>
> Career History:
> Minnesota Vikings (1990–2000)
> Seattle Seahawks (2001–2003)
>
> 2010 Inductee Pro Football Hall Of Fame

College Choice
It was called Texas A&I Kingsville when I got there. My junior college coach, Keith Waters, was hired at Texas A&I as the linebackers coach. I followed him down there a year later.

Describing the City of Kingsville, I will put it in the words of Tom Moore, the former offensive coordinator for the Indianapolis Colts. He went down to Texas A&I one time and said, "If a man had six months to live and he went down to Kingsville, Texas, that would be the longest six months of his life."

It's a town of about 2,000 people down in South Texas. There wasn't anything to do but play basketball, lift weights, and watch cars pass by.

Visiting Brother Playing For Tampa Bay Buccaneers
Going down to Tampa and seeing my brother, who played for Tampa Bay, at camp was kind of like a high school moment. I faced the same thing in high school. My brother started high school before me and everybody was telling me, "This is where your brother did this, this is where your brother did that." It kind of reassured me that going down there wasn't the right idea for me.

Basically they did me a favor by telling me I was too small to play defensive line. I went down to Tampa Bay and said, "I want to play defensive line." They responded, "No, you're going to play linebacker like your brother." I said, "Okay, I can see why you guys are putting me in his category." But, I knew in my mind I was a defensive lineman. It didn't take long for me to make up my mind and leave.

I thought I would be drafted. Coming out of a small school, you don't really know what teams are thinking about you, especially in the late '80s. I thought I had a chance to be drafted, though. I sat around for two days, all day, waiting for somebody to call and tell me I was drafted. At some point, I felt embarrassed. I just said, "You know what, if it doesn't happen, it doesn't happen."

My first contract was about $50,000 before taxes. They gave me a signing bonus of about $5,000, which was basically $3,000 after taxes. It wasn't all about the money, it was just being able to make it. I knew in the back of my mind that I wanted to give it a try, because I said to myself, "If I don't try this, I will regret this for the rest of my life." I've said that to myself a few times in life, but this time I said, "You know what, starting today, I'm going to change. I'm not going to be that kid who grew up in a town of 150 people. I'm going to be a guy that all of a sudden says you know what, I'm going to stand for something." I'm going to at least try out.

Transition To NFL
It was a huge transition, because the year before, I was watching some of these guys on TV. These guys played at schools with their names on the back of their jerseys, and I'm a Division II player coming into this big place, not a draft pick, but as a free agent. I thought that I was going to a new school on the first day. I just felt completely out of place.

I knew one place that I kind of felt everybody had a decent shot was on the football field. I had faced that when I went to a junior college, then when I went to Texas A&I. I felt out of place at those two places, but the one place that I felt comfortable at was on the football field. On the football field, it didn't matter where you came from or who you were, your athletic ability and your talents would give you a better chance of playing. It didn't matter where you came from, it was just about who you were on the football field.

Vikings Defensive Line
When I got to Minnesota, they had Keith Millard at defensive tackle, Henry Thomas at nose guard, Chris Doleman at defensive end, and Al Noga. These guys would sit around with each other like they had known each other for 10 years.

The two things I looked up before going to Minnesota were the guys' weights and heights. Al Noga was about 6' tall, Henry Thomas was around 6'2", Chris Doleman was 6'5", and Keith Millard was about 6'6". They all weighted about 260, and I said to myself, you know what, I can at least kind of fit in with these guys' weights. When I got there and saw those guys, I knew I had a long way to go.

Goals As Player
I see things differently than most people do. Most people sit around, calculate, and say, "I accomplished this; I accomplished that." At the end of the 1993 season, I was looking forward to 1994. I wanted to prove that I was the best defensive tackle in the league. Every year I wasn't looking back, I was looking forward. I said to myself, "What can I improve on from 1993, to make 1994 even better?"

John Teerlinck, our defensive line coach, had similar thoughts about always looking forward and getting better. Just because the guys that are in the room one year, doesn't mean all of those same guys are going to be the next year. That was kind of how I was looking at things.

Practicing Against Randall McDaniel
In practice all I did was go against Randall McDaniel. In games teams were going against both Randall and Gary Zimmerman. My mindset was if you can't do it in practice, there's no way in hell you can do it in a game. My mamma taught me this saying, "Responsibility starts at home." So my thing was, it starts at home practice, everything starts there.

I remember my first year with Paul Wiggin, the Vikings defensive line coach. I was going against Randall and maybe once every two weeks, I would win a drill against Randall. Paul Wiggin came to me and said, "What are you doing? Why are you going against Randall?" I said, "He makes me better." He said, "But you're not beating him." He told me to go against one of the other guys. I did and I just clobbered them. I just started taking these guys and tossing them to the side, left and right. Paul Wiggin comes back over and says, "Go back to going against Randall McDaniel. I see what you're doing and I like it."

That was what I was doing, I was always looking to get better. Going against Randall, I didn't win a lot. I knew if I could do something against Randall that was very productive, in the game it was surely going to work.

Playing Against Green Bay Packers
The state of Minnesota and the state of Wisconsin are side by side. I still live in Minnesota. Every year during Packer week, you see people driving from Green Bay with Packers flags on their cars. That just pissed off my teammates and me. To me, it felt like they were almost invading our state. When we played against Green Bay, it was almost like that Texas-Oklahoma rivalry coming up again. When we played the Packers, it was the bright lights and the State of Minnesota versus the State of Wisconsin.

When I went in the stadium every time we played against Green Bay, I got booed, but I liked it. I liked getting booed by the Packers fans because that just made it even more special for me. Here I am, a kid from Mumford, Texas with a population of 150 people, and I'm walking onto Lambeau Field and they're calling my name. I'm going, "Wow, they know who I am." To me it was like being the villain in Wisconsin.

Reggie White and I used to talk about it all the time. Reggie would tell me, "Take it easy on our quarterback." I would respond "Reggie, if you were back there, I would take you down." I'm sorry, Reg, you're a Packer, I'm a Viking. We're not supposed to get along. That's the way it is."

I always loved going against Brett Favre because he was a true competitor. He was like the neighborhood kid who was always beating everybody. You always looked forward to going against that guy, trying to take him down since he was that good; he was that talented.

Trash Talking

I didn't really trash talk a lot on quarterbacks. I got Trent Dilfer kicked out of a game at the Metrodome one year because we kept messing with him and talking trash to him. Trent thought we were trying to hurt him. Somebody tripped me (or something) and all I could do was just try to reach out and grab his shoe. He thought I was trying to take his leg out. He dropped down on the ground and started punching me, and they kicked him out of the game.

My way of thinking was to get in the head of the offensive linemen. I would say little things to get him unfocused. I knew offensive linemen have a tendency of not listening to everything that's going on, especially when the quarterback is calling out the cadence.

Every Monday, the opposing team's media guides would come out. The team would give you a stack of 200-300 pages containing stories about the team you were going against. I would sit there and read the stories about the offensive linemen. I would take the information and put it in my memory. I could remember all the stuff about these guys. As the game was going on, I could bring it up at the right moment. You could tell a guy something, and all of a sudden he would seem like he was in total shock that you knew his wife's name, his kid's name, his dad's name, the name of his car, and where he got his car from. All of a sudden the offensive lineman is asking you questions like, "How do you know that?" I'd just look at him and smile. The lineman would keep asking me, "How do you know that?" All of a sudden the quarterback is trying to pull the offensive lineman in the huddle, and the offensive lineman is shoving the quarterback, telling him to get out of the way. The next thing you know, those two guys are fighting or arguing in the huddle, and I would go, "Hey, my job is done." I would do things like that. It was fun to do stuff like that.

For example, a guy said in the media guide that his wife goes to every game and sits at the 50-yard line. This guy's playing really physical and I would say, "Nice job, really nice job. I can really tell that you really have been practicing all week, anticipating me coming out here and playing against you. I can also see that your wife Susan is over there at the 50-yard line, and she's really enjoying it. You know what? If I beat you on one play, Susan is going to be disappointed. What do you think Susan's going to think about that?"

All of a sudden he's going, "How do you know my wife's named Susan?" I'd say, "Don't worry about that." Again he's asks, "How do you know my wife's named Susan?" In would respond, "I don't know, maybe because ... she grew up in ... what was that town? She grew up in Michigan, right? She went to the University of Michigan. You know what, I spent some time up at the University of Michigan, hanging out there." Then the quarterback is trying to get him back in the huddle. He's saying, "No, no, no. I want to know how he knows my wife is named Susan and that she went to the University of Michigan." I was like, "I'll tell you later. I'll tell you later."

Every couple of weeks, you'd get a guy who says, "You're not going to get in my head." "Okay. No. I'm not trying to get in your head. I'm not trying to get in." He was like, "You can't talk to me." I would be already in his head.

It was just getting guys pissed off. The quarterback sometimes wouldn't want to give up a sack and he'd just throw the ball and throw an interception. The quarterback would say, "I didn't give you a sack." I would respond, "No, you didn't, but it was an interception, so thank you anyway."

First Career Interception
When I was running after intercepting the ball, my teammate Eddie McDaniel, was yelling, "Toss me the ball." He yelled again, "I told you to toss me the ball." I said, "Dude, listen. This is my first interception, and you want me to toss the ball to you? No, no. I don't get many of these, so I'm not going to toss this." I got run down, and I told the guy I was going in slow motion. I felt like I was in quicksand. It was the most unusual feeling in the world.

Best Running Back
The best running back I played against was Barry Sanders. Monday morning was when you went into the team's facility for film review. Everybody would hope they didn't make Barry's highlight tape. You'd have a guy do a 360, trying to keep up with Barry.

Barry could be backed up on the goal line, and all of a sudden run 25 yards. It was as if Barry was running to classical music, his shoulders would move and it was just ... it was like the guy with the flute and the cobra. Barry's running style would almost lull you to sleep.

Emmitt Smith had a great offensive line. Emmitt wasn't a pushover, but his offensive line was devastating. Dallas had Larry Allen, who bench pressed 692. I'll never forget that. When I read that in those media guides, I said, "This dude bench pressed 692 pounds." Then we were talking about Nate Newton. I said, "Man, Nate Newton. He's big, but Nate can't bench press 692 pounds."

Daryl Johnston, the Dallas fullback wasn't any joke either. If Barry had Dallas offensive linemen, Barry would be still running today.

Pro Football Hall Of Fame Induction
The Pro Football Hall of Fame Induction was unbelievable. Growing up in Texas, Sunday was a day of going to church and then watching football. It was unbelievable. To be inducted was a dream come true for a kid from Texas. It's hard to explain, but it's unbelievable, because I have found myself among my childhood heroes. When I want go back for inductions now, most of the older guys sit up front and talk about old times. Sitting there with Roger Staubach, Dick Butkus, Earl Campbell, and those guys, it's almost like going back in time.

For me, I grew up loving the game and appreciated watching the game. It's like when a person goes to Disney World and they're walking around, looking at everything and they're going, "My God." To me, being around those guys is almost the same thing, because they're all sitting over there. I was sitting there one year with Franco Harris, John Madden, and Lynn Swann. All of the guys are talking. It's like going back in time. I'm a history guy, so I am fascinated with history. Going to Canton and sitting around with these guys, is like a childhood dream.

Chris Doleman
Chris Doleman taught me a lot my rookie year. He taught me how to respect the game and be professional. He was almost like my big

brother on the football field because he taught me so much. I have so much respect for Dole. I was lucky to be around Chris Doleman, Henry Thomas, Keith Millard, and Al Noga when I came into the league. It was like business on Sundays with those guys, but any other day, we were having fun. Later on in my career, I tried to teach and show the younger guys who I played with, the same thing.

Playing For Seattle Seahawks
It was completely different. I had to get used to drinking a lot of coffee and just being in a different world. At the same time, I had so much fun out there and met so many people. The organization was great to be around. I was welcomed with open arms. I still talk to a lot of guys out there in Seattle. That's even where my wife learned to cook. I just had to get used to the rain. It was so different, but at the same time, my wife and I had a chance to discover Seattle together, and it was fun.

Mike Holmgren
Mike Holmgren had so much respect for me. When I got to Seattle, he said he couldn't believe that Minnesota let me go. I said, "One person's junk is another man's treasure."

I had just gotten married, and he taught me a lot about being a dad. It was great to see, because I had always wondered what he was like from watching him on the other side of the field. Being there with him, I got to see what he was all about, and I was lucky to get the chance to do that.

Comparing Playing Defensive End To Defensive Tackle
When a defensive end gets double-teamed, he's getting double-teamed by a tight end and the offensive tackle. When you're a defensive tackle getting double-teamed, it's by the center and the guard or it's the guard and tackle. I don't want to make anybody mad, but it's definitely harder to get a sack inside than it is outside.

Photograph copyright Associated Press

Chapter 44

Aeneas Williams

> College:
> Southern University
>
> Career History:
> Phoenix/Arizona Cardinals (1991–2000)
> St. Louis Rams (2001–2004)
>
> 2014 Inductee Pro Football Hall Of Fame

College Choice
I started playing football when I was four years old, playing all the way through high school. After I graduated high school, I immediately started summer school at Southern University. The reason I didn't play is because my brother Achilles, who was two grades ahead of me, wasn't playing football. My entire goal was to get to Southern and really just follow and do everything that my brother did. He graduated with his degree in accounting in three and a half years because he went to school year-round, attending summer school. I was on pace to graduate in three years.

After Achilles graduated, he called me and said, "Little brother, slow down. You'll be working the rest of your life." It was then that I began to attempt to discover whom in the world I was. Prior to that time, I was Achilles's little brother and I was satisfied with that.

Two things happened that were instrumental in my life at that time; number one, I ended up committing my life to Jesus Christ. In that commitment, I began to understand the nature of [my] purpose as it relates to human beings and other things that are in the world. I also realized, in my heart, I always loved playing football.

The second thing that happened was it entered into my heart, to go walk on the football team. So a week before the season started, I joined the team. The coach allowed me to do it, and the rest is history.

Tying NCAA Record For Most Interceptions In A Season
It was studying, working hard, and working on catching the ball. My second year playing in college I had seven interceptions. The first year after walking on, I had two. I always loved catching interceptions and the impact of how it changed a game.

Joining Cardinals
When the Cardinals drafted me, I knew what to expect. I graduated high school in 1986. Maurice Hurst graduated in 1985, and was one of my mentors. Maurice also played at Southern. He was drafted in the fourth round, as a cornerback by the New England Patriots. Kevin Lewis, valedictorian of the class 1984, the same graduating class as my brother, signed with the 49ers as a free agent cornerback.

Every summer, I got to train with those guys and all the players who were in college or playing in the pros, because they came home to New Orleans during the summer. We would all train at Tulane University. I would compete against professional players. I spent the most time around Maurice and Kevin. They helped acclimate me to the climate and speed of the NFL.

When I got to the Cardinals, it wasn't a culture shock for me at all. It was actually an environment that I was already familiar with.

I didn't understand the magnitude of all the draft choices in 1991. Our first round pick was Eric Swann, who was one of the more dominant interior defensive linemen during the time that he played. Larry Allen, who's a Hall of Famer, told me how difficult it was for him when he had to compete against Eric Swann. Our second round pick was Mike Jones, a defensive tackle from NC State. We wanted to be a draft class that would come in and make our mark, and more importantly be the best that we could be individually, and hopefully collectively.

Focus Not On Money
Money, honestly influences a lot. I learned quickly that if I worked to develop my potential, understood what I was doing, was an asset to my

team, helped us win or did whatever I could to help us win, and exceled, the money would come. So if I developed my potential and became one of the best and reliable players, I always knew the money would come. So my focus was never the money.

Having Two Interceptions Against Troy Aikman In A Playoff Game

My number one goal was to prepare myself, and prepare our team, to beat one of the best teams of our day who had beaten us, literally every time. We had to win the last four games of the season to get in the playoffs, and we weren't expected to win against Dallas. So all I wanted to do was to compete. I knew my assignment was to be matched up on Michael Irvin the entire game. If he went to the restroom, I had to go to the restroom with him.

I knew what my assignment was, and I just wanted to make sure my teammates could trust that I would be able to compete with Michael. It wasn't that he wouldn't make some plays, but when I had the opportunity to make plays, I was able to. We were able to upset Dallas in that game. Then everybody was on notice. That's just the natural bi-product of excellence.

So my goal or my thoughts were never, "Man, now people are going to recognize me." That never was a conscious thought in my mind. It was a conscious thought in my mind to reach my potential, and that was what you were going to see.

Gill Byrd

I had some mentors, particularly Gill Byrd who played cornerback for the San Diego Chargers. He had already played for ten years when I befriended him my second year in the league, after we played the Chargers. I asked Mr. Byrd (I called him that at the time) if he would help me learn how to play the cornerback position. From that time on, my wife Tracy and I would go to San Diego every off-season, and stay at their home. He would take me to the Chargers facility and help me understand how to play the cornerback position at an excellent level.

Hit On Steve Young That Ended Steve's Career

The first thought that occurred to me was to pray that Steve Young would get up and be fine. Even today, from what I've been told, it still would have been called a clean hit. I knew the competitive nature of Steve and more importantly, the great player that he was and I always respected that.

Pat Tillman

I knew Pat Tillman and was a part of the leadership structure that was in place, when the Arizona Cardinals drafted Pat. I spent time with him as he transitioned from college to the pros. Knowing the type of person Pat was, I wasn't surprised he went to the military, fought for the country, and was willing to leave the NFL.

His life ended much too early. Our military is fighting wars that allow us to have the freedom that we have in this country, including playing football. That was a sad moment for me. I get tears in my eyes knowing that Pat won't have the opportunity that I have, to have his children raised by their father.

I know his children and family know, as well as the NFL and teammates, what type of true hero he was. People sometimes call us heroes. I don't think we're heroes at all. Pat and all the servicemen are true heroes.

Playing For Cardinals During Losing Seasons

It wasn't hard. Certainly you want to win, but I always try to keep things in perspective. I would hear people say, "Aeneas, you're playing for the bad Cardinals, on a bad team." One thing I know, I was a part of one of the 32 teams, and it was an honor to be on one of them. I knew what my responsibility was, and I wanted to make sure that I was doing my job and I wasn't part of the reason we were losing.

Trade To St. Louis Rams

When I got traded to the Rams, I realized they already had a winning structure in place; they were already winners. Their team was the second worst team of the decade of the nineties. Dick Vermeil came in, built the foundation, and had got the organization and all of management turned around.

I came in to a team that had already won a Super Bowl, had just come off the playoffs, and was now restructuring the defense with new coaches and new players. I was excited because I knew this wasn't something starting from the ground up. It was a part of something that was already structured and built. I had an expectation that we weren't trying to make the playoffs. Our goal was to win the Super Bowl.

Having Two Interceptions Against Brett Favre In Playoffs
Unfortunately whenever I see a Packers fan, they haven't forgotten it. It was certainly a moment in the history of my career, as well as the history of the St. Louis Rams. The Packers came in our dome, and I think we picked off Brett Favre six times in that particular game. It was a tremendous blessing and a tremendous game. I was proud of how we played collectively as a defense and an entire team.

Favorite Coach
My favorite coach was Lovie Smith, when he was my defensive coordinator. I played in the Senior Bowl coming out of college, and the staff that coached our team was the Kansas City Chiefs. Marty Schottenheimer was the head coach and the defensive backs coach was Tony Dungy. I experienced Tony's demeanor, his expectations, and his ability to communicate with players. Because of that, I always wanted to play for Coach Dungy.

When the Rams hired Coach Lovie as defensive coordinator and I found out that they were implementing the defense that I always wanted to play in under Coach Dungy, and that Coach Lovie was a disciple of Coach Dungy, I wanted to play there. Then I met Coach Lovie, and it was like I finally got a chance to play for Coach Dungy. Coach Lovie was just a spectacular, accountable person, and he helped my career. Coach Lovie is just one of the best that I've ever been around.

St. Louis Ram Aeneas Williams breaks up a pass in the end zone intended for San Francisco 49er Terrell Owens. Photograph copyright Associated Press

Chapter 45

Willie Roaf

> College:
> Louisiana Tech
>
> Career History:
> New Orleans Saints (1993–2001)
> Kansas City Chiefs (2002–2005)
>
> 2012 Inductee Pro Football Hall Of Fame

College Choice

Back then, the Arkansas Razorbacks were kind of rebuilding. I'm from Pine Bluff, Arkansas, the same hometown as Torii Hunter, the baseball player. What happened was we had three guys who were very good football players go to Oklahoma. There was a quarterback named Eric Mitchel, Danny Bradley, and Curtice Williams, a defensive tackle. When those guys did that, Arkansas got a little bit pissed off with the program and didn't recruit us as heavily. My problem was I was playing basketball and weighed about 225 coming out of high school, and had big hands and big feet. I didn't get recruited very heavily.

My bloodline was definitely football. I was kind of raw at basketball and had some potential. I probably had a little more of a love for basketball, but things happen for a reason.

I went to basketball camp and there were about 400 campers there. I was a real good rebounder. They named me 'Mr. Rebound' at camp. I was offered a scholarship to UCA.

One of the biggest All-Star games in the country was called the King Cotton Classics and that was on ESPN. Back in '87 and '88, a couple of games were televised on ESPN. Dick Vitale came and broadcast the tournament in Pine Bluff. We even got to meet him at our luncheon.

We played the King Cotton and got a lot of exposure. Teams from all over the country played in it. Jason Kidd, Dennis Scott, and JR Reid played in that tournament. It was a huge high school basketball tournament. I started playing basketball in seventh or eighth grade. I started playing street ball. I don't know how old I was when I started playing that. When I was about 10 years old, I started playing organized football. I'm maybe 6'5" and I thought it was better just to take the football scholarship and go down to Louisiana Tech. It ended up being a blessing in disguise.

I got a letter from Connecticut when basketball coach Jim Calhoun got there. I guess they had heard about me at the camp in 1988. My basketball coach eventually let me know that he didn't show me all of the letters I had gotten, so I don't know how many offers I had in basketball. My dad knew that I was really a football player, so they didn't give me the letters I got for basketball. So, I took the football scholarship.

Louisiana Tech
I ended up going down to Louisiana Tech. Joe Ferguson was on the staff there. We ran a pro sets offense, so we flip-flopped. I had to know how to play both tackles, and we passed the ball a lot. That system was basically the perfect situation for somebody with my skill set. My basketball skills helped my foot movement. I blossomed in the football program.

Hokie Gajan was with the Saints and asked about me when I was a redshirt freshman. They always told me, "If you do what you're supposed to do, you'll be wearing diamonds." Coach Joe Raymond Peace always told me, "Willie, you've got a lot of potential." When I first got there, they knew I had a lot of potential. I didn't understand it. I said, "Man, I'm 235 pounds. I'm never going to be 300 pounds."

During my redshirt sophomore year, we played against Maryland in the Independence Bowl. We were 8-3, and they had a really good team. They had Larry Webster, Scott Zolak, and Clarence Jones, who ended up playing with me on the Saints. They had three or four pro prospects on that team. We ended up tying them in the Independence Bowl. I think at that time, I was maybe in the Top 40 tackles, and I was 20 or 21 years old. I realized that if I do what I've got to do in school and stay in college, I'm going to have a chance to go pro.

After my junior year, I accepted an invitation to play in the Hula Bowl. Eddie Robinson, the legendary coach from Grambling, and Lou Holtz were my coaches in the Hula Bowl. Eddie Robinson and I became real good friends.

Going into my senior year, there was Todd Perry, Brad Hopkins, and a couple of more guys; all bunched up together after Lincoln Kennedy on teams draft boards. My deal was to go out, establish myself, and work my way up the ladder. The beginning of the year, I couldn't get an insurance policy from Lloyd's of London for $500,000.

We played Alabama and they had top ten prospects in George Teague, Antonio London, Eric Curry, and all of those guys on defense ended up going pro. After the game I had against Eric Curry, my stock went up. The next week in practice there were 10 scouts following me around practice just watching me on the practice field. After that game, I got an insurance policy and my stock went up. Louisiana Tech ended up having four guys drafted because we were ranked the number two defense in the country, behind Alabama. We had a real good program, so it was a lot of fun back then. I didn't realize I had a chance to go pro until my sophomore year, but it was during the course of my senior year when my stock rose.

NFL Draft
Prior to the draft, I was sliding from being drafted anywhere between fifth and eighth in the first round. It was either going to be Tampa Bay, Cincinnati, the Bears, or Detroit drafting me. What happened was Detroit traded their pick to the New Orleans Saints. That's how I ended up becoming a Saint.

Jim Mora
Jim Mora pulled up to his house and there was an intruder in his house. I don't even know if he called the police. Jim went into his house and his wife was there. Jim confronted the intruder and got the intruder out of the house. Jim Moore was a tough, hard man, and had that marine mentality.

We were going to be in shape when we got out of training camp. It is hot and humid in New Orleans. If we got back and we were being a little lackadaisical in practice, he wouldn't even stop to say he didn't like what was going on and start over. We would start practice up from scratch.

We would also practice long and hard with Dick Vermeil in Kansas City. It was tough. We were in shape.

The only problem is when you do a lot of banging and you use your body like that, it gets you in shape and ready to play, but for the first couple of weeks of the season you're tired. You're trying to get your legs back underneath you when you're playing.

Mike Ditka
We worked hard with Mike Ditka, but I don't remember it being as hard as it was with Jim Mora. By that time, I had been in the league for four or five years. I was used to the routine, but it was hard. We had tough years in 1996 and in 1997. Jim Mora left during the 1996 season. The losing gets to you. In 1996, we were three in 13. Then, Mike Ditka came on as head coach.

For me, 1997 was a tough year. I wasn't in the best shape. It was a transition year for me. I either had to get myself together and really become a pro, or I was going to be out of the league. I needed Ditka and I needed 1997. The old legendary coach Dick Stanfel was on that staff in 1997 and 1998. He would get in there and run on the treadmill. I would see him working out. The way he pushed his body and the shape he was in was incredible. He was a real clean-cut man.

In 1998, I played a lot of basketball and was doing a lot of running. I got in real good shape and played really hard. I really didn't want to let the team down. I wanted Coach Stanfel to be proud of me after that 1997 year.

Ricky Williams
It was tough when Ricky came in 1999. It felt wrong when the Saints traded the whole draft for Ricky and then he was in that wedding dress. Master P. had him sign the worst contract in NFL history. Then Ricky was saying, "I'm going to reach these numbers …", which were

crazy numbers to get those incentives. Those were astronomical numbers they put on him. Ricky got a lot of money upfront so he wouldn't think he got picked.

After watching Ricky play college football and the way he was perceived on TV, I thought Ricky was a lot more mature than what he was. Ricky was a very immature, sensitive kid, and got himself in a situation where he was lashing out. The whole time he was there, because of the contract, he was lashing out, doing stuff, and acting aloof. He realized what had been done. What was he going to do about it?

He really couldn't do anything about the situation with the contract. They had him and it was bad. You try to take a positive spin on it, but they put that kid in a real tough situation.

In 1999, before Mike Ditka left, was another tough year. I do remember going to Baltimore and playing against Michael McCrary. Johnny Unitas was standing on the sideline and I was excited to be playing in front of him. That was a circus, a whole lot of hoopla.

Ricky had a good year in 2000, and then he got hurt. I think he had 1,000 yards in 10 games. He was having a hell of a year. We went to the playoffs and won the first playoff game that year. We had really good offensive and defensive lines that year, and they carried our team. We had taken Darren Howard from Kansas State in the draft that year. La'Roi Glover had 17 sacks that year, and we also had Joe Johnson. I don't think Ricky really became a pro until he got to Miami.

It was a tough deal for that kid. I use to go check on him because he lived close by. He would have people over at his house, driving his cars. He just wasn't ready for the pros.

Trade To Kansas City Chiefs
I was in a tough predicament in 2002. There were some innuendos about some family situation going on. I had been with the Saints for nine years and we won a playoff game, but I think that was the best thing for me. With the situation the way it was, I wasn't going back to New Orleans and playing football. I kind of forced the Saints

hand. They paid $500,000 to trade me, and I had to go take a new contract with incentives from the Kansas City Chiefs. I went from close to signing a three-year $13 million contract with the Saints, to a three-year $8 million contract that was mostly incentive based. I wouldn't have it any other way.

I had to start over in Kansas City. I saw Dr. James Andrews, and had ACL surgery. I just felt blessed to come out of that surgery. I had a knee scope in 1998, and came back in 12 days. The scope was a little different than ACL surgery, but I knew I came back from the knee scope pretty quick. I was looking forward to that challenge. I knew I didn't want to end my career limping off the field, trying to play with a bad knee. I knew I didn't want to end my career like that in 2001.

I just was looking forward to an opportunity. I think playing on grass in Kansas City helped me play a couple more years. So, it was a blessing in disguise that I went to play in Kansas City. We had one of the best lines in the NFL. I think over time, we were the best line in the league.

I was very fortunate that the Houston Texans took Tony Boselli that year in the expansion draft, and not me. They said they didn't want to take anybody over 30 years old. I was over 30 and coming off a knee surgery, so they didn't take me.

Being Named To All-Decade Teams of 1990s & 2000s
I didn't know if I was going to make the All-Decade team for the '90s. I was anticipating getting a chance to make it. Someone from ESPN called my agent and let him know that I made the 1990s First Team All-Decade Team. I was just so ecstatic that I made it. You have to come in at a certain point early enough in a decade that you get to play most of the decade. Then you have to play a long time so you get to play in the next decade.

If I hadn't gone to Kansas City, I wouldn't have made the Second Team All-Decade Team for the 2000s. I had four really good football seasons in Kansas City.

Kansas City Offensive Linemen

The Kanas City starting five offensive linemen didn't miss a game the first two years I was with the team. John Tait left and went to the Chicago Bears as a free agent. So next year, the other four of us didn't miss another game for three straight years. I got hurt my last year with the Chiefs in 2005.

My teammate in Kansas City, Will Shields, beat me for the Outland Trophy my senior year in college. He didn't miss a game for 14 years after he got in the lineup his rookie year. Casey Wiegmann started 10 or 11 years without missing a down between Kansas City and Denver, and then back to Kansas City. Brian Waters made the Pro Bowl six times with the Patriots and the Chiefs.

Treating His Body

I took anti-inflammatory shots during the week and on game day. My body hurt after the game. I got on a routine. I would go to the practice on Wednesday, and had a massage every Wednesday night. If we played on the road, it would be on Friday night. If I played at home, I would have a lighter massage on Saturday.

My first four or five years, I looked at teammates going to the chiropractor and I remember saying, "Why do these guys need to go to a chiropractor to get massages?" I could just bounce back then. As I got older, I started to realize why they want to get that done every week. I didn't understand it when I was young, because I was blessed with so much ability. As I got older, I realized that your body starts hurting, and you need this. Those massages are key for you, especially when you get older.

Photograph copyright Associated Press

Chapter 46

Will Shields

> College:
> Nebraska
>
> Career history
> Kansas City Chiefs (1993–2006)
>
> 2015 Inductee Pro Football Hall of Fame

<u>College Choice</u>
I had a couple of colleges that were looking at me. I actually had a hard time qualifying to play college football because of my ACT scores. I had different schools that sort of dropped out of recruiting me. A coach from Oklahoma told me that I could use a combination of ACT scores to qualify. Big tests were not my forte. I ended up qualifying and there were four or five schools recruiting me. Nebraska was one of the top schools on my list of what was going to be the best fit for me as far as where I wanted to go to school.

The schools all had the same regulations of what you needed to get in. I was always close enough to qualifying that schools knew I could qualify. They maybe saw me as being a kid who wouldn't leave the Midwest or wasn't as talented as some of the guys that they were looking at. Nebraska fit what I wanted to do and how I played the game.

Coach Dan Young and Coach Milt Tenopir were the two Nebraska assistant coaches who recruited me. Coach Young came down and spent some time talking to me about different things, and then Coach Tenopir came down and talked a little bit. Coach Tom Osborne came down of course on that last visit to talk.

The thing that was really unique is that they were already ahead of the game as far as the academic side of it. That was very important for me since I felt like I was struggling a little bit to get started. I discovered Nebraska already had academic support in place that would help me get to where I needed to be.

Nebraska Offense
Nebraska was the best option for me. I already knew their offense, because my high school had put in the same offense as Nebraska in my junior year. So that gave me a leg up. And, it wasn't that hard of a transition as going somewhere else and basically learning things from scratch.

Playing Both On The Offensive & Defensive Lines At Nebraska
I like playing on both the offensive and defensive lines. The thing I really liked is that I could play on both. My first year at Nebraska, I actually spent the preseason practicing pass rushing and playing on the defensive line during scout team.

After practice I was helping a teammate rehab his knee. The coach had me pass rushing the rehabbing teammate, and things of that nature. That gave me an opportunity to play on the other side of the ball.

Tom Osborne
Coach Tom Osborne was a lot of fun to play for. The thing most people don't realize is that Coach Osborne let his coaches coach. You really developed a relationship with the coaching staff because of this. Coach Osborne never really sat down and went through the Xs and Os with you. He had meetings with the assistant coaches and they talked about things, and then the assistant coaches came back and implemented everything.

Adjustment To Living Away From Home In College
It was fairly easy. At home I was sort of a homebody, so it made it easy to be a homebody on the college campus. There are always some growing pains here and there, just getting used to being away for a little bit, that kind of stuff; nothing really difficult. The simple fact is I saw my team as my family.

Draft
I was projected to be drafted in the third round. I was hoping that I might be drafted in the first or second round. At one point, I was thinking I am the Outland Trophy Winner. I should be drafted in the

first two rounds since I won a prestigious award. That's not necessarily the case and I learned that fairly quickly when I talked to scouts and agents. It's not where you go in the draft; it's what you do after you get drafted.

I got skipped for two rounds and then was drafted in the third round. I got an opportunity to go in and prove what I could do. I thought, now it's time to provide for my family.

I looked at it as a job. I did not want to be a flash in the pan. It was good that I had good coaches when I first came in. They sort of set the tone of what it was going to be like to be a Pro.

I had great players around like Joe Montana and Marcus Allen. I had a chance to sit and watch them prepare, and to see how they did things. I thought, "You know what? I want to be like those guys." I want to be able to say, "Hey, I had a good career." I had a coach who actually brought that up one of the first meetings we were ever in. He said, "If you can make this a true career, that means you've done something right." From that point forward, I was always looking for that next goal and that next round, so that I could keep performing better and better on a higher level.

Joe Montana
Joe Montana was very cool and relaxed in the huddle. That was the one thing about him, you never knew if he was rattled or if anything bothered him. He was the same regardless if we were down by 21 or up by 21.

There were times he would walk in the huddle and all he'd say is, "Give me a little more time." That's when you knew he saw something the last play, and that he was going to make something happen.

I liked having guys who understood the game from the inside out because they saw certain things and were be able to say, "You know what, give me two more seconds and I know this guy will beat that guy, and we'll make it happen."

When Realized Could Play In NFL

It wasn't until right before we went into training camp. We had a couple of mini-camps, and my first mini-camp was terrible. I had no idea what I was doing. I was sort of lost trying to catch up. The game was so fast at that point, and I was trying to figure out how could I get better.

Then one of my agents came out and we played one on one basketball. He explained to me, "You know you're making this way too complicated." I said, "What do you mean?" He said, "The goal is the quarterback and you're going to keep me away from him. Just like you play basketball, you're going to play football." He sort of made it simple. I said, "Is that how easy it is? It's not complicated? I don't have to stay focused and do this and do that?" He responded, "Nope."

I show up to the next camp, show some flashes, and the coach started giving me some tips and different things to work on when I went home. At that point I said, "You know what? I think I can do pretty well in this league if I just can keep moving forward and keep working on what I need to do to get better."

Toughest Defensive Lineman

John Randle was tough and gave me fits all the time. Next was Trevor Pryce. Trevor's rookie year, our line coach said, "I hope nobody teaches that kid how to pass rush because he's going to be something special." Lo and behold, guess who ends up leaving? My line coach ends up leaving, going to Denver, and teaching this kid how to pass rush. He could tell what guys could do just by seeing them on film.

John Randle tried to talk trash to me, but I had enough problems with him physically without even worrying about the mental part. I really didn't care what he was saying. I was more or less worried about the physical part. He would say, "Oh, you're not going to talk to me now, huh, you're not going to be my friend. You're not going to …" You can fill in the blank. I just looked at him like he was crazy. John is a great guy. What's really cool is you hate playing against him, but off the field talking to him, he is an awesome guy to be around.

Marty Schottenheimer

Marty Schottenheimer and I had a couple of meetings but we really didn't have a relationship. Marty is a defensive coach, so he was very tied into his defensive players and things like that. We got along but I ended up becoming closer with a couple of the other coaches.

Key To Success

I think it's constantly working on your game. I think you've got to work on different things. Also, learning what everyone else is doing really helps.

You need to push yourself. You've always got to be your worst critic so that you know you're always working to get better. If you can see where your downfalls are before somebody else does, that's always a better thing than waiting for someone else to tell you what you're doing wrong. You need to be open enough to take other people's criticism, and use it to make yourself better.

Not Missing A Game In 14 Seasons

Luck was one of those keys to me not missing a game in 14 seasons. I never thought, "I don't think I'm going to play." I also had a great staff around me, with a great chiropractor. The chiropractor would try some things that would get my body back on track. With that and the training staff we had at the Chiefs on top of that, it was amazing some of the things they could do to get you to be able to perform that next week.

There is a threshold of pain of what you can and can't do, but it's also recovery time; being able to recover enough to say okay I can push through it. You want to be able to get through it, one way or the other. On the other hand, you don't want to be a detriment to the team because you can't do what you need to do to help the team. That's the key. There's a difference between being hurt and being injured. If you're just hurting, you push your way through. If you're injured, you need to sit down and let somebody else in, who will play and perform at a higher level.

Derrick Thomas Dying During NFL Career

Derrick Thomas dying was hard on the team. He was a key player to what we were trying to do and what we were trying to accomplish.

We had a future built around him and what he did as a player. When we lost him, it was tough. The simple fact is that the guy was in the locker room with you, showed up to your charity event and things of that nature, and now he's gone. It leaves a void.

Herm Edwards
Herm Edwards didn't shout while coaching. He liked to talk and was very boisterous in a sense. You knew when he was coming down the hallway.

When I first met Herm he was really quiet. He was here when I was a rookie. He was a defensive back coach at that point, and didn't say a whole lot.

Then for him to come around full circle and be a head coach, it was different. He was a very nice guy and did a great job. Some players liked him and some players were not sure how to take him. I'm one of those guys in between. I liked him; he's a great guy. It's part of fitting the right scheme and the right people in the right place.

Decision To Retire
I knew it was time to quit when they said they were going young. I was sore every week and fighting to get back every week. That was one of those tough years that we fought through, and then when they said, "Hey, we're going to go young." I was like, "Yeah, it's time for me to move on." My knees hurt and my back hurts. For me to keep fighting a battle and we're not looking for a championship, I really didn't have that time on my body to keep fighting that old thing called age.

You always think you've got one good play left in you. As long as you can still walk, talk, and move, you've got that one good play in you. That's just sort of the mentality that you have; that's what kept you playing as long as you played. That's what kept you being the person that you are, the competitive nature of it.

Photograph copyright Associated Press

Chapter 47

Larry Allen

> College:
> Sonoma State
>
> Career History:
> Dallas Cowboys (1994–2005)
> San Francisco 49ers (2006–2007)
>
> 2013 Inductee Pro Football Hall Of Fame

College Choice
I went to a junior college in Chico, California until I had the grades to transfer to a four-year college. I was sleeping on my mom's couch when the Sonoma State coach, Frank Scalercio, called to say that he could get me into school. I took recruiting trips to the University of Texas at El Paso, Weber State, and UCLA.

Playing In The Senior Bowl
When I played in the Senior Bowl, I wanted to show my best to get noticed by the NFL teams.

NFL Draft
It was great when I found out I was drafted. Jerry Jones called me up when he drafted me. I was happy. I just ran out of my apartment and jumped into the swimming pool with all my clothes on.

Learning To Play Offensive Line In The NFL
With Mark Tuinei, Nate Newton, Ray Donaldson, and Erik Williams being on the offensive line, it was a great learning experience for me coming from such a small school.

My first day of Cowboys training camp, I got into a fight with defensive lineman Leon Lett. I was just tired and getting frustrated, and Leon and I just got into it I guess. After that day, he just took me under his wing. He said I was a fighter and a scraper. He felt I could help the team win.

My father always told me the Charlie Chaplin saying, "Never get mad; get even." Do it the right way.

Hardest Defensive Lineman To Block
During my rookie year, Reggie White was the hardest player to block. He was just a strong man. After playing against him, Reggie told me I had to get in the weight room and get stronger.

A Lot Of Turnover In Dallas Cowboys Head Coaching Position During Career
Even though there was turnover in the Dallas Cowboys coaching position during my career, I still had my offense line coach, Hudson Houck with me for eight years. He was such a great coach. He taught me everything I needed to know. The head coaching changes really did not bother me much.

Induction Into Dallas Cowboys Ring Of Honor
Being inducted into the Dallas Cowboys Ring of Honor was great. I grew up, watching the Dallas Cowboys on Thanksgiving. I have been a big Cowboys fan since I was a young kid. Being honored with all those guys like Roger Staubach, Troy Aikman, and Emmitt Smith, was a great feeling. Tony Dorsett was one of my favorites growing up.

Preference Run Blocking Or Pass Blocking
I had no preference of run or pass blocking. Both were fine for me. I was just as aggressive a pass blocker as I was a run blocker. So it really did not make a difference to me.

I liked playing guard. You can be more physical at guard than tackle. With tackle, you have all those fast, quick guys you're blocking and you have got to control yourself a little bit more. I just wanted to keep my job. That is the reason why I played so well.

Emmitt Smith
Emmitt Smith was a great running back. People give him a lot of credit. He was a smart back. He was durable. I was happy to play with him.

Troy Aikman
Troy Aikman was a great leader. I did not want to disappoint him.

Leader Of Dallas Cowboys
A whole group of guys were the leaders of the Cowboys. They were Troy Aikman, Emmitt Smith, Michael Irvin, Nate Newton, and Charles Haley.

Michael Irvin Sleeping In Pro Football Hall Of Fame Gold Jacket After Receiving It
I slept in mine too.

Pro Football Hall Of Fame Induction
It is a great feeling being inducted into the Pro Football Hall of Fame. I am not a big public speaker; so giving my enshrinement speech was a little rough for me. I cannot describe the feeling. It is a great feeling.

Favorite Moment In NFL
My favorite moment in the NFL was winning the Super Bowl. I was young. Most guys do not even have a ring. For me, just to get a ring was amazing. It was a great game and a great feeling to win.

Photograph copyright Associated Press

Chapter 48

Jerome Bettis

> College:
> Notre Dame
>
> Career History:
> Los Angeles/St. Louis Rams (1993–1995)
> Pittsburgh Steelers (1996–2005)
>
> 2015 Inductee Pro Football Hall of Fame

College Choice
My choice of which college to attend was between Notre Dame and Michigan. What it boiled down to was I played fullback. Michigan had just signed the number one tailback in the country. I knew he was going to have to get the football. I was a fullback and could run the football, but Michigan's office was based around the tailback running the football. So, I knew that my best opportunity was going to be at Notre Dame where Lou Holtz's system was really predicated on the fullback having success. Notre Dame was the perfect fit for me and who I was.

Lou Holtz
Lou Holtz was amazing. Coach was a dictator; make no mistake about it. If you got on his wrong side, you were in big trouble. He expected you to be disciplined, play with respect, and give one hundred percent. He helped develop me into the player that I became. He was great, but if you got on his bad side, watch out.

I never got on his bad side because I always knew I had to be on time. That was the number one rule. Being late was the quickest way guys got in big trouble. I always knew I had better be early to ensure my success. Because if you are late for a meeting, you'd better believe it's going to affect your football performance. That was the last thing I wanted to do. I was always smart enough to know I had better be sitting when he closed the door, or else I was in trouble.

Only Carrying Ball 15 Times During Freshman Season

I knew as a freshman I wasn't going to get too many opportunities. I understood what the hierarchy was and how everything went. I knew I was a freshman and Lou Holtz hated freshman carrying the football. Coach Holtz told us, "I only do it if I have to do it." He did this because we had veteran players, and at that time, we had All-Americans at every position. I was playing behind some great fullbacks already. I knew that I was going to have to be patient. The fact that I was able to crack into the starting lineup as a freshman, spoke volumes as to what he thought of me. In the bowl game, he gave it to me a couple of times, and that made a big difference.

Sophomore Season

Coach Holtz made up for it my sophomore year, by giving me the football every which way possible. He had the ball thrown to me, had me rush from the fullback position, and also put me at tailback sometimes. When he wanted to go with three wide receivers, I became the tailback. He gave me a lot of opportunities to carry the football starting my sophomore year.

I weighed about 250 pounds in college. I understood that it was best for me to keep it on the ground and not be a receiver. Also, I couldn't jump that high. I knew it was in my best interest to run it every chance that I got.

Notre Dame Rivalry Against Michigan

Notre Dame and Michigan was a big rivalry. It was usually the first game of the season, so the games were very heated, not only because it was the first one, but also because if you lost, you pretty much lost your chance of winning the national championship. They were huge games.

Coach Holtz was always in an uproar when it was Michigan week because he understood the significance of the games. As 18-20-year-old players, we never truly understood the significance of that game.

Convincing Lou Holtz To Allow Me To Tape My Shoes

I put that into the deal when Coach Holtz was recruiting me. I told him that in order to get me to go to Notre Dame, I wanted to have the ability to tape my shoes like I did in high school. It took a little while, but Coach Holtz finally decided to let me do it. So, I was able to tape them up before every game.

Nobody ever really said anything to me about it, and it actually never became a huge issue. It was something I wanted to make sure I had in the deal, that's for sure.

Decision To Forego Senior Year To Declare For The NFL Draft

It wasn't that hard of a decision to forego my senior year and declare for the NFL Draft. After my junior year, Coach Holtz wanted to meet with my parents and me. So, they came to Notre Dame and we all met. Coach Holtz told me that I had done all I could do in college football, and that I should go and test myself in the NFL. He gave us his blessing and that was the end of it.

NFL Draft

There were only two teams in the top ten picks of the NFL Draft who wanted a running back. The two teams were the Arizona Cardinals and the Rams. The top two running backs were Garrison Hearst and I. I had an idea once Arizona took Garrison Hearst, that I was probably going to the Rams.

I didn't know much about either franchise because they are in the western part of the country. I didn't really follow either team, so I didn't know much about either one. I really had no preference at that point.

Team Followed Growing Up

I was a Dallas Cowboys fan growing up. I didn't watch a lot of football because I grew up as a bowler. I didn't play football until high school. So the only games I really watched were on Thanksgiving, and it was either the Lions or Dallas playing. Dallas usually won so I watched them as opposed to watching the Lions.

Rams Change In Head Coach From Chuck Knox To Rich Brooks

It was a big adjustment from Chuck Knox to Rich Brooks. The adjustment was more in Coach Brooks' philosophy than on the field. Coach Brooks came in and he felt as though I had lied to him. You see, he had asked all the veteran players to come to training camp early, because he was putting in a new system.

I was in the middle of a contract dispute with the team, so I held out. He felt that I had lied to him, because I didn't come to camp on time while I was going through the hold out. At that moment, that was pretty much the end of our relationship.

So, he would pretty much put me in the game for a series, or two series, and take me out for the rest of the game. He pretty much ended the relationship I had with the Rams.

Trade To Pittsburgh Steelers

I was hoping a trade would come about. I had told management that if I didn't get a trade, I was going to retire. I was serious about that. I had re-enrolled in school and was committed to not coming back. Once the Rams management saw I was serious, they gave me permission to seek a trade, and that's how I ended up in Pittsburgh.

It was a great move for my career. The Steelers had just come off losing a Super Bowl to the Dallas Cowboys. I was going to a Super Bowl caliber football team. I just felt that it was going to be great for me and for my career. As it turned out, it was. It made a big difference.

Bill Cowher

Bill Cowher was great. He was a player's coach. He was the kind of coach who related to the players well. He knew what we were thinking, and he also gave us leeway to go out and take care of business. He was definitely a championship coach. They've also mentioned his name for the Pro Football Hall of Fame. He is somebody that I'd vote for.

Being Demoted From Being Starter With Pittsburgh Steelers

I'll never forget what I said when I found out I was demoted. I said that I had been on the other side of most of Coach Cowher's decisions. This time I was not on the positive side, but I handled it like I handled the other times. I thought, I'll deal with it, and I'll work my way to hopefully change his mind. By the end of the season, I was able to change his mind and become a starter again. I was patient, but I also understood that you deal with the ups and the downs with the same humility. I think that's what makes you a professional.

Thanksgiving Day Overtime Coin Toss Mistake By Referee (Caused Rule To Be Changed, Now Team Makes Call Before Toss & Not During)

I guess he misunderstood, or didn't hear what I called on the coin toss. I wish I could tell you what happened. What I do know is the referee gave the Detroit Lions the ball. The Lions went down, kicked a field goal, and won the game. After that, Coach Cowher fired me. That was the last time I ever called the coin toss.

It had never happened before where the referee misheard the call, so they didn't have a protocol for that. They took the referee's word for it and that was the end of it, which I can understand. It was devastating for us, because we lost that game and I believe the rest of the games that year. That was the sad part.

Ben Roethlisberger Convincing Me Not To Retire After 2004 Season

Ben Roethlisberger promised me that he would get me a championship. We were talking on the sidelines after we lost the championship game during the 2004 postseason, and Ben said to me, "Give me a chance. You come back, give me one more year, and I'll get you to a championship." He was a man of his word. We won a championship.

2005 Steelers Win Versus Chicago Bears

The 2005 win versus the Chicago Bears was a great game because it really propelled us to winning the championship. We went on a four game winning streak and went into the playoffs hot. We then won four playoff games, and became the champions. The Bears game was like a playoff game. If we lost, we were out of it. We won and then we kept winning. Next thing you know, I was holding the Lombardi Trophy in my hometown of Detroit.

Being A Finalist Five Consecutive Years For Pro Football Hall Of Fame Induction

I was hoping that I would be inducted into the Pro Football Hall of Fame. It is a very, very exclusive club to be in and so I understood that it was a process. I was just hoping that my time would come soon.

I was patient and I understood that if I didn't get in, it just wasn't my time. It wasn't that I wasn't worthy, it just wasn't my time, and that's how I was able to keep my sanity about it. I understood that there were some great players who went in before me who deserved to be in. Every guy that went in … when you look at those lists, they all deserved to be on there. When I look at the group I went in with, there were also another ten guys on that list that deserve to be in. It's just not their time yet, and that's how I had to look at it.

It's difficult waiting every single year. Make no mistake about it, that's the difficult part but you have no choice, it's out of your hands. If I could score a touchdown and make getting inducted happen, you better believe I would've been through the hole and there wouldn't have been anybody to stop me. Unfortunately you're not in control of it. You can't determine the outcome, so you have to hang on and hope that it happens.

Photograph copyright Associated Press

Chapter 49

Derrick Brooks

> College:
> Florida State
>
> Career History:
> Tampa Bay Buccaneers (1995–2008)
>
> 2014 Inductee Pro Football Hall Of Fame

College Choice
Florida State was my primary choice for a college when I was being recruited. I chose Florida State. When I was being recruited, so many colleges were starting to sound the same. I said no matter where I go I need to get a good education.

I was laying down one day and I thought, 'If something happens to me, my parents need to be able to get to me. So the closest university to Pensacola, Florida was Florida State and that's why I ended up at Florida State.

Miami was on my list to visit, but at the end of the day when it got down to it, Miami was 10-11 hours away. Florida State was only two hours and 10 minutes away. So, that helped me boil it down to Florida State, too.

Bobby Bowden
Florida State Head Coach Bobby Bowden was awesome. He had the principles to live his life with religious faith in the industry of college football for 50 plus years. That is amazing. He set the tone for the team thru his principles. Playing for Mickey Andrews, the Florida State defensive coordinator, allowed me to develop the mental toughness that I have today. That was awesome. I had fun there with the linebacker coaches, Wally Burnham and Jim Gladden. I really enjoyed my time at Florida State with all the coaches.

Winning National Championship Against Nebraska

Winning the National Championship against Nebraska wasn't bad either. That's another thing that I'm grateful for. I was on the team that brought Coach Bowden his first National Championship after he coached for so many years. It was great to be a part of that team and be able to say, "We did it for Coach Bobby. We were part of his first championship team." All of those things are important to me. I was blessed to obviously win it and to be a part of it.

We were heavy favorites in 1993, against Nebraska. Going into the game most people had us blowing them out. We knew it was going to be a lot tougher game than what people were projecting. Nebraska was a tough opponent. We made plays down the stretch to win, but we knew going in how tough the game was going to be, and we didn't take Nebraska lightly at all. I played to win and at no point did I doubt that we were going to win that game.

NFL Draft

Was I the 28th best player in the first round? Not in my mind. Obviously I was expecting the best, but I just wanted an opportunity to play and go in and prove myself. I thank God that the Tampa Bay Buccaneers moved back into the first round to draft me at number 28. I'm grateful that I was able to play my entire career in the state of Florida.

At that time, I was just thankful that I had got drafted. I wasn't a guy who was bitter, saying I should have been this pick or that pick. I was drafted where I was meant to be drafted, and I embraced the opportunity that was before me.

Tony Dungy

Tony Dungy was tough. He coached us tough, but yet it was fun. He brought discipline, consistency, and a way of doing business that changed the Buccaneers culture. He came in talking about changing our community and making us all winners on and off the field. Coach Dungy set the tone for my attitude towards making a difference in the community.

Tampa Bay Buccaneers Lack Of Success Until Late '90s
That's the intriguing part of the position that we were in to turn the franchise around. Now, I can say that was part of my Hall of Fame resume.

Tampa Bay Defense
The defenses architect was actually Chuck Noll of the Pittsburgh Steelers. Tony Dungy obviously put his principles on it and installed it, and he brought it to Monte Kiffin. Monte Kiffin and Tony Dungy had worked together before being with the Buccaneers. I like to think it was honestly the head coach's influence, and trusting the coaches to get the teaching over to the players.

When Coach Dungy talks about the Tampa defense, he always gives credit back to Chuck Noll and what the Steeler defense was able to do. Obviously, he changed things out depending on the talent level we had at Tampa. It all dates back to Chuck Noll when you talk about some of the principles that Tony Dungy ran defensively for us.

Leader Of Tampa Bay Buccaneers Defense
Each position had its own leadership within its position. At times, different leaders spoke up. Generally my teammates looked at me asking who was the leader. Then, I stepped up and embraced that role. I was the type of leader where the stage was big enough for everyone to shine. I like to think we did it together, to be honest.

Toughest Opponent
There really wasn't just one guy. I had my battles with all of my opponents. I looked at tough battles as an opportunity to shine. I embraced the joy in going up against the likes of Marshall Faulk and Barry Sanders, and determining how could I step my game up. Going against my opponent, I used that as motivation to bring out the best in me.

Personal Stats
My stats were pretty good every year. To be honest, I wasn't asked to sack the quarterback, so that's why I don't have a lot of sacks. I like to think that I had a complete game, and whatever the defense asked me to do, I believe I had the skill set to do it.

Playing Philosophy

I modeled my game after myself. I try to get better every single year. "Stay in the moment" was my playing motto, and it still is today. When I first came into the NFL, Junior Seau was in the league and as far as 4-3 linebackers go, you looked at him. Hardy Nickerson was on my team and set a standard for my position. At the end of the day, I wanted to make my game, my game and just try to get better every year.

2002 NFL Defensive Player Of The Year

I like to celebrate 2002, because when I received that individual award for being the best defensive player, we won the Super Bowl. That's special to me.

Winning Super Bowl vs. Oakland Raiders

I think the Super Bowl win gave validation to the Tampa Bay Buccaneers and the Tampa Bay area. The Buccaneers went from 0-26 when they first started in the league, to Super Bowl champion years later. I think it was a combination of a lot of hard work, a lot of disappointments, and obviously a lot of joy. I think the Tampa Bay area celebrated the championship because that's how much it meant to our city.

Feelings On Tony Dungy Not Winning A Super Bowl With The Tampa Bay Buccaneers

I felt bad every year we lost in the playoffs and didn't go further. Coach Jon Gruden came in and brought a different dynamic to our football team. Obviously, that dynamic helped us win a championship. At the time, we were blessed with the challenge of looking forward, not backward. I think Coach Dungy went on to have a pretty good career after Tampa.

Lee Roy Selmon Not Getting A Chance To Play In A Super Bowl

That's part of the Tampa Bay Buccaneers' history. It's overcoming those types of moments. Everybody doesn't get a chance to play in the Super Bowl. There are other Hall of Fame players who never played in the Super Bowl. So, you just understand how special the opportunity to play in the Super Bowl is, and when you win, it's even more special.

Favorite Play In Career

I didn't have a favorite play. I tried to appreciate all the plays I made individually. Obviously, some plays meant more in the game than others. You tend to gravitate toward those and I do that as well. But, I kind of appreciate them all. I was blessed to play a lot of football in the NFL, and I don't want to take any play that I made or didn't make for granted.

Decision To Retire

I just knew it was time to retire. I got some calls from teams after I was released from the Buccaneers, but I was just trying to wait for the right situation for me. There were situations that came close, but there was never one that I felt comfortable accepting as a total package.

It wasn't really one moment or one day when I decided to retire. It was just things added up over time while I started transitioning into life after football. Before I knew it, I had a full schedule. I had no regrets. It was time to move on.

Being Named Walter Payton Man Of The Year

Winning the award recognizes not only me, but also the work of a lot of people behind the scenes who are making changes in the community, and making life better for people. I was just grateful that we won the first year they renamed the award after Walter Payton. I was one of the co-recipients. That is life's work. That's where I feel the game gives you a platform to make a difference, and I thank God that I was able to do it.

Pro Football Hall Of Fame Induction

I was joyous, ecstatic, and emotional all at once. Sometimes you experience emotions that you can't describe. That was one of those moments.

I'm blessed that I was a first ballot Hall of Famer. I'm also blessed that I got a chance to be a part of history. I was enshrined with Ray Guy, the only full-time punter in the Hall of Fame. Claude Humphrey is one of the best defensive ends, and I saw how appreciative he was to be enshrined the same year as me. Whether you get in on the first ballot or you get in after many years, doesn't matter. The fact is they went into the Hall of Fame, and I got a chance to share that with them. I appreciate that I was a part of the 2014 Hall of Fame Class. God blessed me to be a part of it with those guys.

Photograph copyright Associated Press

Chapter 50

Walter Jones

> College:
> Florida State
>
> Career History:
> Seattle Seahawks (1997–2009)
>
> 2014 Inductee Pro Football Hall Of Fame

<u>College Choice</u>
Being from Alabama people ask me about my college choice all of the time. "Why didn't you go to Alabama?" I joke around and say, "Florida State's check was bigger." When I was being recruited, Florida State was one of the dominant teams in college football.

I went to Florida State for a visit and I said, "This is where I want to play my college ball." I was going to do whatever it took for me to get there and play at Florida State.

I was an Alabama fan growing up. Alabama was the team everybody in Alabama loved. When I was attending junior college, it was hard to choose Florida State because I still had an opportunity to go to Alabama. I had to go where I thought there was a better opportunity for me to get into the NFL.

Coming out of high school, I think everybody has a story of not doing as well in school I they would have liked. I had a high school coach that kind of got me on track. He took me around to college games and stuff.

I made a visit to Florida State and other colleges and went to major college football games. Coming from a small town, I figure, "This is my way out. This is something that I want to do, this is something I want to be a part of."

I'm not saying that it was a lot different, but there are more people. You get to meet all types of people. For me, that was something I wanted to be a part of. I wanted to be part of a big time school, playing football. I did everything I could to get to that point. I think the transition was more like I can't wait to get there. It was something that I had been working hard for. I worked through high school and junior college to get to Florida State. I wanted to be walking on that campus and I wanted to be a part of the whole school scene.

I came from a small rural town and didn't have much. I watched football and thought, "I got the potential to be good at this." For me, I just decided that football was something I wanted to pursue, so I kind of put all my marbles in one basket and said, "Hey, this is what I want to pursue."

Before I got into football, I wasn't doing that well in school. School wasn't something that was important to me. Once I got into football, I realized that I had to improve in school. I should have been doing my schoolwork, but I wasn't. I was doing other things. I had to put the other things that weren't helping me out, behind me and I had to concentrate on school. I was ineligible to play my senior year of high school. That's why I had to go to a junior college.

I had to do all my own recruiting. I had make all of my videotapes, send them out to teams, and let teams know that I was out there because I wouldn't be playing football my senior year.

I had to go the junior college route. At the junior college, my recruiting started all over again. Colleges found out I was from the state of Alabama, and I had already said that I was going to go to Florida State when I was in high school.

Bobby Bowden
Bobby Bowden is a hometown favorite. For me to get a chance to play for a great coach like that was fine. He was very family-oriented, where he knew everything about your family. Florida State had become a big powerhouse, so Coach Bowden was relying more on his assistants to make his team accomplish his goals. For him, it was more about getting to know you as a player.

Now that I think about it after being in the NFL, it was more like he was preparing you for the NFL. In the NFL, you don't see the head coach as much as you see the assistant coaches and the guys who are relaying the information down to you. You have to get it done on the football field. At Florida State, players were kind of getting that feeling of how things are done in the pros.

Florida State's Biggest Rival

That's tough, but when I was playing, it was Florida. Miami was their biggest rival back in the early '90s. I got a chance to play against Florida twice. My first year at Florida State, I was a redshirt, so I didn't get a chance to play. That game was so good. We came back and tied the game up. Just being on the sidelines and seeing that game was great.

Then the next year I played against Florida. Florida was the number one team in the country going into the game and we were number two. That game was so hyped, and we came out on top. That was our last regular season game and we had to see who we would play for the championship.

Florida went on and won the SEC championship, and we ended up playing those guys again for the championship. In that two-year span, Florida was the team that we knew we had to beat. We shouldn't have played them in a championship game since we had already beaten them, but those guys kind of figured out what we were doing to them. Danny Wuerffel kind of showed why he was the Heisman Trophy winner. He threw the ball all over the field and stuff. The game kind of got out of hand pretty fast, and we lost.

Redshirting

It's one of those situations where I learned a lot. I was doing everything except playing in the game on Sunday, so it kind of humbled me a little bit. I just had to wait my turn.

A lot of classes that I had taken at the junior college weren't transferring. There was so much paperwork to do to get those classes transferred, and making sure those classes counted with the Division I schools. I was preparing myself to play by practicing every day, doing everything, and hoping I would get in the game. It was about game six of the season when all my classes from my junior college had cleared. I sat down with the coaches, and they told me the best thing for me to do was to redshirt and it would be a learning year for me.

In the grand scheme of things, it helped me out a lot. I was able to play with great guys every day in practice, and hone my skills and preparing myself. The next year I was ready, prepared, and able to go out and play at a high level.

NFL Draft
I didn't know the Seattle Seahawks were going to draft me. When I was coming out in the draft, there was a list of the six elite guys coming out in the draft, and I was on that list.

I didn't think Seattle was going to draft me. Prior to the draft, I went to Seattle on a scouting visit. Even though they were showing interest in me, they just didn't say, "If you're available, we're going to pick you."

I was watching the draft with my family. Once Seattle picked Shawn Springs with the third pick in the draft, I figured I was going to be drafted by Oakland. Then some trades happened, and all of a sudden it was Seattle drafting with the number six pick. With probably a minute left on the draft clock for Seattle to make a pick, Seattle Head Coach Dennis Erickson called me and said, "How would you like to be a Seattle Seahawk?" I said, "I would love to be a Seattle Seahawk." They made the pick, and the rest is history. At that time, all I wanted to do was to get into the NFL and prove that I could play at the NFL level.

First Training Camp
The coaches put me at left tackle and said, "You're our left tackle. The only way you'll lose your job is if you don't play well." I realized that it was my job to lose, so I put everything into it. I said, "I'm not going to lose the job. I've been working for the last five years to get to this point."

For the Seahawks to draft me that high, I knew that they were pretty confident that I could come in there and be a starter for them. Once they gave me the job, I was thrown into the fire. When quarterbacks are that high of a draft pick, sometimes people say they should not start for a year. But, I think as an offensive lineman playing at that high level, at that high of a pick, you have to take the good and the bad and let the offensive lineman learn the system, learn the plays, and learn on the fly instead of sitting on the sideline. I think as an offensive lineman, you can learn so much by playing and getting a lot of reps at practice and in the game.

Seattle Seahawks Defensive Line
Phillip Daniels gave me fits every day. Phillip and Cortez Kennedy were true professionals. Those guys worked me every day. As a rookie, you have to earn your respect with those guys, so you want to go out there and prove that you can play at the NFL level. Those guys had been playing for a couple of years. For me, it was great work. I wanted to be a part of it, and this is where I wanted to be. I was going to do everything I could to gain their respect, and go out there and prove to them that I could play. It was not just about going against them, going out there on Sunday, fighting and showing that I could fight. I wanted to show why the team picked me and wanted me to be their left tackle.

Realization Could Play At A High Level In NFL
I think the blessing for me is that we ran one offense for about ten years, so that made everything a lot easier for me. A lot of times the game plan for me was, "Hey, block the defensive end." That made it easier for me to go out there and say, "I know I can play this game. Now all I have to do is study the guy I'm going against, and do everything I can to take that guy out of the game."

That made my game plan easy, so all I had to do was go out there and focus on that guy. I'm not saying that wasn't a tough job at times, but as a player you want that competition. You want to go out there and shut a guy out. That's when things started to open up for me.

When I was growing up, Anthony Muñoz was probably one of the best left tackles out there. In high school the offensive linemen watched tapes showing techniques for lineman. Anthony Muñoz was shown as an example of how left tackles should play the game.

There were some great guys who were playing the game at that time. If you go back and look, there was Erik Williams, Jonathan Ogden, Orlando Pace, and Tony Boselli, before he got hurt. I wanted to play just like them. I wanted to be persistent just like those guys.

I had a lot of guys that I could watch and see what made them great. They would go in a game and shut their opponent out. That's how I wanted to be. That's the way I played every year. I wanted to be consistent and be at the top every year. That was something I strived for every year from that point on.

Favorite Running Back To Block For

I didn't really have a favorite running back to block for. Warrick Dunn made a lineman's job a lot easier because he was so small. He knew how to set up blocks, and he knew how to get behind the offensive lineman.

If you've got a great running back, all he wants you to do is to block the guys in front of you and get him to the safety. As an offensive lineman, that's what you want to do. You want to get him to the safety, or get him to the odd block guy. Most of the time, the running back can make those guys miss him. Once those guys get to the second level, they can make a lot of yards and a lot of plays. I never looked in the backfield to see what running back was in the huddle. I knew that the running backs out there understood the offense and knew what we were trying to do.

Mike Holmgren

Mike Holmgren came to the Seahawks and showed us that we could win and be in the big games. He said, "If you do it this way, we can win." I think that's where the Seattle Seahawks 12th Man started and all that. Mike Holmgren went in there and showed the city that this team could win just as well as the Green Bays of the world. He came in with a lot of respect.

For a team that wasn't doing that well, he came in and showed us the way we could become better—how we could be consistent and play at a high level. If you do that, you can be in games, or you can be in the hunt to win a Super Bowl. Getting the chance to play in the Super Bowl was awesome. He told us if we did what he said, and we did it right, we could play for a championship. We did, and it happened. We didn't bring home a Super Bowl victory, but everything that he said to do we did, and we had an opportunity to win the game in the end.

Toughest Defensive Lineman

When I first got into the league, I went against Derrick Thomas, who was playing for the Kansas City Chiefs. Going up there, probably before the 12th Man, I think we experienced the loudest stadium. As a rookie going up there, Derrick got the crowd going. I was thinking, "Oh my God, this is what I signed up for."

I went against great guys all the time. Those guys gave their A game every game, so I had to be out there and stay focused. I had to try my best to not go out there and be lackadaisical and give up a sack. That's part of the game. You don't want to give up a sack, but once you get let down one play, that's when things go wrong.

What A Quarterback Typically Does When Sacked

A lot of times, the quarterback will take on the responsibility and say, "That was my fault. I should have got the ball out." The quarterback understands how tough it is to go out there and block those guys.

A lot of quarterbacks feel that if a lineman gets beat for a sack, then the lineman shouldn't come and help the quarterback up. Most of the time, you see linemen once they give up a sack, go back to the huddle, because the quarterback is probably pissed off. If you got just completely physically beat, and the quarterback got hit, the quarterback doesn't want to see the guy who got beat helping him get up. Most of the time if that happens, the offensive lineman feels, "Well, I don't want to go back and pick him up after that." A lineman has the mindset, "Okay, I don't want to be that guy who goes to pick him up, so I'm trying my best to keep that guy from hitting my quarterback."

Mike Holmgren Said Walter Jones Best Offensive Player He Ever Coached

I love Coach Holmgren for saying that. When I played, I got a chance to be in one offense for ten years, and it made my game a lot easier. It made me say, "Okay, this is what I have to work on." I knew the offense, so it made it a lot easier for me. I wanted to go out there and be dominant and be consistent at what I did. I wanted to set the standard on how a left tackle should play the game of football. For him saying that, and for me now to be inducted into the Pro Football Hall of Fame, I can sit back and I can feel good that a young kid can look at me and say, "That's the way I want to play the game of football." I was honored to hear Mike Holmgren say that I went out there and played the game the way it is supposed to be played.

Pro Football Hall Of Fame Induction
In 2014, the Pro Football Hall of Fame brought the 15 finalists for the Hall of Fame to New York City. I was sitting in a hotel room for 30 minutes trying to figure out if I was going to get in or not. That was a very raw emotion, because at that point, I couldn't do anything. You've got all of these voters picking out five guys from the top 15. All 15 guys deserve to be in. I was sitting with my son, waiting on that phone call to say I got in.

When I found out I was selected, it was very emotional for my son and me. It was great for the city of Seattle. It was incredible. I played my whole career in Seattle. I was consistent during my football career, and then I ended my career as a first ballot Hall of Famer. I will never, ever forget all of the emotions I felt.

Only Penalized 9 Times For Holding In 13 NFL Seasons
If referees don't call it, it's not holding. I think it's a situation where referees always tell you if you keep your hands inside, it's not holding. Most of the time, if the referees call holding, it's because the offensive lineman's hands are outside the shoulder pads of a defensive lineman. For me personally, I tried my best to keep my hands inside. I am not saying that I wasn't grabbing cloth or grabbing pads, but as an offensive lineman, I think you have to learn how to get away with stuff that's part of the game. There's no way you can go out there and say you're not holding, because you probably can get called for holding on every snap. It's all about working on your techniques, and making sure you've got your hands in the right place.

Photograph copyright Associated Press

Chapter 51

Orlando Pace

> College:
> Ohio State
>
> Career History:
> St. Louis Rams (1997–2008)
> Chicago Bears (2009)
>
> 2016 Inductee Pro Football Hall Of Fame

College Choice
Choosing a college was a tough choice. I hate to say it, but it came down to Michigan and Ohio State. I'm from Sandusky, Ohio, which is close to Michigan. You have Michigan fans in Sandusky. Of course there are a lot of Ohio State fans, too.

When I visited Ohio State University, I met some incredible people there like Korey Stringer, who was a great player at the time. Korey took me under his wing a little bit. That kind of sealed the deal for me. It was a great choice for me. Probably one of the best choices I've made in my life.

John Cooper
John Cooper was great. He treated us like young men. He was one of the guys who recruited me really hard. He wanted me to come to Ohio State. The biggest thing he offered me was an opportunity to play as a freshman. That's what I was looking for.

Being Only Second True Freshman To Start Opening Game
I immediately saw the speed of the game was a lot different from high school. The coaches kind of threw me in there with the big boys to see if I could handle it. The first game was a little rough, just because of the speed of the game. Everybody's big and everybody's strong. Being a freshman, I still had some growing up to do and had

to develop my game. You kind of learn as you go out there. Each week got better for me. It was a good experience.

Rivalry With Michigan

When you go to Ohio State, you know that the Michigan game is "The Game". The game is played at the end of the regular season, and normally there's something on the line in that game. You really go to Ohio State to be in the atmosphere and be around that rivalry.

Winning Awards In College

All the awards are really special in their own right. Just to be acknowledged is special. I was the only guy who won two Lombardi Awards in college. I'm not sure if there will ever be another lineman who will duplicated that. I was Ohio State MVP, Big Ten Offensive MVP, and finished 4th in the Heisman Trophy voting. You just don't see offensive lineman finishing 4th in the Heisman voting. You just don't see offensive lineman get that kind of acknowledgement. I was really fortunate and I worked really hard to get those awards.

Key To Success In College

I wanted to be the best. I really did. I wanted to do something that separated me from so many other linemen. I was 30 yards down the field blocking defenders. That was my way of saying "Hey I want to separate myself from any other linemen."

Also, I wanted to break the will of guys. It's an offensive lineman's dream to break the will of the defender. One of the things I really wanted to do was put something on tape where the guy playing against me the following week would experience some fear in his heart.

NFL Draft

I didn't know the St. Louis Rams were going to draft me. To be honest, I only took three scouting trips. I visited the New York Jets, who had the number one pick. I also went to visit the Oakland Raiders and the New Orleans Saints, who had traded up prior to draft day. I thought I was either going to go to the Jets, or at worst, not going to get past the third selection. Then the Rams traded up to the first pick.

I don't even remember the interviewing process with the Rams. Coach Vermeil had broadcast a ton of our games at Ohio State. I think he was familiar with the type of player I was. So as soon as the Rams made that trade, I got a phone call from Coach Vermeil that they would be selecting me with the number one pick.

Missing First Training Camp With St. Louis Rams
I missed the first training camp with the Rams. I was in contract negotiations. The second year training camp was tough. Coach Vermeil was an old school coach who believed in really tough training camps. He wanted to find out who his guys were and what they were made of. The training camps were tough, really tough. The physicality of the camps, the hours on the field, and everything he demanded of us was really tough.

Missing the first training camp wasn't by design. It kind of worked out that way. I didn't know how tough it would be at the time. Looking back on it, I could have missed a couple more training camps and I think I would have been fine.

When I started practicing with the Rams, it was tough for me. When you go in as a rookie and are the number one pick in the league, the expectations are high. The guys are saying, "Hey, where is this guy?" I bought my teammates a lot of breakfasts and dinners. They accepted me once I was practicing with them. Those guys were really great.

Kurt Warner
When Kurt Warner first started, for anybody to say Kurt was going to be an NFL MVP and a potential Hall of Famer, they would be lying. Kurt worked extremely hard, but no one new he would be that good. When he got under center when Trent Green went down, he was phenomenal. He had his opportunity and he made the most of it.

Preference Run Blocking Or Pass Blocking
I came out of Ohio State, the pancake blocker trying to smash defenders. I didn't give a sack up in two years there. I could pass and run block. It didn't make a difference. Mike Martz was named the offensive coordinator in 1999. Mike Martz liked to chuck the ball

down the field, so I had to have my pass technique correct and ready to go.

Pancake Block
I saw Korey Stringer play against Alabama in the Citrus Bowl, and he just crushed this guy. I could see the defenders were scared of him. At that point, I realized I wanted to impose my will on guys as well. I wanted to be able to finish blocks and really separate myself from guys. Guys always block to the man. I really wanted to block through the man. Once the "pancake block" took off and people started noticing it, then you obviously want to do it more.

Realization St. Louis Rams Offense Could Be Special
Going into training camp in 1999, we felt good with Trent Green being the starter at quarterback. Kurt got in there when Trent got hurt. Marshall Faulk had just come in and the guys were healthy. We knew this offense could be special when we beat San Francisco the third game of 1999. San Francisco had beaten us 18 times in a row, I believe. Once we beat San Francisco, we knew we were a pretty good team.

The great thing about that team was everybody was unselfish. They are all good guys. Nobody wanted the credit. Kurt Warner is an awesome guy. Marshall Faulk, Isaac Bruce, and Torry Holt are really good people. Offensive linemen always take pride in their team winning ballgames. That's just the mindset of offensive linemen. We don't really need the credit. We just want to go out there, do our work, and win ballgames.

Playing In First Super Bowl
As a kid, I dreamed of one day running out of the tunnel playing in the Super Bowl. To win that game the way we did, not knowing if the ball crossed the goal line or not, was really special. The first quarter I felt like I was walking on air because I was so excited to get out there and play. I couldn't wait to get out there. I felt faster. Everything felt great at the time.

Dick Vermeil Retiring After Winning Super Bowl
I didn't realize that Coach Vermeil was going to retire after we won the Super Bowl. I was thinking that we could continue our success for

the next two or three years. The difficult part was Offensive Coordinator Mike Martz was so hot at the time. It was impossible to keep him as the offensive coordinator for the following year. Everyone thought he was going to be offered him a head coaching job. If he had been, I think he would have taken it. Coach Vermeil realized that he had the ultimate prize—winning the Super Bowl. He probably felt at that time, he could step away. Had Coach Vermeil stayed on another year, we probably would have won a couple Super Bowls.

Dick Vermeil

Dick Vermeil was great. He was an old school coach who really believed in his players, not as just the football player, but the actual person. His former players from the Philadelphia Eagles would come to our meetings. Coach Vermeil would cry about everybody, but it was genuine. That's one thing I really appreciated about him. He was genuine.

When he said we would rally around Kurt Warner, Coach Vermeil truly believed that. He also believed we were going to be a great team. That year everybody bought into his system. That's really the sign of a good coach. If you have a good coach who the players believe in, you'll have success.

Losing To New England Patriots In Super Bowl

The team felt confident going into the Super Bowl against the New England Patriots. The Patriots were playing with a backup quarterback in Tom Brady, and we thought we would run over the Patriots.

Patriots Head Coach Bill Belichick had a great game plan. They were really stopping our passing game. Had we run the ball, the outcome may have been different. The Patriots dropped a lot of guys in coverage to stop our passing game and we needed to make adjustments.

John Randle's Trash Talking

I played against John Randle a couple of times and the things he would say were just flat out hilarious. I couldn't believe it. He read player bios. He was talking trash to the offensive guard as I was in my stance next to the guard, literally laughing. I'd think, "Oh my gosh, this guy is hilarious." He talked so much trash. It was unbelievable. He told one of my guards the guard's wife's name. I thought, "How in the world does John know the guard's wife's name?" My guard got pretty pissed off about it.

Favorite Game In NFL
Every player will say that the Super Bowl was his favorite game. There were so many good games. One game that stands out is the game against San Francisco, and being able to get that monkey off our backs having lost 18 games in a row to them. When you play for 13 years, there are a lot of games that really stand out in your mind. The NFC Championship game against Tampa was a tough game. It was really tough getting to the Super Bowl.

One special game that really stood out, now that I think of it, was our first playoff game on the run to that Super Bowl against Minnesota. I can remember the city of St. Louis being really excited because the Rams had never been to the playoffs before. The first play of the game we scored. That's the game that really sticks out because the Edward Jones Dome in St. Louis was really rocking. It was good to be in the playoffs. I remember, wow, this is a great feeling to be in the playoffs.

Pro Football Hall Of Fame Induction
Being selected for the Pro Football Hall of Fame was great. That last hour when the decision was being made, was really tough. You try to visualize scenarios where you get in. You just never know how the process will shake out. I had a little nervousness. My initial feelings and reaction after finding out I was going to be inducted, were relief and excitement. Being one of the youngest guys in the Hall of Fame makes it even more special.

When you look at how many guys have actually played in the NFL and realize that there are only 300 guys who are in the Pro Football Hall of Fame, and you are part of that elite group, it's really hard to describe the feeling. It means so much as a player. The ultimate goal as a player is to be known, one day, as one of the best of all time. I'm humbled by the honor.

St. Louis Ram offensive lineman Orlando Pace pass blocks San Francisco 49er Chris Doleman during an NFL game. Photograph copyright Associated Press

www.ingramcontent.com/pod-product-compliance
Lightning Source LLC
Chambersburg PA
CBHW071355160426
42811CB00094B/497